Mrs Bee

Book of

Needlework

Mrs Beeton's
Book of
Needlework

CONSISTING OF

DESCRIPTIONS AND INSTRUCTIONS,

ILLUSTRATED BY

SIX HUNDRED ENGRAVINGS,

OF

TATTING PATTERNS.	POINT LACE PATTERNS.
CROCHET PATTERNS.	GUIPURE D'ART.
KNITTING PATTERNS.	BERLIN WORK.
NETTING PATTERNS.	MONOGRAMS.
EMBROIDERY PATTERNS.	INITIALS AND NAMES.

PILLOW LACE, AND LACE STITCHES.

Every Pattern and Stitch Described and Engraved with the utmost Accuracy, and the Exact Quantity of Material requisite for each Pattern stated.

Beeton's Book of Needlework was originally published in
Great Britain in 1870 by Ward, Lock and Tyler

This facsimile edition published 2007 by Bounty Books,
a division of Octopus Publishing Group Ltd
2–4 Heron Quays, London E14 4JP
Volume copyright © Octopus Publishing Group Ltd., 2007

ISBN-13: 978-0-753714-67-6
ISBN-10: 0-753714-67-1

A CIP catalogue record for this book is available
from the British Library

Printed and bound in India

SAMUEL BUTLER'S
PREFACE

———◆◇◆———

THE Art of Needlework dates from the earliest record of the world's history, and has, also, from time immemorial been the support, comfort, or employment of women of every rank and age. Day by day, it increases its votaries, who enlarge and develop its various branches, so that any addition and assistance in teaching or learning Needlework will be welcomed by the Daughters of England, "wise of heart," who work diligently with their hands.

The recent introduction of Point Lace has brought a finer, and, apparently, more difficult class of fancy work into general favour. Ladies may now, however, confidently commence, with our patterns before them, to reproduce Antique laces; for care and patience, with a knowledge of Point Lace stitches, are alone required to perfect the beautiful work, which, as shown in existing specimens of exquisite Old Lace, constitute the chief glory of women's refined industry in past centuries.

INSTRUCTIONS in TATTING, in EMBROIDERY, in CROCHET, in KNITTING and NETTING, in BERLIN WOOL WORK, in POINT LACE, and GUIPURE D'ART are prefixed to the pages devoted to these separate branches of needlework. The whole work is interspersed with coloured and other Patterns in Point Lace, Guipure d'Art, Tatting, Embroidery, and Designs for Monograms and Initials for marking handkerchiefs and table-linen. The quantity of materials required for each class of work is also given with every pattern.

The idea of combining a series of minute and exact instructions in fancy needlework with useful patterns was conceived some years ago by one whose life was devoted to the inculcation of the practical duties of woman's life, and to assisting her sex in their daily work of HOUSEHOLD MANAGEMENT and REFINEMENT.

Her great wish was that her BOOK OF NEEDLEWORK should be as valuable in its way to her Countrywomen as her work upon Household Management was useful in showing the best mode of providing for the diurnal wants of families. Other hands have brought to a conclusion her original plans. The best attainable workers have contributed to this volume. Only those who knew the extent of the late Mrs. Beeton's design, will miss, in the pages now before them, " the touch of a vanished hand."

S. O. B.

Paternoster Row, 1870.

CONTENTS.

——◦◦——

TATTING.

TATTING

INSTRUCTIONS

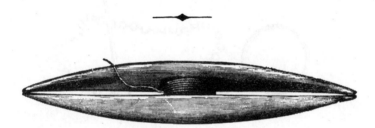

Tatting Shuttle.

The needlework called Tatting in England, *Frivolité* in French, and *Frivolitäten* in German, is a work which seems, from all accounts, to have been in favour several generations ago. Modern ingenuity has discovered some ways of improving on the original plan of tatting, which was, indeed, rather a primitive sort of business as first practised. To Mrs. Mee, one of our most accomplished *artistes* in all matters connected with the work-table, belongs, we believe, the introduction of the plan of working from the reel instead of the shuttle. By this alteration the advantage of the shuttle being constantly kept filled with cotton was gained, and the necessity also obviated for frequently joining the thread ; and to Mdlle. Riego, equally distinguished in all details appertaining to the employment of the needle, ladies are indebted for an arrangement by which the same thread used in the making of the pattern is used for fastening the work. The old plan only provided for the working of the different portions which constituted the pattern, and then these portions had to be

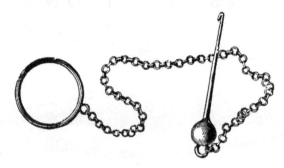

Tatting Pin.

sewn together with a needle and thread. The ingenious workers on the Continent have also given much attention of late to the art of tatting, and our instructions now printed comprise what we consider the best mode of learning and doing this exceedingly interesting and fashionable work.

Tatting differs entirely from crochet, and is composed of stitches forming *knots*. It is intended as an imitation of point lace, and is especially used for trimming under-linen, on account of its strength.

To make the stitches or knots a small instrument is used, called a *shuttle*. This shuttle consists of two oval pieces, flat on one side and convex on the other, and is made of wood or ivory.

The two oval pieces are joined together by a strong cross-piece. The illustration shows the construction of the shuttle. These shuttles are made in ivory, pearl, tortoiseshell inlaid with pearl, and silver; they are also manufactured in coloured bone, black, red, and white. The best to work with are the pearl for a white shuttle, and the inlaid tortoiseshell for a black shuttle; the prices vary from sixpence to one shilling and two-and-sixpence each. In selecting a shuttle be careful to see that the ends close, as if dropped it soon becomes unthreaded, which is very inconvenient. The cotton intended for the work is wound round this shuttle, and the thickness of the cotton varies according to the style of work. It is better to use the proper tatting cotton, because it is stronger than the ordinary kinds; this is manufactured by Messrs. Walter Evans and Co. for the purpose. Their Boar's Head Cotton is also frequently used, and answers very well.

Shuttles.

These are made in 3 sizes :—Finest, No. 1 ; No. 2, useful medium size ; No. 3, the largest.

The Way to Hold the Hands.

Take the shuttle in the right hand, between the thumb and second finger, and allow the forefinger to remain at liberty, and rest the under part of the shuttle *between* the second and third and *on* the middle finger. Place the thread round the three middle fingers of the left hand, so as to form a loop, keeping the second and third fingers a little apart, and bring the cotton again between the thumb and forefinger, letting the end fall within the palm of the hand, while the end of cotton which holds on to the shuttle passes over the thumb-nail.

To Make a Stitch.

Keep the hands in the position above described; pass the shuttle at the back, through the loop—that is, between the second and third fingers. Take the end of the shuttle which comes out from the loop between the forefinger and thumb of the right hand, and strain the cotton very tightly towards the right. When the cotton is drawn through the loop, this cotton must not be impeded by the fourth finger; it should, on the contrary, slide over it, and be drawn tight. It should divide the loop into two parts. After this withdraw the second left-hand finger, which is *above* the cotton, and pass it again under that cotton, so as to draw up the loop. A *half-stitch* is thus formed, and must be tightened by being drawn closely to the forefinger and thumb of the left hand. For the remaining half of the stitch keep the hands in the same position, but, instead of letting the cotton fall over the thumb, pass this cotton over the back of the hand; then let the shuttle fall between the second and third fingers of the left hand, in front, and take it out again at the back, strain the cotton very tightly, withdraw the second finger from the loop, letting the cotton which is behind the hand sweep over the fingers. When this is done, guide with the unoccupied fingers of the left hand this second half-stitch up to the other, thus completing *one stitch.*

The Way to Make a Loop in Tatting.

When a certain number of stitches are made, very tightly draw in the loop by straining the cotton until the first stitch touches the last, and thus a loop is formed. During this process the stitches should be held tightly between the forefinger and thumb

The Way to Make a Purl.

A *purl* is a small loop of cotton often used as an edging in tatting, as, for instance, round the outer edge of the ovals in tatted insertion No. 2. The following is the easiest method of making a purl:—The stitches are not made quite closely together at the place where a purl is to be made; about one-sixth of an inch is left between each. This space is left free until the loop is made by uniting the stitches; then the small piece of cotton in the space bulges out between the stitches, and forms the purl. If several are required a small space is left between every two or three stitches, according to the desired number. Care must be taken in that case that the small pieces of cotton left be all of the same length, so that the purl may be perfectly even. The purl can also be made thus: At the same time with the end of thread take the tatting-pin or a very large darning needle or knitting needle in the left hand, so that the point may come out farther than the row of stitches; if then you wish to make a purl, throw the cotton on the pin before making the stitch; then fasten this stitch, and push it at once close to the preceding; the pin with the cotton should come above the stitches. Do not take out the pin before all the purl and all the stitches are completed and joined together.

Joining the Work.

Place the tatting-pin in the loop that is to be joined, and with the hook draw the thread of the loop—that is, round the hand through it—pass the shuttle through this loop, and draw it up tightly close to the stitches.

A " straight" or double thread is used to join various parts of the work, and forms very beautiful patterns. Without the straight thread we should be unable to imitate point lace patterns, or, indeed, to execute any designs but those composed of circles, ovals, &c.   To use this straight thread 2 shuttles are required ; they should be of different colours. Sometimes one end of thread is left attached to the reel instead of using the second shuttle.   In commencing a loop the straight thread is held between the second and third fingers of the left hand, about 2 or 3 inches from the work ; the other shuttle is held as usual in the right hand, and the stitches and purls worked with it upon the foundation of the straight thread of the second shuttle

TATTING.

1.—*Pine Pattern Collar in Tatting.*

Materials: Messrs. Walter Evans and Co.'s Boar's Head cotton No. 80, or tatting cotton No. 60; tatting-pin No. 3; a small shuttle.

This collar is worked with very fine tatting cotton as follows .—1st circle : 2 double, 1 purl 7 times, 2 double, draw up the cotton. 2nd circle : 3 double, join it to the last purl of the 1st circle, 1 double, 1 purl 8 times, 2 double, draw the cotton up. 3rd circle : 2 double, join it to the last purl of the 2nd

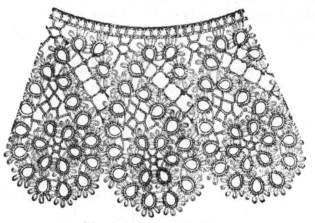

1.—Pine Pattern Collar in Tatting.

circle, 1 double, join it to the 7th purl of the 2nd circle, 1 double, 1 purl 8 times, 2 double, draw the cotton up. 4th circle : 2 double, join it to the last purl of 3rd circle, 3 double, 1 purl, 1 double 7 times, 1 double, draw the cotton up. 5th circle : 2 double, join it to the last purl of 4th circle, 2 double, 1 purl, 1 double 3 times, draw up the cotton. 6th circle : 2 double, join it to the last purl of the 5th circle, 1 double, join it to the 5th purl of the preceding circle, 1 double, 1 purl 6 times, 1 double, join it to the first purl of the 1st circle, 2 double, draw up the cotton. This completes the star pattern in centre of pine.

1st circle of pine : 2 double, 1 purl, 1 double 8 times, 2 double, draw up the cotton. 2nd circle : 3 double, join to the last purl of 1st circle, 1 double, join it to the 7th purl of 1st circle, 1 double, 1 purl 6 times, 3 double, draw up the cotton and join it to the 3rd purl of centre star. 3rd circle : 3 double, join to the last purl of 2nd circle, 1 double, 1 purl 8 times, 2 double, draw up the cotton and join it on to the centre purl of 2nd circle in star. 4th circle : 2 double, join to the last purl of 3rd circle, 1 double, 1 purl 5 times, 3 double, 1 purl, 2 double, draw up the cotton and join it to the 5th purl of 2nd centre circle in star. 5th circle : 2 double, join the cotton to the last purl of 4th circle, 1 double, 1 purl 7 times, 2 double, draw up the cotton, repeat the 5th circle twice more, then join the cotton to the centre purl of 4th circle in star. 8th circle : 2 double, join to the last purl of 7th circle, 1 purl, 1 double 5 times, 2 double, draw up the cotton and join it to the centre purl of 5th circle in star. 9th circle : 2 double, join to the last purl of 8th circle, 1 double, 1 purl 6 times, 2 double, draw up the cotton. Repeat the 9th circle 3 times. 13th circle : 3 double, join the cotton to the last purl of the 12th circle, 1 double, 1 purl 7 times, 4 double, draw up the cotton, turn the work downwards, and work the 14th circle : 2 double, 1 purl, 3 double, join it to the 1st purl of the 1st circle of pine, 1 double, join it to the 2nd purl of first pine circle, 1 double, 1 purl 6 times, 2 double, draw up the cotton. 15th circle : 3

double, join to the last purl of the 13th circle, 1 double, 1 purl 6 times, 3 double, draw up the cotton. 16th circle, 3 double, join to the last purl of the 15th circle, 1 double, 1 purl 4 times, 3 double, 1 purl, 1 double, draw up the cotton, 17th circle : 1 double, join to the last purl of the 16th circle, 1 double, 1 purl 6 times, 2 double, draw up the cotton. 18th circle : 1 double, join to the last purl of the 17th circle, 1 double, 1 purl 8 times, 1 double, draw up the cotton, and repeat from commencement until the collar is the required size. The upper part of the pines is filled in with lace stitches, as clearly shown in our illustration.

2.—*Tatted Insertion.*

Materials : Messrs. Walter Evans and Co.'s tatting cotton No. 30, or Boar's Head crochet cotton No. 12 ; tatting pin No. 2 ; large shuttle.

2.—Tatted Insertion.

This insertion should be worked with coarse cotton. 5 double *, 1 purl, 2 double, repeat from * 4 times, 1 purl, 5 double, draw up the cotton, turn the pattern downward, and work another circle the same as that above described, leaving one-sixth of an inch of cotton between each circle.

3.—*Lace Edging in Tatting.*

Materials : Messrs. Walter Evans and Co.'s crochet cotton No. 10, or tatting cotton No. 20 ; tatting-pin No. 3 ; any sized shuttle. For a finer edging, No. 18.

1st oval : Fill the shuttle, but do not cut it off from the reel, as a double thread is used, and commence by working 10 double stitches, 1 purl, 10 double ; draw up.

Double thread : Putting the thread attached to the reel round the left hand, work 8 double, 1 purl, 8 double.

3.—Lace Edging in Tatting.

2nd oval : 10 double, join to purl in 1st oval, 10 double ; draw up.

The pattern is now complete. Repeat from beginning, taking care that the next oval be close to the last.

Crochet a heading with the same cotton, working 7 chain, 1 double into the purl in double thread. Repeat.

4.— *Lace Edging in Tatting.*

Materials: Messrs. Walter Evans and Co.'s crochet cotton No. 10, or tatting cotton No. 20; tatting-pin No. 3 ; any sized shuttle. For a finer edging, No. 18.

4.—Lace Edging in Tatting.

1st oval : Fill the shuttle, but do not cut it off from the reel, as a double thread is required, and commence by working 10 double stitches, 1 purl, 10 double stitches, draw up.

2nd oval : Close to last oval, work 10 double, 1 purl, 10 double ; draw up.

Double thread : Putting the thread attached to the reel round the left hand, work 12 double, 1 purl, 4 double ; then join the shuttle-thread to the purl in 2nd oval, by drawing it through with a pin. Then do another similar chain of stitches with the double thread, viz., 4 double, 1 purl, 12 double.

3rd oval : 10 double, join to the purl in 2nd oval—the same as that to which the shuttle-thread has been fastened—10 double ; draw up.

4th oval : Close to last oval, work 10 double, join to purl of 1st oval, 10 double, draw up.

The pattern is now complete. Repeat from beginning, taking care that the next oval be close to the last. Crochet a heading with the same cotton, working 4 chain, 1 double into the purl of double thread, 6 chain, 1 double into the next purl. Repeat.

5.—*Border in Tatting with Crochet Edging.*

Materials : Messrs. Walter Evans and Co.'s tatting cotton No. 60, or crochet cotton No. 80; tatting-pin No. 2; a bone shuttle.

5.—Border in Tatting with Crochet Edging.

Work * 4 double stitches (that is, 4 times following 1 purled stitch and 1 plain), 1 purl, four times following 3 double stitches, 1 purl, 4 double stitches, draw up the cotton so as to form an oval, and for the smaller oval, work 9 double stitches, but leave, before beginning the first double stitch, the space of one-sixth of an inch between this oval and the preceding ; repeat from *, leaving the same space between each oval ; join together the larger ovals by the purl.

For the crochet edging, work the 1st row in the following manner :—1 double (followed by 6 chain) in each of the smaller ovals. The 2nd and 3rd rows are composed of short treble stitches, placed one above the other, and divided by one chain. While working the short treble stitches of the 3rd row form the small purl thus :—* 1 short treble in the first short treble of preceding row, let the loop slip off from the crochet needle, insert the needle in the under stitch, from which comes the loop now made into a purl, work 1 double in the first short treble of preceding row, 1 chain, under which miss 1 stitch, and repeat from *.

6.—*Border in Tatting with Crochet.*

Materials: Messrs. Walter Evans and Co.'s Boar's Head cotton No. 20, or tatting cotton No. 40; tatting-pin No. 2. For a coarser size use Boar's Head cotton No. 4, or tatting cotton No. 20.

6.—Border in Tatting with Crochet.

4 double stitches, 1 purl, 4 times following, 3 double stitches, 1 purl, 4 double stitches, draw up the oval, but not quite tight, leave a space about one-sixth of an inch, leave a similar space between this oval and the next, work 3 double stitches, fasten them to the nearest purl of preceding oval, then work twice following 4 double stitches, 1 purl, then 3 double stitches, 1 purl, 3 double stitches, and draw up the oval

7.—*Tatted Insertion.*

Materials: Messrs. Walter Evans and Co.'s Boar's Head crochet cotton No. 18; tatting-pin No. 3.

This strip of insertion is worked with crochet cotton, and

consists of a row of circles, two of which are always joined together, and edged on either side with chain stitches. Work first * 2 double, 4 purl divided by 1 double, 1 double, 1 long purl about one-fifth of an inch long, 10 double divided by 1 purl,

7.—Tatted Insertion.

1 long purl, 4 times alternately 1 double, 1 purl, then 2 double ; join the stitches into a circle ; work close to this a second circle, and knot the end of the cotton together with the cotton with which the first circle has been begun ; repeat from *, but henceforward in the first of the two circles fasten the cotton on to the middle purl of the preceding circle, instead of working the middle purl. When the strip of insertion is sufficiently long, edge it on either side with a row of chain stitches, by working 1 double in 1 long purl and 5 chain between.

8 —*Rosette in Tatting.*

Materials : Messrs. Walter Evans and Co.'s tatting cotton No. 40 ; tatting-pin No. 3.

This rosette is worked with two cottons, viz., 1 plain, 1 purl, 1 plain, 5 double, 1 purl, 10 double, 1 purl, 1 plain ; turn the work downwards, 10 double, fastened on the last purl turned downwards ; this forms one loop turned upwards ; turn work downwards, 10 double, 1 purl, 5 double, fastened on first purl turned downwards ; turn figure thus formed downwards ; 4 double, 1 single, repeat 4 times more from *, joining the figures

8.—Rosette in Tatting.

by means of the purl stitch ; the ends of the cotton are knotted together.

9.—*Star in Tatting.*

Materials : Messrs. Walter Evans and Co.'s tatting cotton No. 50 ; tatting-pin No. 3.

9.—Star in Tatting.

Fill the shuttle, and commencing a loop, work 1 double, then 1 purl and 1 double 12 times, draw into a round ; join the cotton to the 1st purl loop. 1st oval.—Commence a loop close to the joining, work 7 double, join to 1st purl of round, work 7 double and draw close ; reverse the work. Join the thread from reel, and holding it out for a straight thread, commence the scallop :—5 double, 1 purl, 5 double, reverse the work. The 2nd oval same as first. Repeat oval and scallop alternately, until the star is completed.

10.—*Insertion worked in Tatting.*

Materials : Messrs. Walter Evans and Co.'s tatting cotton No. 50; tatting-pin No. 3.

10.—Insertion worked in Tatting.

This strip of insertion is worked with two cottons. Work with the cotton in the left hand over that in the right hand. Both ends of cotton are fastened together at the beginning by a knot. First work one half of the insertion the long way in the following manner :—1 plain, 1 purl, 1 plain (the purl must be very short) ; turn the purl downwards, 6 double, 1 purl, * 6 double, 1 purl, 1 plain, which must all be turned upwards ; then turn the work so that the upper edge is turned downwards ; work 6 double, fastened on to the last purl turned downwards (the fastening of the stitches is made with the thread in the right hand) ; a loop turned upwards is thus formed ; turn the work downwards, draw the cotton in right hand underneath that in left hand, and work 6 double, 1 purl, 6 double, all turned upwards ; fasten these stitches on 1st purl turned downwards. In this pattern 1st of border pattern is thus completed ; turn it downwards, 8 double, 1 purl, 8 double, 1 purl, 1 plain, turn work downwards, 6 double, fastened on last purl of last pattern, turned up.   Repeat from *. When the insertion is of sufficient length, work the other half in same manner, and fasten it on the 1st half by means of purl stitches between the 8 double stitches twice repeated.

11.—*Tatted Insertion for Trimming Lingeries.*

Materials: Messrs. Walter Evans and Co.'s tatting cotton No. 40, or crochet cotton No. 20; tatting-pin No. 3.

11.—Tatted Insertion.

This insertion consists of 2 rows of three-branched patterns which lie opposite each other, and are joined by slanting rows of knots.   A coloured silk ribbon is drawn through these rows which join the patterns.   Each of the 3 branches of 1 pattern consists of 9 double, 1 purl, 9 double, and must be worked close to another.   When the 3rd branch is completed, fasten another piece of cotton on to the middle branch.   Work 12 double over this 2nd piece of cotton, and then work without the 2nd piece of cotton a 2nd three-branched pattern like the 1st.*   Fasten the 2nd piece of cotton on to the middle branch of the just-finished pattern, work 12 double over it, then again a three-branched pattern; in this pattern as well as in the following ones, instead of working the purl of the 1st branch, fasten it on to the purl of the 3rd branch of the preceding three-branched pattern of the *same* row, as can be seen in illustration. Repeat till the strip of insertion is sufficiently long.

12.—*Circle in Tatting.*

Materials: Messrs. Walter Evans and Co.'s tatting cotton No. 80; tatting-pin No. 3.

12.—Circle in Tatting.

Work first 8 ovals, each composed of 5 double stitches, 3 purl divided one from the other by 4 double stitches, 5 double stitches; these ovals are joined together by the purl at the sides, then the circle is tightened as much as possible, and the cotton with which you are working is twisted round the ends of cotton that have been cut: the cotton is then fastened off nearly underneath.

Begin a fresh small oval, composed of 12 double stitches, which should be fastened to the preceding oval after 3 double stitches (to the purl in the centre of the first oval), then fasten it again to the purl which joins together the first and the second oval; leave a space of about one-fourth of an inch, and work an oval composed of 4 double stitches, 5 purl, followed each by 2 double stitches, 4 double stitches. A very little farther off make a very small oval, composed of 8 double stitches, which after the four first double stitches is joined to the centre purl of the second oval, leaving the same space between as before, make another oval of 4 double stitches, 5 purl, each followed by 2 double stitches, 4 double stitches ; but the first purl is *missed,* because at this place the oval is joined to the fifth purl of the corresponding oval ; once more leave a space of one-fourth of an inch, and repeat. At the end of the round the two ends of cotton are tied tightly together.

13.—*Tatted Border with Beads.*

Materials: Black purse silk, or, for white trimming, Messrs. Walter Evans and Co.'s tatting cotton No. 2; tatting-pin No. 3; 3 hanks of beads No. 4 to the yard of border.

13.—Tatted Border with Beads.

This border, edged with beads No. 4, is worked in middling-size purse silk over fine silk cord of the same colour as the silk. Before beginning to work this pattern, thread the beads which take the place of purl stitches, and which are slipped in between two double stitches. When the row of stitches is of the length required, form the trefoil leaves, and sew a few beads over the places where they are joined. These trefoil leaves are made separately, and then sewn together.

14.—*Insertion in Tatting.*

Materials: Messrs. Walter Evans and Co.'s crochet cotton No. 10; tatting-pin
No. 3; any sized shuttle; for a finer insertion No. 18 or 20.

14.—Insertion in Tatting.

1st oval : Fill the shuttle, but do not cut it off from the
reel, as a double thread is used, and commence by working 10
double stitches, 1 purl, 10 double, draw up.   Double thread :
Putting the thread attached to the reel round the left hand, work
8 double, 1 purl, 8 double.

2nd oval : 10 double, join to purl of 1st oval, 10 double,
draw up.   Repeat till the length required is worked, then cut off.

For the fresh length, which will make the other half of the
insertion, the shuttle must still be attached to the reel.   Commence by working—

1st oval : 10 double, join to the purl which connects the first
and second ovals of the piece already worked, 10 double, draw
up.   Double thread : 8 double, 1 purl, 8 double.

2nd oval : 10 double, join to the same purl as last—namely,
the one connecting the first and second ovals of the piece already
worked, 10 double, draw up.   Repeat, joining the two next

ovals to the purl which connects the two next in the piece already worked, and so on.

Crochet a heading each side, working 7 chain, 1 double into the purl of double thread, repeat. With a heading on one side only, this makes a pretty wide edging.

15.—*Border in Tatting and Crochet.*

Materials: Messrs. Walter Evans and Co.'s tatting cotton No. 40, and crochet cotton No. 80 ; tatting-pin No. 3.

15.— Border in Tatting and Crochet.

This lace is rendered stronger by the crochet rows of scallops and treble stitch round the edge. Begin with the tatting as follows : Make a circle of 8 double, 7 purl divided by 2 double, 8 double. This circle is repeated at a distance of about three-fourths of an inch, only instead of the 1st purl each following circle must be fastened on to the last purl of the preceding circle. Then take some crochet cotton, which must be finer than the cotton used for tatting, and work a row of double stitches over the thread which joins the circles. The number of stitches depends on the length and size of the cotton ; work double stitches round the circles at the place where both ends meet. The outer row consists of treble stitches, which are worked with 1 chain stitch between, missing 1 stitch under each chain. The scallops consist of the two following rows :—1 double, with which the last and first purl of 2 circles are joined, 4 chain; in each of the other purl, 1 double, 4 chain, between 2 double stitches.

2nd row: 1 double in each chain stitch scallop, 1 double, 3 long double, 1 double.

16 *and* 17.—*Lady's Veil in Net and Tatting.*

This veil is slightly gathered in front and fastened to the brim of the bonnet. It is tied at the back under the chignon. The

16.—Lady's Veil in Net and Tatting.

veil is of black silk net. The flowrets are tatted with black purse silk, and worked in appliqué over the tulle. The veil is edged round with a tatted lace made with the same silk. For the patterns and lace and instructions, see Nos. 18 and 19. No. 16 shows the way in which the veil is worn upon the bonnet, and No. 17 shows its shape when stretched out.

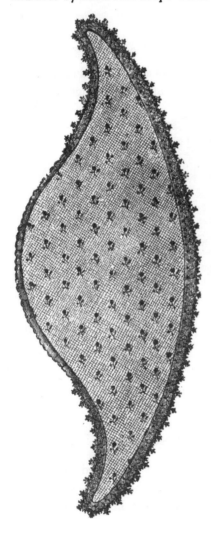

17.—Shape of Veil.

18 *and* 19.—*Patterns in Tatting.*

Materials : Messrs. Walter Evans and Co.'s tatting cotton No. 120 for a white veil; fine black silk for a black veil; tatting-pin No. 2.

18.—Tatting Pattern for Veil (16).

19 —Tatting Pattern for Veil (16).

The patterns Nos. 18 and 19 are meant for ornamenting the veil No. 16. They are sewn upon the net at regular distances.

For working the pattern No. 18, make with black silk or white cotton 6 times alternately 2 double, 1 purl, at the end 1 purl, then join the stitch into a circle, * fasten the silk on to the next purl. Then 1 spot or Josephine knot, consisting of 6 plain stitches, carry the shuttle downwards through the loop, and draw the stitches close together; repeat 3 times more from *. Fasten the silk on to the next purl, and work a circle as follows :—8 times 2 double, divided by 1 purl; fasten the silk on to the next purl, work again 1 spot, after which the silk is fastened, then work 2 more similar circles divided by 1 spot; they are fastened on to the last purl of the preceding circle instead of the 1st purl. Fasten off the silk after the last circle.

For No. 19 work 25 double, divided by 1 purl, join the stitches into a circle, knot the beginning and the end of the cotton together, cut off the ends at a short distance. Then work a smaller circle, consisting of 8 double, divided by 1 purl; at the place of the 1st purl fasten the cotton at a short distance on to the 2nd purl of the large circle. The ends of this circle are knotted together and cut off in the same way. Then work a circle consisting of 11 double, fasten the silk on to the 20th purl of the large circle, work 5 double, and join the stitches into a circle. Then take the ends of the 3 circles, and work close fine stitches with silk round them, so as to form the stem. The completed pattern is sewn upon the net.

20 *and* 21.—*Diamond Pattern and Circle in Tatting, for Trimming Linen Collars, Cuffs, &c.*

Materials: Messrs. Walter Evans and Co.'s tatting cotton No 30; tatting-pin No. 3.

20.—DIAMOND PATTERN.—Work, not far one from the other, four leaves, each composed of 5 double stitches, 7 rather long purl divided one from the other by 2 double stitches, 5 double stitches. Instead of making the 1st purl in each of the 3 next leaves, fasten the cotton to the last leaf of preceding leaf. Fasten off and cut the cotton ; begin a fresh circle by 2 double stitches, 7 purl divided by 2 double stitches, 2 more double stitches ; fasten the cotton to the centre purl of one of the four leaves, and work a very small circle thus :—2 double stitches, fasten the cotton to the last purl of the first circle, 3 double stitches, 1 purl, 2 double stitches ; fasten the cotton * to the 6th purl of the leaf ; work a larger circle thus :—2 double stitches

20.—Diamond in Tatting.

21.—Circle in Tatting.

fastened to the purl of the small circle, 2 double stitches, 4 purl divided by 2 double stitches, 2 more double stitches ; fasten the cotton not far off to the second purl of the second leaf ; work another small circle similar to that above-described ; fasten the cotton to the third purl of the second leaf, then to the fourth purl of the same leaf, and repeat from * three times more, always fastening the first purl of the first circle you are working (each time you repeat the pattern) to the purl of the last small circle last worked ; fasten off and cut the cotton.

21.—CIRCLE.—Begin it in the centre by working a circle of 8 purl, rather long, divided one from the other by 2 double stitches. After you have fastened off and cut the cotton, work * one very small circle composed of 3 double stitches, 1 long purl, 3 double stitches; fasten the cotton not far off to the first purl of the circle, and repeat from * 7 times more, at regular distances. Fasten off and cut the cotton, and begin * a fresh circle of 2 double stitches, 7 purl divided each by 2 double stitches, 2 more double stitches; fasten the cotton to the purl of the very small circle, and work, not far off, a circle of 2 double stitches, 2 purl divided by 2 double stitches, 2 more double stitches; fasten the cotton to the purl of the next small circle, and repeat from * 7 times more. Instead of making the first purl of the next large circle, fasten the cotton to the last purl of the small circle.

22.—*Border in Tatting and Crochet.*

Materials : Messrs. Walter Evans and Co.'s tatting cotton No. 20; tatting-pin No. 3.

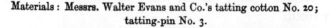

22.—Border in Tatting and Crochet.

Begin this border with one of the smaller circles consisting of * 3 double, 1 purl, 3 double, 1 purl, 3 double; work a large circle at a short distance, 5 double, 4 times 1 purl divided by 2 double, 5 double; close to this circle another as follows :—5 double, fastened on to the last purl of the preceding circle, 5 times 2 double divided by 1 purl, 1 purl, 5 double; a third circle as follows :—5 double fastened on to the last purl of the preceding circle, 3 times 2 double divided by 1 purl, 1 purl, 5 double ; the cotton is fastened a short distance further on to the second purl of the first worked small circle, which must be turned downwards ; then turn the work so that the three circles which are joined together are turned downwards. Work another small circle as follows at the distance of two-fifths of an inch :—4 double, 1 purl, 4 double, leave again an interval of about two-fifths of an inch, and repeat from * till the lace is long enough ; but in working the following figures, consisting of three circles, the 1st circle must be fastened on to the last purl of the 3rd circle at the place of the 1st purl. Complete the tatting with the 2 following rows of crochet :—* 1 slip stitch in the purl of one of the small circles turned upwards, 5 chain, 1 slip stitch in the next purl, 4 chain ; repeat from *. In the following row work 1 double in every stitch.

23.—*Insertion in Tatting and Lace Stitch.*

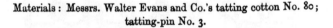

Materials : Messrs. Walter Evans and Co.'s tatting cotton No. 80 ; tatting-pin No. 3.

23.—Insertion in Tatting and Lace Stitch.

This insertion forms a very pretty standing-up collar when worked with fine cotton and a coloured ribbon drawn through. It consists of 2 rows of 3 branched figures turned opposite one

another, which are worked separately and then joined into a row
Work 9 times as follows :—2 double, 1 purl, 2 double, * draw
into a circle and * work at a short distance a 2nd circle as follows :—
2 double fastened on to the last purl of the 1st circle, 8 times 2
double, 1 purl, 2 double, repeat once more from *, knot together the
two ends of the cotton, and fasten them on the wrong side. One
figure is thus completed ; each following figure is fastened on to
the preceding one on the middle purl of a circle (see illustration).
When a sufficient number of such figures have been worked,
work a 2nd row of them in the same manner, and fasten from
illustration each middle circle of one figure on to the corresponding circle of the 1st row.   The circles filled with lace stitch
are worked when the 2 rows are completed from illustration in
the empty places between 4 patterns ; work first 3 double, fasten
them on to a purl on the side of a leaf turned inside, * 3 double,
fasten them on to a purl of the next leaf, repeat 5 times more
from *, work 3 double, join the stitches into a circle, but not too
close, so that the purls keep their natural position ; cut off
the cotton, and fasten the two ends on the wrong side.   The
lace stitch inside of these circles is worked with fine crochet
cotton ; the pattern may be changed for a single or double
wheel.

24 —*Insertion in Tatting.*

Materials : Messrs. Walter Evans and Co.'s tatting cotton No. 3c ;
tatting-pin No. 3.

Begin by working separately a sufficient number of small
rosettes, each composed of six ovals of double stitches and purl.
These ovals are worked first in a straight row, then they are
joined into a circle and united in the centre by button-hole stitches.
The rosettes are joined together with fine cotton.   The crochet

border is then worked on either side in chain stitches and treble crochet, as seen in illustration.

24.—Insertion in Tatting.

25.—*Centre of a Tatted Couvrette.*

Materials : Messrs. Walter Evans and Co.'s tatting cotton No. 20, or crochet cotton No. 1 ; tatting-pin No. 2.

This illustration shows the centre of a tatted couvrette in full size, and measuring 12 inches across. Separate rosettes like the pattern may be joined together with smaller ones, and form a very pretty couvrette. The pattern is worked in rounds. Begin the rosette with a circle, consisting of 4 double, 1 purl, 6 double, 1 purl, 6 double, 1 purl, 4 double. Take up another shuttle, and work over the cotton on it, fasten the end on the last double of the circle and work over it, beginning close to the circle, 6 plain ; 1 circle like the 1st worked with the 1st shuttle, and which is fastened on the last purl of the 1st circle at the place of the 1st purl ; 6 plain, and continue to work so alternately till you have 7 circles divided by 6 plain stitches. Draw up very tightly the cotton over which you work, so that the circles form a rosette, which is closed by sewing together the two corresponding purl of the first an last circle. Both the ends of the cotton over which you have worked are knotted together. For the 2nd round, fasten the cotton on one shuttle on the middle purl of a circle, work a circle like those of the 1st round, take up the 2nd shuttle, and work on exactly as in the 1st round, only work 8

25.—Centre of a Tatted Couvrette.

plain between the circles over the cotton on the 2nd shuttle. The 2nd round consists of 15 circles ; the cotton with which you work must be fastened at the required places on the middle purl of a circle of the preceding round. The 3rd and following rounds are worked in the same manner ; the number of circles must be such as to keep the couvrette quite flat. In the pattern the 3rd round has 26 circles. Fasten the cotton well after each round.

26.—*Tatted Lace.*

Materials: Messrs. Walter Evans and Co.'s tatting cotton No. 30;
tatting-pin No. 2.

26.—Tatted Lace.

This very simple lace consists of scallops which look as if
they were slightly gathered. It must be worked with tatting
cotton. Each scallop consists of 5 plain, 1 purl, 5 plain, then
alternately 5 purled stitches, draw up these stitches till the cotton
between the 1st and last stitch is two-fifths of an inch long,
and work a 2nd similar scallop at a short distance from the
1st. But in the following scallops fasten each to the last purl
of the preceding scallop instead of working the 1st purl.

27.—*Tatted Lace.*

Materials: Messrs. Walter Evans and Co.'s tatting cotton No. 50 or 80;
tatting-pin No. 3.

27.—Tatted Lace.

This pretty lace is worked with fine tatting cotton. Work
with 2 threads; the knots are worked over the cotton, which is
held in the right hand. Work first the outer scallops of the lace

Fasten both ends of cotton together and make 10 double, divided by 1 purl, turn the work so as to turn the wrong side upwards, fasten the cotton over which you work on to the last purl, go back over the same row, miss 1 purl next to the cotton with which you work, 9 double divided by 1 purl, fastening the cotton over which you work on the next purl of the 1st row after every double stitch. This forms 1 scallop. * Turn the work downwards (that is, the purl stitch must be turned downwards), make 4 times 2 double, 1 purl, 1 purled stitch : this is the straight row between 2 outer scallops of the lace. Then work a scallop like the preceding one, fastening it from illustration after the first row on the middle one of the 9 outer purl of the preceding scallop, with the cotton over which you work ; repeat from * till the lace is long enough, and fasten the cotton. Knot both ends together again, fasten the cotton over which you work on the first purl of the first scallop, make 9 double, 1 short purl, 1 double, turn so that the upper edge of the row is turned downwards, and the scallops upwards, 5 double, fasten the 2 middle purl of the 4 of the next straight row together by drawing the cotton, with which you are working through the 2nd purl, so as to form a loop, draw the cotton over which you work through this loop and draw up the latter ; work 5 double, fasten the cotton over which you work on to the short purl worked after 9 double, turn the work so that the outer scallops of the lace are turned downwards, 10 double, fasten the cotton over which you work on the first purl of the next scallop, repeat from *, and fasten the cotton. After having fastened both ends together again, turn the work the right side upwards and the outer scallops upwards also, fasten the cotton over which you work on to the short purl which is under the first loop ; * work 4 times 2 double, 1 purl, 2 double, fasten the cotton over which you work on tne purl under the next loop, and repeat from * till the lace is completed.

28.—*Collar in Tatting and Darned Netting.*

Materials: Messrs. Walter Evans and Co.'s tatting cotton No. 40; tatting-pin No. 3; Messrs. Walter Evans and Co.'s French embroidery cotton No. 60; square netting.

28.—Collar in Tatting and Darned Netting

The pattern is worked with very fine cotton ; the netted grounding over a mesh measuring two-fifths of an inch round. The collar is ornamented round the outer edge with a tatted lace. Work a straight strip of netting for the grounding; begin with 2 stitches, work 18 rows backwards and forwards, increasing 1 at the end of each row, so that the last row has 19 holes ; work 1 row without increasing ; then continue to work with the same number of stitches, increasing 1 at the end of one row and decreasing 1 at the end of the other. When the strip is sufficiently long, work I row again without increasing or decreasing, and form the side by making 18 rows, decreasing I stitch at the end of each, cast off the 2 last stitches on I stitch without forming a new stitch on the needle. Trace the outline of the collar on the grounding with thick cotton, and begin to darn it from illustration. When the darning is completed work the tatted lace with the same cotton, as follows :—6 double, I short purl, alternately, 3 times 3 double, I purl, 6 double, draw up the stitch so as to form a scallop leaving one fifth of an inch between the first and last stitch ; work a second scallop at a short distance from the first, and so on ; every scallop is fastened on to the preceding one after the first 3 double stitches. Work a row of double overcast stitch between the darned netting and the tatted lace ; work this row over the cotton tracing, marking the outline of the collar on the grounding and over the cotton between the tatted scallops. Work also a row of double overcast round the neck part, gathering in the collar a little if necessary. Cut away the netting on the wrong side close to the row of overcast stitches.

29.—*Mignardise and Tatting.*

Materials : Messrs. Walter Evans and Co.'s tatting cotton No. 40 ; fine mignardise braid.

Patterns formed of mignardise and tatting are of quite new style, and look very pretty. The insertion is easy to work by the following process :—Make first a circle, as follows : I plain stitch, 2 double, I purl, 6 double, I purl, 2 double, I plain ; fasten the cotton on to one side of the mignardise, at the distance of about five-eighths of an

29.—Mignardise and Tatting.

inch, by taking 2 loops of it together ; work a second circle at a
short distance from the first, and so on.   When the strip of
insertion is sufficiently long, work in the same manner on the
other side of the mignardise.   This kind of work is destined to
become very popular, and nothing can be more light and graceful
than the union of mignardise and tatting.

30.—*Linen Bag for Cotton.*

Materials : Fine linen, 6 inches square ; Messrs. Walter Evans and Co.'s
tatting cotton No. 40.

30.—Linen Bag for Cotton.

The bag seen in illustration No. 30 is meant to keep the
cotton for working a couvrette ; it consists of a round piece,
measuring 6 inches across, which is hemmed all round, and
trimmed with a tatted lace.   It is drawn together at top.

31.—*Tatting Insertion.*

Materials : Messrs. Walter Evans and Co.'s cotton No. 30.

The insertion shown in illustration No. 31 is composed in
two similar halves.   Begin the first in the following way :— 10

double, 1 purl, 3 double, 1 purl, 10 double, join the stitches into a circle, and work a second similar circle at a distance of one-third of an inch; instead of the 1st purl, draw the cotton through the 2nd purl of the first-worked circle; leave an interval of one-eighth of an inch, and repeat the two rounds till

31.—Tatting Insertion.

the insertion is sufficiently long. Then tat round the pieces of cotton which join the two rounds, work round the longest 10 double, and round the shortest 4 double, inserting the shuttle alternately once upwards and once downwards, but for the rest proceeding as in the common button-hole stitch. When the first half is completed, work the second in the same way, and fasten it on to the first with the purl.

32.—*Tatting Insertion.*

Materials: Messrs. Walter Evans and Co.'s cotton No. 30.

32.—Tatting Insertion.

The pretty effect of the insertion shown in illustration No. 32 is obtained by means of longer and shorter purl. Work as follows :—Join 9 double into a circle, 1 long purl, 3 double, 1 long purl, 4 double *. After an interval of five-eighths of an inch, begin the large figure of the pattern : 2 double, 1 small purl, 2 double, draw the cotton through the last purl of the small circle, 2 double, drawn through the 1st purl of the same circle, 2 double, 1 small purl, 2 double, 1 long purl, 2 double, 1 small purl, 2 double, repeat 6 times more from *, and draw up. After an interval of five-eighths of an inch comes another small circle : 4 double, draw the cotton through the last purl of the large figure, 3 double, draw the cotton through the next long purl of the same figure, 2 double, 1 long purl, 3 double, 1 long purl, 4 double. Repeat the pattern for the length of insertion required. The threads which join the small circles are worked over with 7 double in the manner described above, only the cotton at the principal figure must be left loose the width of a straw, so as to imitate a long purl. Complete the insertion from illustration by tatting round the small circles of 16 double on the other side (but in the contrary direction), form no purl, but draw the cotton through the long purl of the large figure ; the threads which join the 2 circles are likewise drawn through the middle long purl of the large figure ; this thread is then tatted over with 7 double, like the opposite outer edge.

33.—*Tatted Square or Diamond..*

Materials : If for couvrettes, Messrs. Walter Evans and Co.'s tatting cotton No. 20, or crochet cotton No. 4 ; tatting-pin No. 3. For d'oyleys, tatting cotton No. 50 ; tatting-pin No. 2. For headdresses, tatting cotton No. 80 ; tatting-pin No. 2.

The square is composed first of nine 4-branched patterns, worked in 3 rows of 3 patterns each, and joined on one to the other with purl. Each pattern consists of 4 branches close to each other, and each branch consists of 7 double, 1 purl, 7 double ; when the 4 branches of one pattern are completed, cut off the cotton, and fasten both ends together so as to form a small circle in the centre. Then work a second pattern, which is fastened on to the first and second branches of the first pattern, instead of working the purl stitch; work a third pattern, which is fastened in the same manner on to the second pattern. Then work 2 more rows exactly the same as can be seen in illustration.

33.—Tatted Square.

* For the border of the square, fasten the cotton on the first purl of the first pattern, work 4 double, 13 purl divided by 2 double, 4 double, draw up the stitches close, fasten the cotton again on to the same purl of the first pattern *, and work the following scallop at a short distance:—4 double fastened on the last purl of the preceding circle, 10 purl divided by 2 double, 4 double, draw up the stitch, leaving an interval of two-fifths of an inch between the first and the last; fasten the cotton on to the next purl which joins two patterns, repeat twice more from *, and continue to repeat from *.

34.—*Tatted Rosette.*

Materials : Messrs. Walter Evans and Co.'s tatting cotton No. 40, or crochet
cotton No. 60.

34.—Tatted Rosette.

This rosette is very pretty for trimming *lingeries* ; it is worked with very fine crochet or tatting cotton. Begin in the centre and work one circle : 16 times alternately 2 double, 1 purl, then 1 purled stitch. Fasten the cotton on to the first purl and work the 2nd round : 1 small circle, consisting of 6 double divided by 1 purl. Fasten the cotton on to the next purl of the middle circle, and repeat in rounds. 3rd round : Fasten the cotton on the middle purl of the first circle of the preceding round, * work at a short distance 8 double divided by 1 purl, join the stitches into a circle, fasten the cotton at the same distance on to the middle purl of the next circle of the preceding round, and repeat in rounds from *, after which the cotton is fastened off.

35.—*Rosette in Tatting.*

Materials : Messrs. Walter Evans and Co.'s tatting cotton No. 40 ;
tatting-pin No. 3.

35.—Rosette in Tatting.

Begin this rosette with the circle in the centre, and work 8 times alternately 2 double, 1 purl, 1 double, join the stitches into a circle and fasten the cotton. Take a second shuttle and work over the cotton on this shuttle ; knot the two ends of cotton together * and work 5 plain, fasten the cotton over which you work on a purl of the circle which is completed, and which must be turned downwards; 5 plain, 1 purl; repeat 7 times more from *, and fasten the cotton. Work now with one of the shuttles the small circles on the outside; * fasten the cotton on to a purl of the second round, and work a circle as follows :—6 double, 1 purl, 6 double, fasten the cotton on to the same purl of the second round, work a similar circle at a short distance, and a third at the same distance. Repeat 7 times more from *, and fasten off the cotton neatly.

36.—*Diamond in Tatting.*

Materials : Messrs. Walter Evans and Co.'s tatting cotton No. 40; tatting-pin No. 2.

36.—Diamond in Tatting.

This diamond is suitable for trimming collars, cuffs, &c., when worked with fine cotton. Work first the four corner patterns separately, as follows :—7 double, 3 purl divided by 3

D

double, 6 double, join the stitches into a circle, work close to
this circle a second one consisting of 6 double fastened on the
last purl of the 1st circle, 4 double, 2 purl divided by 4 double,
6 double; then a 3rd circle consisting of 6 double fastened on
the last purl of the preceding circle, 3 double, 2 purl divided by
3 double, 7 double. Take a second shuttle, fasten the cotton on
the end of the cotton of the 1st circle, throw the cotton of the
1st shuttle over the fingers of the left hand, and work with this
cotton over the cotton on the other shuttle in the right hand.
Work 5 double, and then one circle as follows with the cotton in
the left hand only :—8 double fastened on the last purl of the
3rd of the 3 circles worked close to each other, 5 double, 1 purl,
5 double, 1 purl, 4 double, 1 purl, 6 double, then again over the
cotton on the other shuttle, 5 double, 4 purl divided by 5 double,
5 double, then with one shuttle only one circle as follows :—6
double, 1 purl, 4 double, 1 purl, 5 double, 1 purl, 5 double
fastened on 1st purl of the circle worked at the beginning, 8
double; then again with two shuttles 5 double. Fasten the
cotton on the piece of cotton before the 5 double worked with
two shuttles, so that the stitches worked over two shuttles form
a circle, and cut off the cotton. When three of these patterns
have been worked, work the centre pattern of the square. It
consists of 4 leaves touching each other at the lower points ; each
leaf is formed of 3 double, 5 purl divided by 3 double, 3 double ;
each following leaf is fastened on to the preceding one at the
place of the 1st purl. Then work first 1 round of the oval circles
of the square, with which the corner patterns are joined. Fasten
the cotton on one purl of one corner pattern, make 7 double, 1
purl, 8 double ; fasten on the corresponding purl of another
corner pattern, work 8 double, 1 purl, 7 double, join the stitches
into a circle, fasten the cotton on to the same purl to which the

cotton has already been fastened, carry the latter on to the next purl of the same corner pattern, fasten it, then work three more circles like the first, which are fastened on to each preceding circle, at the place of the first purl ; fasten the cotton on the two cross purl of the centre pattern, and work four similar circles on the other side of the same. The 8 circles which go across the square in the opposite direction are worked in the same manner. When the square is completed, draw two threads on each side of each corner pattern on to the other side of the square along the cotton which joins the circles together.

37.—*Tatting for Cap Crown.*

Materials : Messrs. Walter Evans and Co.'s tatting cotton No. 100 ; tatting-pin No. 1.

This pattern is very pretty for the crown of a cap like the one described on page 36, and also for covers, toilet cushions, &c. The size of the cotton depends upon the use you

37.—Tatting for Cap Crown.

wish to make of the pattern. The pattern is worked with fine tatting cotton. It consists of eight-branched rosettes joined together with small circles. Each rosette is worked as follows : Work 8 loops or branches close to each other, consisting of 7

double, 1 purl, 7 double ; fasten both ends of the cotton
together, and cut them off. Each of the small circles which joins
the rosettes together consists of 2 double, 8 purl divided by 2
double.   It is easy to see from the illustration how the patterns
are joined together by means of the purl stitches

38 and 39.—Cap in Tatting.

Materials : Messrs. Walter Evans and Co.'s tatting cotton No. 100
tatting-pin No. 1.

38.—Cap in Tatting.

This very pretty cap consists of an oval crown in tatting, edged all round with a tatted lace ; the lappets are made in tatting also. The cap is trimmed with large and small rosettes of narrow blue velvet. A narrow velvet ribbon is drawn through the straight open-work edge of the lace, as can be seen in illustration.

39—Border for Cap No. 38.

No. 39.—Border for Cap.—The upper part of the border consists of 4 rows of circles worked at a distance of three-fifths of an inch from each other. The circles of the 1st row consist of 3 double, 3 purl divided by 3 double, 3 double. In the following 3 rows each circle is fastened on to the cotton, which joins 2 circles in the 1st row, instead of working the middle purl, the cotton between 2 circles in the last row must only be two-fifths of an inch long. Then work a certain number of six-branched rosettes, each branch consisting of 9 double, 1 purl, 9 double. Each rosette is fastened on to every other circle of the

1st row, as can be seen in illustration.   The border is completed
as follows :—* 1 double, 6 purl divided by 1 double, 1 purled
stitch fastened on to the middle purl of a circle of the 1st row,
1 plain, 6 purl divided by 1 double, join the stitch into a circle,
turn the lace so that the rosettes are turned upwards, fasten the
cotton on to the purl of the next branch of the next rosette, work
1 double, 7 purl divided by 1 double, 1 double; fasten the
cotton on to the purl of the next branch, * work 1 double, 8 purl
divided by 1 double, 1 double ; fasten the cotton on to the next
branch, repeat once more from *, work 1 double, 7 purl divided
by 1 double, 1 double, and repeat from * to the end of the lace.

40.—*Lace in Tatting and Crochet.*

Materials : Messrs. Walter Evans and Co.'s tatting cotton No. 50;
tatting-pin No. 2 ; crochet cotton No. 60.

40.—Lace in Tatting and Crochet.

The beauty of this lace depends entirely upon the regularity
of the tatting.   The purl stitches must be very regularly made,
the circles must be drawn up tight.   Make * 1 circle, consisting
of 4 double, 8 purl divided by 2 double, 4 double ; close to
this circle a second one ; 5 double fastened on the last purl of
the preceding circle, 8 times 2 double divided by 1 purl, 1 purl

5 double, close to the 2nd circle a third one similar to the first, but instead of working the 1st purl fasten it on the last purl of the preceding circle ; leave an interval of about $1\frac{2}{5}$ inch, and repeat from * till the lace is sufficiently long. The rest is worked in crochet. Take the fine crochet cotton and work the straight row at the top to join the patterns together. Crochet 1 double in the 3 first and last purl of the first and last circle of one pattern, then a sufficient number of double stitches under the piece of cotton which joins 2 circles. At the place where the circles are drawn together, join the two pieces of cotton (the beginning and the end) in such a manner that the top of the lace forms a straight line (see illustration). The 2nd row consists of 1 treble in every other stitch, 1 chain after every treble. Then work on the other side of the lace * a row of treble stitches divided by chain. The treble stitches are worked in the purl stitches of the circles. Work 1 long treble in the 1st purl left free of the 1st circle (4th purl of the circle), 3 chain, * 1 treble, 3 chain, 1 treble, 3 chain, 2 treble in the next 2 purl, but cast off the 1st treble only so far as to keep 2 loops on the needle. When the 2nd treble is completed cast off all the loops on the needle, 3 chain, 5 treble divided by 4 chain, 3 chain, 2 treble in the 2 following purl, which are cast off like those above described, 3 chain, 2 treble divided by 3 chain in the 2 next purl of a pattern, 1 chain, 1 long treble with which you must join the last purl and the first one of the next pattern, 1 chain ; repeat from *. The next row consists of small scallops worked round the chain stitch scallops of the preceding row ; work in each 1 double, 4 treble, 1 double, 1 double in the first and last chain stitch of every pattern.

41.—*Insertion in Tatting and Crochet.*

Materials : Messrs. Walter Evans and Co.'s tatting cotton No. 40;
crochet cotton No. 60 ; tatting-pin No. 2.

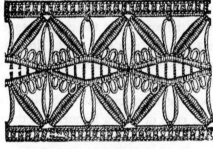

41.—Insertion in Tatting and Crochet.

Begin the tatting with fine cotton and 2 shuttles.
Work with the cotton on one shuttle over the cotton on the
other in the following manner :—Knot the 2 ends of cotton
together * 4 times 2 double divided by a short purl, 3 long purl
divided by 1 double ; the 1st and 3rd purl must be three-fifths of
an inch long, the 2nd one two-fifths of an inch ; 4 times 2 double
divided by a short purl, 1 purl two-fifths of an inch long ; repeat
from * till the strip of insertion is sufficiently long.   Then work
a similar row of tatting, and join the two rows before working
the 1 long purl, by fastening the cotton on the corresponding
long purl of the 1st row, so that the 2 rows are joined closely
together, and the purl stitches of either are turned outwards.
At the top and bottom of the tatting work the 3 following
rows of crochet :—* 1 double in the middle one of the 3 long
purl, 8 chain, 1 double in each of the 3 following long purl, 8
chain ; repeat from * to the end of the row. 2nd row . 8 double
in each scallop, miss the 3 double stitches of the preceding row
under 3 chain.   The 3rd row consists of treble stitches in every

other stitch, 1 chain after every treble. Lastly, the leaves are worked with thick cotton by filling up the first and last long purl of a pattern with darning stitch from illustration; the cross stitches between the two rows of tatting are worked with very fine cotton.

42.—*Purse in Tatting and Beads.*

Materials: Grey purse-silk; steel beads; scarlet glacé silk; a steel clasp with chain.

This purse is worked in tatting with grey silk and beads. The beads are threaded on a piece of silk, with which you work over another piece of the same. Begin each of the second halves of the purse with the circle in the centre, which consists of 1 purled stitch, 1 purl (all the purl of this circle are three-tenths of an inch long, and are covered with six beads, which must be drawn up close together before working the purl), 12 double divided by 1 purl. Join the stitches into a circle by knotting together the two ends of the silk.

2nd round: Begin again and work one of the small circles; * 2 double, draw up one bead after each, 1 double, 1 short purl without beads, 2 double, 1 bead after each, 1 double, fasten the silk on the purl of the middle circle, so as to let it come between the 3rd and 4th bead of the 6 beads on that purl; 2 double, 1 bead after each, 1 double, 1 short purl, 2 double, 1 bead after each, 1 double, join the stitches into a circle; draw up 2 beads; work a larger circle without fastening the silk belonging to the smaller one; 3 double, 1 bead after each, 1 double, 1 purl with 4 beads, 3 double, 1 bead after each, 1 double; 1 short purl, 3 double, 1 bead after each, 1 double, 1 purl with 4 beads, 3 double, 1 bead after each, 1 double; draw up 2 beads close to this large circle and repeat from *. Each following small circle must be fastened on the next purl of the circle which forms the centre; they are also fastened on to each other, instead of working the 1st purl, by fastening the piece of silk

42.—Purse in Tatting and Beads.

over which you work on the preceding small circle; in the larger circles, instead of working the 1st purl with 4 beads, the piece of silk must be fastened on the last purl of the preceding circle, so that it comes between the 2nd and 3rd beads. At the end of the round, the ends of the silk are knotted together and fastened off.

3rd round: * 3 double, 1 bead after each, 1 double, 1 short purl, 3 double, 1 bead after each, 1 double fastened on the middle purl of the 1st circle of the preceding round, 3 double, 1 bead after each, 1 double, 1 purl with 2 beads, 3 double, 1 bead after each, 1 double ; join the stitches into a circle, and work at a short distance a 2nd circle ; 3 double, 1 bead after each, 1 double, fastened on the last purl of the just-finished circle of this round, 3 double, 1 bead after each, 1 double fastened on the purl of the preceding round which is between 2 circles ; the loop must come between the 2 beads ; 3 double, 1 bead after each ; 1 double, 1 purl with 2 beads ; 3 double, with 1 bead after each ; 1 double ; leave a small interval, and repeat 11 times more from *, then fasten the ends.

When two similar parts have been worked, line them with scarlet glacé silk ; fasten them together round the outside, and sew on the clasp. A round of large circles edges the purse round the outside. The 1st of these circles consists of 12 double, 1 bead after each, 1 double, 1 purl with 2 beads, 4 double, 1 bead after each, 1 double. Work a 2nd circle at a short distance from the 1st : * 4 double, 1 bead after each, 1 double fastened on the purl of the 1st circle of this round ; 7 double, 1 bead after each, 1 double, 1 purl with 2 beads, 4 double, 1 bead after each, 1 double ; leave a short interval, and repeat from * till a sufficient number of circles have been made. The last purl is not worked in the last circle.

43.—*Insertion in Tatting and Crochet.*

Materials: Messrs. Walter Evans and Co.'s tatting cotton No. 40; crochet cotton
No. 60; tatting-pin No. 3.

43.—Insertion in Tatting and Crochet.

This pattern is composed of leaves and flowers.   Each of the
six leaves forming a circle is composed of 4 double, 2 purl,
separated by 2 double, 4 double (the first and last purl of each
leaf must be joined in the manner before explained), and the
centre of each circle forms a wheel.   The flower has four leaves ;
each leaf consists of 6 double, 11 purl, separated each by 1
double, and again 6 double ; each leaf is filled up with button-
hole stitches in fine cotton.   To form the circle in the centre of
this flower, turn several times the thread which joins the leaves,
and work button-hole stitches round it.   Join the flowers and
the circles by knotting them together, or by making 1 purl longer
than the others, and by drawing the next figure through.   The
crochet border on each side of the tatting consists of six rows,
which are plainly seen in the illustration.

44.—*Border in Tatting and Lace Stitch.*

Materials : Messrs. Walter Evans and Co.'s tatting cotton No. 20 and 40.

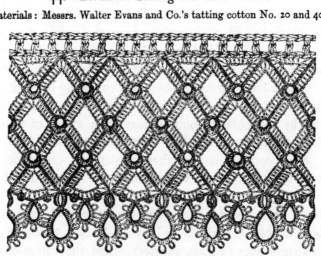

44.—Border in Tatting and Lace Stitch.

This mixture of tatting and lace stitch is a style of work not only entirely new, but very pretty and effective when cotton of very different sizes is used. The tatting is begun with a row of circles two-thirds of an inch distant from each other ; each circle consists of 13 stitches of plain tatting. Fasten a 2nd row to the 1st, and a 3rd to the 2nd, by working a circle of 13 stitches of plain tatting at one-third of an inch distance, * then at the same distance ; fasten the cotton on the next circle of the preceding row, work a circle at the same distance again, and repeat from *. The cotton is fastened on the circles by drawing it through the circle with a crochet-needle, so as to form a loop, and then drawing it out of the loop. Take care to keep the distance between 2 circles always the same. Between the circles of the 3rd row draw another piece of cotton, by fastening the cotton on each circle of the 3rd row at distances of two-thirds of an inch. Then work the lower edge of the border in the following way :—1 small spot called a *Josephine knot* (for which work 5 stitches of plain tatting, draw the cotton downwards through the loop which fastens the stitches, and draw up the whole), fasten the cotton between the next two circles of the 3rd row, * and a little further make a spot consisting of 8 stitches of single tatting, close to this a circle formed of 3 double, 9 purl divided by 2 double, 3 double ; then again a spot of 8 stitches of plain tatting, turn the 2 last spots so as to make their round sides come opposite one another ; fasten the cotton on again between the 2 next circles of the 3rd row. Then a little further off work 1 small spot (5 stitches of plain tatting), 1 circle of 3 double, 1 purl, 2 double fastened on the last purl of the preceding circle, 2 double, 5 purl divided by 2 double, 3 double ; then again a small spot (5 plain stitches), fasten the cotton on again between the next 2 circles of the 3rd row, and repeat from *, always fastening each new circle to the corresponding purl of the preceding one. On the other long side, the border is completed by 2 rows of crochet. The 1st row is formed by working 1 double under the piece of cotton between 2 circles of the 1st row, with 5 chain stitches between.

2nd row : 1 treble in every other stitch, 1 chain stitch after every treble. The strip of insertion is then tacked on a piece of cardboard or oil-cloth, and the lace stitches are worked between the circles, as is seen in illustration.

45.—*Tatted Rosette.*

Materials : Messrs. Walter Evans and Co.'s tatting cotton No. 30 for large rosette, No. 80 for small rosette ; tatting-pin No. 3.

This rosette forms a very pretty trimming for lingerie—cravats, caps, handkerchiefs, &c. The raised pattern in the centre consists of 4 rounds, consisting of 5 circles each, which are sewn together and then fastened on the rosette. The 5 circles of each round must be worked close to each other : after working the last circle of each round, knot the beginning and end of the cotton together. Each circle of the smallest round has 9 double, the circles of the next round each 15, the circles of the following one 21, and the circles of the last and largest round 27

45.—Tatted Rosette.

double stitches. When these circles have been sewn on one to another as in illustration, work a large circle consisting of 4 double, 1 purl, 9 times alternately 5 double, 1 purl, then 1 double. The purls of this circle are fastened on to the circles of the next round of the rosette. Fasten the cotton on to the next purl of the middle circle, and work a circle as follows :—4 double, 1 purl, 4 double, 1 purl, 3 double, 1 purl, 3 double, 1 purl, 4 double, 1 purl, 4 double. Repeat 9 times more from *, but now, instead of working the 1st purl of every circle, fasten it on to the last purl of the preceding circle. Then fasten the cotton. For the last round, which consists of scallops and rounds, fasten the cotton on to the middle purl of a circle of the preceding round, and work a circle consisting of 3 times alternately 4 double, 1

purl, then 4 double.   Then fasten a second thread on to the
same purl on which the just completed circle has been fastened,
and over which all the scallops are to be worked.   Work over it
5 double, fastened on to the last purl of the preceding circle, 4
double, 1 purl, 4 double, 1 purl, 5 double.   Fasten the cotton
on to the middle purl of the next circle of the preceding round,
and repeat from * till the round is completed ; but in working
these circles, instead of the first purl, fasten them on to the last
purl of the preceding scallop.   Lastly, the raised pattern is
sewn on.

46.—*Linen Bag for Tatting, &c.*

Materials : Fine linen; Messrs. Walter Evans and Co.'s tatting cotton No. 30
or 40 ; tatting-pin No. 2.

46.—Linen Bag for Tatting, &c.

   This pretty linen bag is meant to keep tatting and such work
from being soiled before it is completed.   The bag is drawn
together round the top.   Its size depends upon what you wish to

put into it. The original pattern is 3¾ inches deep, and 3 inches wide; it is hemmed round the top, and trimmed with a narrow tatted lace, consisting of large and small circles.

47.—*Tatted Border.*

Materials: Messrs. Walter Evans and Co.'s tatting cotton No. 40; tatting-pin No. 2.

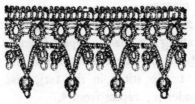

47.—Tatted Border.

Begin this elegant border with 2 rows of tatting, in the following manner :—

1st row : 2 double, 1 purl, 3 double, 1 purl, 3 double, 1 purl, 2 double ; draw these stitches up into a circle, and repeat the circle at a very short distance, till the border is long enough ; but instead of working the first purl of each circle, you must join the circle to the preceding one ; the purl on the sides of the circle must therefore be longer than that in the middle.

For the 2nd row take another shuttle, make a loop on the left side with the cotton, and work with this end of cotton over the cotton in the right hand, which is also to be held between the thumb and forefinger of the left hand. Then work in the following way :—2 double, then 1 circle consisting of 3 double, 1 purl, 3 double ; to form this circle, let the cotton in the left-hand shuttle fall downwards, and make a loop round the left hand with the cotton on the shuttle of the right hand. Then take up again the left-hand shuttle, and join the circle to the middle purl of the 1st circle of the 1st row by drawing the cotton through the purl like a loop, and then drawing the cotton in the right hand through this loop. * 7 double, 1 circle, 7 double, joined to the middle purl of the next circle of the 1st row; 1 circle, 5 double, 1 circle joined on the middle purl of the following circle; repeat from *.

The upper edge of the border is worked in 2 crochet rows, in the following manner :—

1st row : * 2 treble, divided by 1 chain in the 1st circle of the 1st row of tatting; 2 chain; repeat from *.

2nd row : * 1 treble in the 1st chain of the preceding row, 1 purl (3 chain, 1 slip stitch in the 1st), miss 1 stitch of the preceding row under it; repeat from *.

48.—*Rosette in Embroidery and Tatting.*

Materials for trimmings: Messrs. Walter Evans and Co.'s knitting cotton No. 20; tatting cotton No. 50; tatting-pin No. 3. For couvrettes, crochet cotton No. 4.

This rosette, joined to other similar ones, forms a very pretty trimming for articles of fine linen, or even for small couvrettes; if used for the former, they must be worked with very fine cotton. The centre of the rosette is formed of an embroidered raised pattern worked in *point de minute;* round this centre there are small circles worked in button-hole stitch; the embroidery is worked with knitting cotton, the circles with crochet cotton. Before beginning the circles, make a circle consisting of a foundation chain of 80 stitches, in order to be able to fasten the button-hole stitch; in each of the stitches of the foundation chain work 1 double, then fasten the cotton. In the 2nd round of these circles fasten the cotton on every 5th stitch of the crochet circle. Work 1 round of open-work treble stitch in the double stitch of the crochet circle, work in tatting the border of the rosette as follows in 1 round :—* 2 double, 1 purl, 2 double, fastened on to 1 chain stitch between 2 treble stitch, 2 double ; 1 purl, 2 double, ; join these stitches into a circle ; turn the work so that the wrong side

48.—Rosette in Embroidery and Tatting.

lies upwards, and work a second larger circle at a short distance consisting of 4 double, 5 purl divided by 2 double, 4 double, turn again and repeat from *. The smaller circles must be fastened after every other treble stitch ; the larger and smaller circles must be fastened above one another at the place of the 1st purl.

49.—*Linen Collar trimmed with Tatting.*

Materials : Messrs. Walter Evans and Co 's tatting cotton No. 60 ; tatting-pin No. 2.

The diamond pattern placed in the corner of the collar is commenced in the centre. For each of the four centre leaves work 6 double stitches, 6 purl divided one from the other by 3 double stitches, then 6 more double stitches. Fasten off the

49.—Linen Collar trimmed with Tatting.

cotton, cut it, and begin a fresh leaf by working 2 double stitches,

10 purl divided one from the other by 2 double stitches, then 2 more double stitches. (This small leaf forms one of the corners of the diamond pattern.) Fasten the cotton to the fourth purl of one of the four centre leaves, and work another leaf similar to the preceding. Join this leaf by its two centre purl to the two last purl of the corner leaf (see illustration). After two more similar leaves, work one corner leaf, and continue the pattern in the same manner until you come back to the first corner leaf, then fasten off, and cut the cotton. Place the diamond pattern upon the point of the collar, and cut away the material under it ; fold back the edges, sew them neatly, and cover them with the following crochet edging :—Make alternately 2 chain, 1 purl (the latter composed of 3 chain joined together by 1 slip stitch). It will be easy to work the circles in tatting from our illustration ; they form an elegant border round the collar. We shall merely say that the centre circle is always worked separately, and that the cotton is fastened on afresh to work the eight outer leaves. The upper edge of this border is worked in crochet. It is composed of two rows—one formed of chain stitches, and a few slip stitches worked in the purl of the circles in tatting, the other worked in open treble crochet.

50.—*Cravat in Cambric Muslin and Tatting.*

Materials : Messrs. Walter Evans and Co.'s tatting cotton No. 100;
tatting-pin No. 3.

This cravat consists of a strip of cambric muslin 1 yard long, 6 inches wide, hemmed on both sides. The ends of the cravat are ornamented with patterns in tatting, worked with tatting cotton No. 100. A rosette in tatting is sewn on in the middle of the end of the cravat. The end of the cravat is pointed, lined on the wrong side with a strip of the same material as the cravat, and edged with a tatted lace. Begin the rosette in the centre with a circle worked in the following manner.—I double, I purl, * twice 2 double divided by I purl, I purl, 3 double, I purl, twice

50.—Cravat in Muslin and Tatting.

4 double divided by I purl, I purl, * 3 double, I purl; repeat from * to * once more, 2 double. At the beginning of the 2nd round fasten the cotton on the Ist purl of the Ist round, and

work as follows :—* I circle consisting of 10 double, 1 purl, 2 double, 1 purl, 10 double ; fasten the cotton on to the next purl, 1 circle like the preceding one, fastened on to the next purl, 1 circle consisting of 9 double, 1 purl, 9 double fastened on to the next purl, 2 circles consisting each of 7 double, 1 purl, 7 double ; between the 2 fasten the cotton on to the next purl ; 2 similar circles fastened also on to the next purl, 1 circle consisting of 8 double, 1 purl, 8 double, fastened on to the next circle ; repeat once more from *, and fasten off the cotton. Fasten on the cotton afresh for the 3rd round, worked in the following manner :—* 1 circle consisting of 6 double, 1 purl, 5 double, 1 purl, 6 times 2 double divided by 1 purl ; 1 purl, 5 double, 1 purl, 6 double ; fasten the cotton at a short distance on to the 1st purl of the 2nd round, 1 circle worked as follows :—5 double fastened on to the last purl of the preceding circle of this round, 4 double, 1 purl, 4 times 2 double divided by 1 purl, 1 purl, 4 double, 1 purl, 5 double fastened on to the next purl of the 2nd circle of the 2nd round ; 6 similar circles, between each of which the cotton is to be fastened on to the nearest purl of a circle of the 2nd round ; repeat once more from *, and knot the beginning and the end of the cotton together. When completed, the rosette is sewn on the material of the cravat with button-hole stitches, taking up one purl with each stitch ; the muslin is cut away underneath the rosette ; then work a round of knotted stitches underneath the button-hole stitch. For the lace, make a row of circles one-fifth of an inch distant from each other, consisting each of 6 double, 1 purl, 2 double, 1 purl, 4 times 2 double divided by 1 purl, 1 purl, 2 double, 1 purl, 6 double, which are fastened together by the purl of each circle, and are sewn on the cravat over the cotton between the circles in overcast stitch.

51.—*Cravat in Cambric Muslin and Tatting.*

Materials: Messrs. Walter Evans and Co.'s tatting cotton No. 100;
tatting-pin No. 3.

51,—Cravat in Muslin and Tatting.

The end of this cravat is formed by a long rosette or
médaillon in tatting. This rosette is likewise begun in the centre,
and consists of 4 rounds, the 2 first of which are worked like

those of the rosette in illustration 50, with this difference only, that in the 2nd round each of the circles nearest to the top and to the bottom of the rosette consists of 8 double, 1 purl, 2 double, 1 purl, 8 double. 3rd round : * 1 circle, consisting of 6 double, 1 purl, 5 double, 1 purl, 6 times 2 double divided by 1 purl, 1 purl, 5 double, 1 purl, 6 double, fastened on to the next purl of the 2nd circle of the preceding round ; 1 circle as follows :—5 double, the last of which is fastened on to the last purl of the preceding round, 4 double, 1 purl, twice 2 double divided by 1 purl, 1 purl, 4 double, 1 purl, 5 double fastened on the next purl of the preceding round ; 8 more similar circles, between each of which the cotton is fastened on to the next purl of the preceding round ; repeat from * once more, fasten the two ends of the cotton together. 4th round : * Fasten on the cotton afresh with a circle consisting of 7 double, 1 purl, 4 double, 1 purl, 6 times 2 double divided by 1 purl, 1 purl, 4 double, 1 purl, 7 double, fastened on to the middle purl of the 1st circle of the preceding round ; a 2nd circle worked in the same way, only instead of working the last purl, fasten the cotton on to the last purl of the preceding circle, then on to the 1st circle of the preceding round ; 10 more similar circles, between each of which the cotton is fastened on to the middle purl of a circle of the preceding round, and then on to the 2nd purl of the larger circle at the bottom of the medallion ; repeat once more from *. The pattern is sewn on the cravat with button-hole stitches, as can be seen in the illustration.

52.—*Border in Crochet and Tatting.*

Materials : Messrs. Walter Evans and Co.'s Boar's Head cotton No. 26.

This border is formed of circles in tatting and crochet leaves, which are joined together by rows of crochet work ; a narrow border in tatting forms the lower edge. Omitting this edge, the border forms a strip of insertion. Each of the rosettes or circles is begun in the centre; work first 2 double (a double stitch is formed by passing the thread over the back of the hand, and then passing the shuttle upwards between the forefinger and second finger, and drawing it up, then work a stitch of plain tatting; this completes the double stitch, and whenever so many double

52.—Border in Crochet and Tatting.

stitches are directed it means the 2 stitches), I purl, repeat 9 times, join the stitch into a circle, work at a small distance * a smaller ring consisting of 3 double, 5 purl, divided each by 2 double stitches, 4 double, draw the cotton through the purl of the first circle, and repeat 8 times more from *, only each following circle must be fastened on to a purl of the preceding circle after 3 double stitches, and having completed each circle the thread must be drawn through the purl of the first circle, which forms the centre of the rosette. The beginning and the end of the thread are knotted together. For the tatted border, make at short distances 1 loop with 5 double, 1 purl, 5 double; after having worked a sufficient number of such loops, wind another thread round the thread between the loops, turning always 1 loop on the right side and 1 on the left. Now begin the crochet part with the leaves. Make for each of these a foundation chain of 12 stitches, crochet back over this chain 2 double in the last stitch but one, 1 double in the next stitch, 1 treble in each of the following 7 chain, 2 treble in the next stitch, 2 treble, 1 long treble, and 2 treble in the next following stitch of the foundation chain. Work on the other side of the chain the same pattern, only the reverse way; then 3 double in the point of the leaf thus formed, and edge the whole leaf with a round of double stitches, always working 2 double in each stitch of the preceding row, and 3 in the long treble stitch. In working this last round, the circles must be joined to the leaves by taking up the purl stitch of the circle before casting off the corresponding double stitch of the leaf; then work the stem which joins the 2 rows of circles and leaves with a row of chain stitches, on which a row of double is worked. Then comes the border which forms the upper edge. Make a row of chain stitches, joining leaves and circles together, then work 3 rows of treble, work 3 more rows over the tatted border, the first row entirely in chain stitches, after every fourth stitch take up the purl of the loops on one side. 2nd row : 1 treble in the middle stitch of the 3 chain, 2 treble, divided by 3 chain. 3rd row : 1 treble, 1 chain, miss 1 under the last. In the last row the leaves and circles must be fastened on the border, as seen in illustration.

53.—*Diamond in Tatting.*

Materials: Messrs. Walter Evans and Co.'s crochet cotton No. 10; tatting-pin
No. 2; any sized shuttle.

53.—Diamond in Tatting.

1st oval : Fill the shuttle, but do not cut it off from the reel,
as a double thread is required, and commence by working 5
double stitches, 1 purl, then (3 double, 1 purl 10 times), 5 double,
draw up.

Double thread : Putting the thread attached to the reel round
the left hand, work 7 single stitches, taking care to do them
tightly.

2nd oval: 4 double, join to the last purl of 1st oval, then (3
double, 1 purl, 5 times) 4 double, draw up.

Double thread ₁ 12 single stitches tightly worked.

3rd oval : 4 double, join to last purl of 2nd oval, 3 double,
join to next purl of 2nd oval, then (3 double, 1 purl 5 times) 4
double, draw up.

Double thread : 12 single stitches.

4th oval : 4 double, join to last purl of last oval, 3 double, join to next purl, then (3 double, 1 purl, 8 times) 4 double, draw up.

Double thread : 12 single stitches.

5th oval : 4 double, join to last purl of last oval, 3 double, join to next purl, then (3 double, 1 purl, 5 times) 4 double, draw up.

Double thread : 12 single stitches.

6th oval : 4 double, join to last purl of last oval, 3 double, join to next purl, then (3 double, 1 purl, 4 times) 4 double, draw up.

Double thread : 7 single stitches.

7th oval : 5 double, join to last purl of last oval, then (3. double, 1 purl, 10 times) 5 double, draw up.

Double thread : 7 single stitches.

8th oval : 4 double, join to last purl of last oval, then (3 double, 1 purl, 5 times) 4 double, draw up.

Double thread : 12 single stitches.

9th oval ; 4 double, join to last purl of last oval, 3 double, join to next purl then (3 double, 1 purl, 5 times) 4 double, draw up.

Double thread : 12 single stitches.

10th oval : 4 double, join to last purl of last oval, 3 double, join to next purl, then (3 double, 1 purl, 8 times) 4 double, draw up.

Double thread : 12 single stitches.

11th oval : 4 double, join to last purl of last oval, 3 double, join to next purl, then (3 double, 1 purl, 5 times) 4 double, draw up.

Double thread : 12 single stitches.

12th oval : 4 double, join to last purl of last oval, 3 double, join to next purl, then (3 double, 1 purl, 3 times) 3 double, join to 1st purl of 1st oval, 4 double, draw up.

Double thread : 7 single stitches.

Now cut off both threads, and with a needle fasten off neatly at the back of first oval by sewing 1 thread over the other.

The diamond is now finished. The centre must be filled up with lacework, using fine sewing-cotton.

Arranged in groups of 7 or 8, 3 diamonds form a very pretty trimming for the skirts of silk dresses, the body being trimmed with single diamonds.

54.—*Linen Collar trimmed with Tatting.*

Materials : Messrs. Walter Evans and Co.'s tatting cotton No. 100, tatting-pin No. 3 ; 1 piece of very fine cord.

This collar is ornamented with a triangle and a border of a very effective pattern. The triangle is begun in the centre, by working for each of the three leaves 5 double stitches, 5 purl divided one from the other by 2 double stitches, and 5 more double stitches. When the third leaf is completed, fasten off and cut the cotton. Now take, instead of the cotton wound upon the shuttle, a piece of extremely fine cord, over which work with the cotton from the reel the following row of stitches :—1 double stitch, fasten the cotton to the centre purl of one of the three leaves, * 2 double stitches, 5 purl divided one from the other by 2 double stitches, 3 double stitches, fasten the cotton to the centre purl of the nearest leaf, 2 double stitches, 9 purl divided one from the other by 3 double stitches, 2 double stitches fastened to the same purl as before. Repeat from * twice more, then fasten off, and cut the cord and the cotton. Begin afresh, and work 3 small circles, each composed of 12 plain stitches placed quite close together (these form one of the corners of the triangle), then at

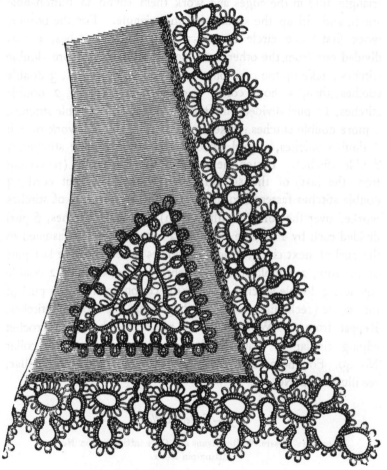

54.—Linen Collar trimmed with Tatting.

small distances one from the other work 13 similar circles, every second one of which is fastened to one purl of the row of

stitches worked over the cord (see illustration). Cut away from
the collar the piece of linen which is to be replaced by the
triangle, fold in the edges and work them round in button-hole
stitch, and fill up the space with the triangle. For the border,
work first * one circle composed of 3 double stitches, 4 purl
divided one from the other by 2 double stitches, 3 more double
stitches; take up the cord once more and work over it, 3 double
stitches, then, without cord, 1 circle composed of 2 double
stitches, 12 purl divided one from the other by 2 double stitches,
2 more double stitches; take up the cord again and work over it
3 double stitches, 4 purl divided each by 2 double stitches, 3
double stitches. Fasten the cotton to the third purl (reckoning
from the last) of the second circle worked without cord; 3
double stitches fastened to the fourth purl of the row of stitches
worked over the cord (illustration), 2 double stitches, 6 purl
divided each by 2 double stitches, 3 double stitches fastened to
the purl of next circle, 3 double stitches fastened to the last purl
of the row, 2 double stitches, 3 purl divided each by 2 double
stitches, 3 double stitches; fasten the cotton to the sixth purl of
the circle (reckoning from the beginning), 4 double stitches.
Repeat from *. Work over the top of the border a crochet
edging similar to that round the diamond pattern of collar
No. 49. For the point of the border, at the corner of the collar,
see illustration No. 54.

55.—*Tatted Collar.*

Materials : Messrs. Walter Evans and Co.'s tatting cotton No. 100;
tatting-pin No. 1.

This collar is worked with very fine tatting cotton. It
consists of four branched tatted patterns and of separate tatted
circles, fastened on to one another as seen in illustration. The

four branched patterns are worked as follow :—3 double, 1 purl, 7 times alternately 2 double, 1 purl, then 3 double, and join the knots into a circle. Work 3 similar leaves close to this

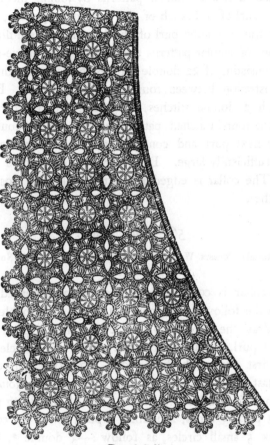

55.—Tatted Collar.

1st leaf, but instead of working the 1st purl, fasten them on to the last purl of the preceding leaf ; besides this, instead of

F

working the last purl of the 4th branch, fasten it on to the first purl of the 1st branch. When 1 such four-branched pattern is completed, knot both ends of the cotton together and cut them off. Make a row of similar patterns by joining them on to the 2 middle purl of a branch of the preceding pattern, instead of working the 2 middle purl of the last branch (see illustration). Two rows of similar patterns are joined by the above-mentioned circles, consisting of 32 double stitches, by fastening these circles from illustration between four branched patterns. Begin each circle with 2 double stitches, fasten it on to the corresponding purl of the four-branched pattern,. work again 2 double, fasten on to the next purl, and continue in the same manner till the circle is sufficiently large. Each circle is ornamented with lace stitch. The collar is edged round the neck with close button-hole stitches.

56.—*Tatted Collar.*

Materials: Messrs. Walter Evans and Co.'s tatting cotton No. 60; tatting-pin No. 3.

This collar is commenced at the top, and worked with fine cotton in the following manner :—1st oval: 2 double, 1 purl, 9 times, draw the cotton into a circle, 3 double, 1 purl, 1 double, 5 times, 1 purl, 3 double, draw the cotton into a circle, and join it to the first purl of the first circle ; work two more circles the same as last. 2nd oval: 2 double, 1 purl, 7 times, join the third purl to the third purl of the centre circle of preceding pattern, 3 double, 1 purl, 3 times, 2 double, 1 purl, draw the cotton up, and work 5 small circles, as follow :—3 double *, 1 purl, 1 double, 4 times, * 1 purl, 3 double, joining each circle to the purl of the 2nd oval. 3rd oval : 2 double, 1 purl, 8 times, joining the 3rd purl to the 2nd purl of the centre circle of the preceding

56.—Tatted Collar.

pattern, 3 double, 1 purl, 4 times, 2 double, 1 purl, draw the cotton up, and work 7 small circles, similar to the small circles described in 2nd oval.

57.—*Circle in Tatting.*

Materials: Messrs. Walter Evans and Co's tatting cotton No. 50; tatting-pin No. 2.

57.—Circle in Tatting.

This circle is worked with fine cotton, and will be very pretty for ornamenting cravat-ends and different articles of lingerie.   It is commenced in the centre with 2 double, 1 purl, repeated 8 times, draw the cotton into a ring, and work 8 small circles, as follow :—3 double, * 1 purl, 1 double, repeat from * 6 times, 1 purl, 3 double, draw up tbe cotton, and join it to the purl of centre ring and corresponding circle.   Large circle : 3 double, * 1 purl, 2 double, repeat from * 14 times, 3 double, draw up the cotton, and join it to the 4th purl of small circle. The centre of ring is filled up with lace stitches.

58.—*Tatting Medallion for Trimming Lingeries, &c.*

Materials : Messrs. Walter Evans and Co.'s tatting cotton No. 50 for cravats and collars, 100 for pocket-handkerchiefs, 20 for petticoats ; tatting-pin No. 2 or 3.

This pattern is suitable for trimming cravats, collars, pocket-handkerchiefs, petticoats, &c., according to the size of the cotton with which it is worked.   Work first the round of circles which incloses the leaves, overlapping each other in the centre ; begin with the smallest circle, which is at the top of the pattern ; it consists of 3 double, 1 purl, 7 double, 1 purl, 7 double, 1 purl, 3 double.   Then work at a short distance another circle like the preceding one, only work 8 double instead of 7, and instead of working the first purl, fasten the circle on to the last purl of the preceding circle ; all the other circles are fastened on to each other in the same manner.   The next circle, worked again at a distance of about one-fifth of an inch, has 4 double ; fasten it on to the preceding circle, 9 double, 1 purl, 9 double, 1 purl, 4 double.   The following four circles are worked like the preceding one ; only work in the first of these circles 10 double instead of 9, in the second 11 double, in the third 12 double. The piece of cotton which joins the circles together must also be somewhat longer between the larger circles.   Then work a circle

as follows :—5 double, fasten the cotton, 13 double, 1 purl,
13 double, 1 purl, 5 double ; then a similar circle, but always
working 14 double instead of 13. The next circle consists of
6 double, fasten the cotton, 15 double, 1 purl, 15 double, 1 purl,
6 double ; the two following circles are worked in the same

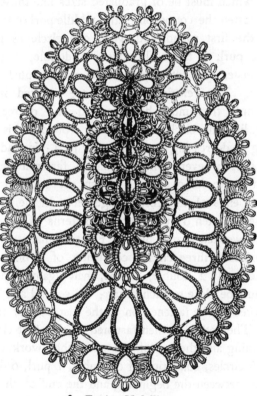

58.—Tatting Medallion.

manner, working 16 double instead of 15. Then comes the
largest circle of the round, which consists of 6 double, 17 double,
1 purl, 17 double, 1 purl, 6 double. Work 11 circles more

like the 2nd to 12th of those just described (the 13th circle forms the middle), only the order of sizes must be reversed, so that the round closes with the smallest circle. Then fasten both ends of the cotton together, so that the circles are joined into a circle. Then work round this row of circles another round, the circles of which must be of graduated sizes like those of the first round. Fasten the cotton on to the middle purl of the first small circle of the first round, and work one circle as follows :—3 double, 1 purl, 6 times alternately 2 double, 1 purl, then 3 double ; fasten the cotton on to the middle purl of the next circle, &c. The remaining circles are worked in the same manner, only they must be increased and decreased in size gradually like the circles of the first round ; this is done by increasing or decreasing the number of purl ; instead of working the first purl of every following circle, fasten it on to the last purl of the preceding circle. When the round is completed, fasten both ends of the cotton together. In the centre of the oval pattern, fasten 6 five-branched patterns of graduated size, which are worked in one piece. For the smallest of these patterns work first three circles, consisting of 5 double, 1 purl, 5 times alternately 2 double, 1 purl, then again 5 double (these circles must be close to each other ; the second and third circles must, moreover, be fastened on to the last purl of the preceding circle). The cotton is then fastened on the first circle between the beginning and the end of the same, then work close to them two small circles, consisting of 6 double, 1 purl, 6 double, fasten the cotton between the beginning and the end of the third circle. The other five-branched patterns are worked in the same manner at intervals of about three-tenths of an inch ; but the separate circles of each pattern must become gradually larger. In the largest pattern the three large circles consist of 5 double, 1 purl,

8 times alternately 2 double, 1 purl, 5 double; the two smaller circles consist each of 15 double, 1 purl, 15 double; the size of the other patterns can easily be worked from this; the cotton which joins these last together is covered by over-casting with a needle and thread, so as to imitate double stitches. The five-branched patterns are then fastened in the oval pattern; they must overlap each other to half way, as seen in the illustration.

59.—*Tatted Diamond.*

Materials: Messrs. Walter Evans and Co.'s tatting cotton No. 40, or 80 if required finer; tatting-pin No. 3.

59.—Tatted Diamond.

This pattern is meant to ornament lingerie; it is worked with fine tatting cotton in the following manner :—Work a * circle consisting of 6 double, 1 purl, 6 double, turn the circle downwards and work at a short distance another circle consisting of 5 double, 4 purl divided by 2 double, 5 double; at a similar distance a circle of 5 double fastened on to the last purl of the preceding circle, 2 double, 5 purl divided by 2 double, 5 double; then again a circle consisting of 5 double fastened on to the last purl of the preceding circle, 2 double, 3 purl divided by 2 double,

5 double : fasten the cotton on to the first circle. Then turn the work so that the last three circles are turned downwards, leave an interval of at least three-fourths of an inch, and repeat three times more from *, fastening the circles on to each other from illustration. Knot together the beginning and end of the cotton, work button-hole stitches round the cotton which joins the circles, as shown in illustration. The purl stitches of the four middle circles of the diamond are knotted together.

60.—*Tatted Cravat End.*

Materials : Messrs. Walter Evans and Co.'s tatting cotton No. 50 ; tatting-pin No. 3 ; 2 shuttles.

This cravat end is given in full size. It is ornamented with a tatted medallion, edged with lace. The tatting is worked with tatting fine cotton and two shuttles. Make first the two rosettes which form the centre of the medallion, then the insertion-like part which edges the rosettes. The larger rosette is worked as follows :—Knot the cotton of both shuttles together and work with 1 shuttle only 1 circle consisting of 10 double, 1 purl one-fifth of an inch long, 10 double ; * close to this circle, which is turned downwards, work over the cotton with the other shuttle, 1 double, 1 purl, 8 double ; this forms one of the scallops joining two circles. Then turn the work again and work close to the just completed scallop another circle like the first, but which is joined to the first circle instead of working the purl. Repeat 4 times more from *. Then work another scallop and fasten both ends of cotton on to the cotton over which the first scallop has been worked, at the place where the scallop is joined to the first circle. The first round of the rosette is thus completed. Work then the 2nd round over the cotton on the 2nd shuttle, beginning to work where the two ends of cotton have been fastened, ∗ 6 double, 1 purl, 5 double, fastened on to the

60.—Tatted Cravat End.

purl of the next scallop of the preceding round, 5 double, 1 purl, 6 double fastened on to the cotton between two scallops of the

preceding round; repeat 5 times more from *. The larger
rosette is now completed. The smaller rosette is worked like
the first, only without the second round. The insertion-like
border is worked in two halves as follows :—The half which
touches the edge of the medallion is worked as follows :—Knot
both ends of cotton together and *, work with 1 shuttle only 1
circle consisting of 8 double, 1 purl one-fifth of an inch long, 8
double; turn the circle downwards and work close to it over the
cotton on the 2nd shuttle 6 double, 1 purl, 6 double; this forms
a scallop of the border. Then turn the work again and work
close to the scallop another circle like the first, but which is
fastened on to the first circle instead of working the purl. Turn
the work again, work a scallop like the preceding one, and repeat
15 times more from *, only the scallops at the lower edge of the
medallion must have a few double stitches more, as can be seen
in illustration. After working the last scallop fasten the two ends
of the cotton on to the 1st circle; then cut them off. The second
inner half is worked like the first; only the circles are worked
without any purl stitch, and fastened on to the circles of the first
half from illustration; the scallops of this half are somewhat
smaller; each consists of 5 double, 1 purl, 5 double. The
completed border is sewn on to the rosettes from illustration; the
different pieces must be first fastened on cardboard. The cotton
must be wound several times round the long threads, as seen in
illustration. The medallion is then sewn into the muslin at the
top only; the remaining border is edged, before joining it to the
muslin, with a straight row of knots to be worked over cotton,
and fastened on to each outer scallop of the border at regular
intervals. The number of double stitches between two purl is
different, as distinctly seen in illustration. For the lace knot both
ends of cotton together, * work with one shuttle only 1 circle

consisting of 8 double, 1 purl, 8 double ; turn the work and make another circle consisting of 2 double, 9 times alternately 1 purl, 2 double ; then fasten this circle on to the preceding one, where it has been joined into a circle, so that both circles meet as seen in illustration. After having turned the work again, work 9 double over the cotton on the 2nd shuttle, which form a scallop between the circles, and repeat from *. The lace is then sewn round the edge of the muslin.

61.—*Rosette in Tatting and Embroidery.*

Materials : Messrs. Walter Evans and Co.'s tatting cotton No. 50, or No. 40 if desired in a larger size.

61.—Rosette in Tatting and Embroidery.

This rosette is suitable for ornamenting lingeries, cravats, &c. It is worked in white embroidery and lace stitch, and edged all round with a tatted lace. For the latter work with very fine cotton * 1 large circle, consisting of 5 double, 1 purl, 7 times alternately 2 double, 1 purl, then 5 double. At a short distance from this circle work a smaller one, consisting of 5 double fastened on to the last purl of the large circle, 5 double. Leave again an interval as small as the last, and repeat from * 11 times more. But in working the large circles, instead of working the 1st purl, fasten them on the same purl of the large circle on which the small circle has been fastened ; besides this, in working the last (12th) large circle, instead of working the last purl, fasten it on the 1st purl of the 1st circle ; the last small circle is fastened on to the same purl. The lace is thus joined into a circle, and is sewn round the outside of the rosette with button-hole stitches.

62.—*Cravat End in Tatting.*

Materials : Messrs. Walter Evans and Co.'s tatting cotton No. 60 ; tatting-pin No. 3.

62.—Cravat End in Tatting.

The illustration shows the end of a tatted cravat. Work first the middle row of the cravat at the same time with the row of circles on the left side of the middle row in illustration ;

begin with the first circle of the middle row. It consists of 7 times alternately 3 double, 1 small purl, then 3 double. Work close to this circle, which must be turned downwards, a Josephine knot, consisting of 5 plain stitches, then a circle consisting of 5 double, 1 purl one-fifth of an inch long, 5 times alternately 3 double, 1 small purl ; 3 double, 1 long purl, 5 double. * Turn this circle (which is the first of the side row) downwards, work close to it a Josephine knot, then a circle consisting of 12 double, 1 small purl, 12 double. Turn this circle downwards, work a Josephine knot, and then again a circle like the first of the side row, but instead of working the first long purl, fasten it on to the last purl of the preceding circle of the same row. Then hold the work so that the circles of the side row are turned downwards, work a Josephine knot, 1 circle like the first circle of the middle row, turn the work, make 1 Josephine knot, and then a circle like the second circle of the side row. Repeat from * till the cravat is sufficiently long. The last circle of the middle row must correspond to the first circle of the same row. Then begin to work the lower edge at the same time with the last circle of the middle row, * 1 Josephine knot, then a circle like the circles of the side row, again 1 Josephine knot, fastened on to the next purl of the last circle of the middle row ; repeat 3 times more from *. Then continue as before, and work on the right side of the middle row a row of circles exactly like those which have been worked at the same time with those of the middle row.

The fastening on of the cotton between two Josephine knots is seen in illustration. The circles at the other end of the cravat are fastened like those of the first-described end. The cravat is edged all round with a row of circles with Josephine knots worked exactly like those of the preceding row, and the manner of fastening which is seen in the illustration.

63.—*Rosette in Tatting and Embroidery.*

Materials: Messrs. Walter Evans and Co.'s tatting cotton No. 60, or 40 if required larger; tatting-pin No. 3.

63.—Rosette in Tatting and Embroidery.

The centre of this rosette is worked in lace stitch on muslin, edged round with button-hole stitch and trimmed with a tatted lace, which is worked at the same time with the centre. Work first * a small circle consisting of 5 double, 1 purl, 3 double, fastened on to the button-hole stitch edging of the rosette, then 3 double, 1 purl, 5 double. Then turn the just-completed circle downwards, and afterwards work at a short distance a large circle consisting of 7 double, 6 times alternately 1 purl, 2 double, lastly 1 purl, 7 double, then 1 Josephine knot consisting of 7 plain. Then turn the work again, so that the last large circle is turned downwards, and repeat from * 12 times more; the large and small circles must be fastened on to one another, as seen in illustration. The fastening of the small circles on to the centre is likewise done from the illustration.

64.—*Cravat End in Tatting and Darned Netting.*

Materials : Messrs. Walter Evans and Co.'s tatting cotton No. 50 ; tatting-pin
No. 3 ; square of netting ; fine Mecklenburg thread No. 80.

64.—Cravat End in Tatting and Darned Netting.

The end of this cravat is ornamented with a square of darned
netting, edged with a tatted border, and sewn on to the material
of the cravat. But the diamond in tatting (page 18), or the
square (page 31) will look very pretty with this border. The

square is worked in diamond netting, and has seven holes in length and breadth. They are darned in linen stitch, darning stitch, and *point d'esprit*, with Mecklenburg thread. The ground is worked over a mesh measuring three-tenths of an inch round. For each square one more row than is needed must be worked, and the cast-on stitches are cut off, as they are longer than the stitches of the other rows. The tatted border is worked with fine tatting cotton. Fasten the cotton at one corner of the square and work * a circle consisting of 7 double, 1 purl, then six times alternately 2 double, 1 purl, 7 double, fasten the cotton on to the same stitch of the ground where it was first fastened; † work a second circle like the first, but fasten it, instead of working the first purl on to the last purl of the preceding circle; fasten the cotton again on to the same stitch, then on to the next stitch, and work a small circle, consisting of 5 double fastened on to the last purl of the preceding circle, 4 double, 1 purl, 5 double. The cotton is fastened on to the same netted stitch as before, and then on to the next stitch; repeat twice more from †, and then repeat from * in all three times more, so that the square is edged all round. It is sewn into the material from the illustration.

65. – Tatted Antimacassar. (See pages 574-5.)

Materials: Messrs. Walter Evans and Co.'s Boar's Head cotton No. 30, or tatting cotton No. 24, or for a larger size tatting cotton No. 20; tatting-pin No. 1; large shuttle.

The illustration shows the fourth of the antimacassar and the whole of the rosette which forms the centre. Begin with the latter, with the five-branched pattern in the centre, at the same time with the following round of circles :—* Work first one circle of this round, consisting of 3 double, 1 purl, 4 times alternately 2 double, 1 purl, 3 double; then at a short distance a circle like the one just made, in which, however, instead of working the first purl, the cotton must be joined on to the last purl of the preceding circle. Then work at a short distance the first leaf of the five-branched pattern, which consists of 4 double, 1 purl, 4 double. When this branch is completed, repeat at a short distance 4 times more from *; but in working the branches of the five-branched pattern, instead of working the purl, join it on to the purl of the first branch of the five-branched pattern (this purl forms the centre of the pattern), All the circles must also be joined one to each other, as can be seen from illustration. Then work the scallops round the border of the rosette, * fasten the cotton on to the purl which joins the two next circles of the preceding round, and work one scallop consisting of 11 times alternately 2 double, 1 purl, then 2 double. Repeat 9 times more from * When the rosette is completed, work eight rosettes in the same manner and join them into a circle from illustration by means of small three-branched patterns, and then join them on to the middle rosette.

The strip of insertion which comes next is worked in two halves as follows :—Work first, for the half turned towards the centre, two rows of circles lying opposite each other ; begin with one of the largest circles, consisting of 4 double, 1 purl, 3 times alternately 2 double, 1 purl, then 4 double ; * at a short distance work a smaller circle of 4 double, 1 purl, 4 double ; after another short distance, a circle like the first joined on to it ; then again a smaller circle, which at the place of the first purl is joined on to the purl of the preceding small circle. A short distance from this work again one of the larger circles just described, which is fastened on to the preceding similar circle ; then repeat from * till the double row has nine larger and eight smaller circles. The first half of the strip of insertion is completed ; the second outer

G

half is worked like the first, only the small circles must here be worked without any purl, and two of them together must always be fastened on to the two joined small circles of the first half, as was done for the five-branched pattern of the rosette; besides this, each of the large circles has 4 double, 1 purl, 4 times alternately 2 double, 1 purl, then 4 double. When eight similar patterns have been worked, join them into a circle from illustration by means of small rosettes; this circle is then joined to the already-finished part of the cover. The small rosettes and remaining patterns of the antimacassar are easily worked from illustration. The completed patterns are joined together in the course of the work.

TATTING COTTON

Is supplied by Messrs. Walter Evans and Co., of Derby, in all sizes from 20 to 120. Crochet Cotton, which is preferred by some Tatters, is sold in all sizes from 0 to 120.

The following table will assist ladies in selecting the size of either tatting or crochet cotton. All these cottons are on reels containing 100 yards:—

	Tatting.	Crochet.
Petticoat Edgings and Insertions . .	20	0 and 12
Night Dress Trimmings	40	60
Lingerie Trimming	50	70
Collars and Cravats	50	70
Pocket Handkerchiefs	100	120
Parasol Covers	100	120
Antimacassars	20, 30	0 and 20
Pincushions	60	80
Caps	100	120
Lace	60, 80, 100	80, 100, 120
Insertions	20, 40, 80	40, 80, 100

Ladies at a distance from town or on the Continent will be glad to have some guide as to the quantity of cotton required to complete their work. The quantity of tatting or crochet cotton used by an average worker is found to be two yards to the square inch with a single shuttle; three yards to the square inch with two shuttles.

EMBROIDERY

INSTRUCTIONS.

———◆———

THE art of embroidering with cotton on linen, muslin, cambric, piqué, &c., is very easy to learn by strictly attending to the following instructions.

The size of the thread and needle must correspond to that of the material on which you embroider ; the needle must not be too long, and the cotton must be soft. Messrs. Walter Evans and Co.'s embroidery cotton is the best. Skilful embroiderers never work over anything, because when you tack the material on paper or cloth each stitch shows, and if the material is very fine, leaves small holes ; but for those that are learning we should advise them to tack the material to be embroidered upon a piece of *toile cirée*. If you work without this, place the material straight over the forefinger of the left hand ; the material must never be held slantways. The three other fingers of the left hand hold the work ; the thumb remains free to give the right position to each stitch. The work must always, if possible, lie so that the outline of the pattern is turned towards the person who works. For the sake of greater clearness one part of the following illustrations is given in larger size than nature. Preparing the patterns is one of the most important things in embroidery, for the shape of the patterns is often spoiled merely because they have not been prepared with sufficient care.

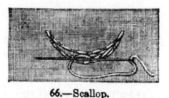

66.—Scallop.

ILLUSTRATION 66 shows how to prepare a scallop. Take thicker cotton than that with which you work ; never commence with a knot, and do not take a thread longer than sixteen or eighteen inches. The outlines of the scallops are first traced with short straight stitches. In the corners particularly the stitches must be short. The space between the outlines is filled with chain stitches, as can be seen from illustration ; they must not be too long, otherwise the embroidery will look coarse. It is in this way that every pattern to be worked in button-hole or satin stitch is to be prepared.

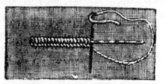

67.—Double Overcast Stitch.

ILLUSTRATION 67 shows the double overcast stitch or button-hole stitch in a straight line. After having traced the outline begin to work from left to right ; fasten the cotton with a few stitches, hold it with the thumb of the left hand under the outline, insert the needle downwards above the outline, draw it out under the same above the cotton which you hold in the left hand, and draw it up. Repeat for all the stitches in the same manner; they must be regular and lie close to one another Great care should be taken that the material on which you embroider is not puckered.

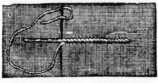

68.—Overcast Stitch.

ILLUSTRATION 68 (*Overcast Stitch*).—The double overcast and the button-hole stitches are worked from left to right, whilst back stitches, knotted and satin stitches are worked from right to left. The stitch is worked in the same way as the double overcast, only the needle must never be drawn out *above*, but *below*, the cotton with which you work, and which you keep down with the thumb of the left hand.

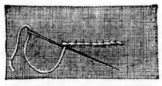

69.—Slanting Overcast Stitch.

ILLUSTRATION 69.—The slanting overcast stitch is worked without tracing the outline, always inserting tne needle downwards—that is, from top to bottom. The needle must be inserted in the manner shown in illustration—that is, not straight, but slanting; insert it a little farther than the last stitch, and draw it out close to it. The wrong side of the work must show back stitches. This sort of stitch is used for the fine outlines in patterns or letter.

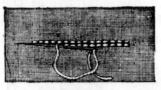

70.—Back Stitch.

ILLUSTRATION 70.—This shows the back stitch, the working of which is well known; it is worked in several rows close to each other.

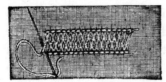

71.—Point Croisé.

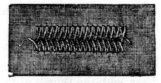

72.—Point Croisé.

ILLUSTRATIONS 71 & 72 show another kind of back stitch, called *point croisé*, which is only used on very thin and transparent materials. This stitch forms on the wrong side a sort of darned pattern, which is seen by transparence on the right side, and gives the embroidered pattern a thicker appearance, contrasting with the rest of the work (see the lower leaves of the flower on illustration 110). For this stitch insert the needle into the material as for the common back stitch, draw it out underneath the needle on the opposite outline of the pattern, so as to form on the wrong side a slanting line. Insert the needle again as for common back stitch; draw it out slanting at the place marked for the next stitch on the opposite outline, as shown in illustration 71.

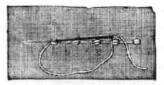

73.—Knotted Stitch.

ILLUSTRATION 73 shows the knotted stitch; the simplest way of working it is to work two back stitches at a short distance from each other over the same thread.

The knotted stitch seen in ILLUSTRATION 74 is worked thus :—Take about four threads of the material on the needle, draw the needle half out, wind the cotton twice round the point of the needle, hold it tight with the thumb, draw the needle out carefully and insert it at the place where the stitch was begun, and draw it out at the place where the next stitch is to be worked.

74.—Knotted Stitch.

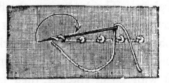

75.—Knotted Stitch

The knotted stitch seen on ILLUSTRATION 75 is worked in nearly the same manner as the preceding one. Before drawing the cotton out of the material hold it tight with the left-hand thumb; leave the needle in the same position, wind the cotton twice round it, turn the needle from left to right, so (follow the direction of the arrow) that its point arrives where the cotton was drawn out (marked by a cross in illustration), insert the needle there, and draw it out at the place of the next stitch.

ILLUSTRATIONS 76 & 77.—Raised satin stitch is principally used for blossoms, flowers, leaves, letters, &c. After having traced the outlines of the pattern, fill the space left between them with chain stitches in a direction different from that in which the pattern is to be embroidered; begin at the point of the leaf, working from right to left, make short straight stitches, always

76.—Raised Satin Stitch.

inserting the needle close above the outline and drawing it out below. The leaves on the flowers, as well as on the branches, must be begun from the point, because they thus acquire a better shape. If you wish to work a leaf divided in the middle, as seen in illustration 77, you must trace the veining before you fill it with chain stitches, then begin at one point of the leaf and work first one half and then the other.

77.—Raised Satin Stitch.

78.—Point de Plume.

ILLUSTRATION 78 shows the so-called *point de plume* on a scalloped leaf. It is worked like the satin stitch, only the needle is drawn through the material in a slanting direction.

79.—Point de Minute.

ILLUSTRATION 79 (*Point de Minute*).—This stitch is often used instead of satin stitch when the patterns must appear raised. Wind the cotton several times round the point of the needle, which is inserted into the material half its length (the number of times the cotton is to be wound round the needle depends on the length of the pattern), hold fast the windings with the thumb of the left hand, draw the needle and the cotton through the windings, insert the needle into the material at the same place, and draw it out at the place where the next stitch is to begin.

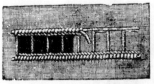

80.—Ladder Stitch.

81.—Ladder Stitch.

ILLUSTRATIONS 80 & 81 show the *ladder stitch*, often used in ornamental embroidery. Trace first the outlines as seen in illustrations ; mark also the cross stitches between the outlines, so that the first touch the outlines only at both ends. The outlines are embroidered in overcast stitch or double overcast ; the material is cut away underneath the ladder stitch between the outlines

H

We have now shown the different kinds of stitches used in embroidery; the following illustrations show them used for different patterns.

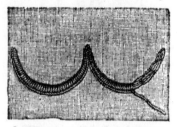

82.—Button-hole Stitch Scallop.

83.—Button-hole Stitch Scallop.

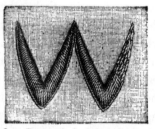

84.—Button-hole Stitch Scallop.

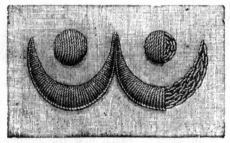

85.—Button-hole Stitch Scallop.

ILLUSTRATIONS 82 TO 85 (*Different Batton-hole Stitch Scallops*).—These scallops are prepared as above described. Take care to have the stitches even and regular; the scallops must be wide in the centre and very fine at both ends.

ILLUSTRATIONS 86 & 87 (*Button-holes and Eyelets*).—This kind of embroidery is used only in round or long patterns. Trace first the outline of the hole, cut away a small round piece of material, not too close to the outlines (when the button-hole is very small merely insert the point of the scissors or a stiletto into the material), fold the edge of the material back with the needle, and work the hole in overcast stitch, inserting the needle into the

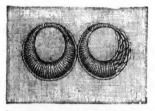

86.—Button and Eyelet Holes.

87.—Button and Eylet Holes.

empty place in the centre and drawing it out under the outline. Some button-holes are worked separately ; sometimes they are in a row ; if so, take care to begin to work each button-hole at the place where it touches the next. In the following button-holes the outside must be traced double, so as to reach as far as the next one, but each button-hole is finished at once. Illustration 86 shows a button-hole worked round in button-hole stitch, 87 an eyelet-hole worked in overcast.

88.—Shaded Button-hole.   89.—Shaded Button-hole.

ILLUSTRATIONS 88 & 89.—Shaded button-holes are worked like the others, only they are prepared, as can be seen in illustration 89, so as to mark the thickness. The stitches must gradually get narrower or wider, and be worked very close to each other.

90.—Leaf in Raised Satin Stitch.

ILLUSTRATIONS 90 & 91 (*Two Leaves in Raised Satin Stitch*). —In a leaf like the one seen in 90 work first the outline and veining in overcast stitch; work one half of the leaf in satin stitch, and the other half between the overcast outline and veining in back stitch. The stem of a leaf is always worked last.

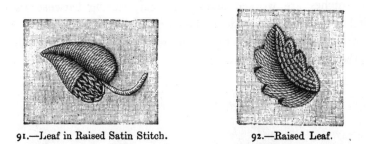

91.—Leaf in Raised Satin Stitch.   92.—Raised Leaf.

ILLUSTRATIONS 92 & 93 (*Two Leaves in Satin Stitch and
Point de Plume*).—For leaves like the one seen in 93 begin with
the veinings, then work the inner points, then the outer ones,
and lastly the raised spots in the centre. The leaf seen in 92 is
worked, one half in *point de plume*, the other half in back stitch
or *point d'or.*

93.—Raised Leaf.

94.—Leaf.

ILLUSTRATION 94.—The outline of this leaf is embroidered
in overcast stitch; the open-work veining consists of eyelets;
one half of the leaf is worked in back stitch, the other half in a
kind of satin stitch worked without chain stitches underneath ;

the stitches are worked across the leaf, leaving between two stitches an interval as wide as the stitch itself. The next row is then worked in these intervals, and each stitch begins half-way up the one before and after it.

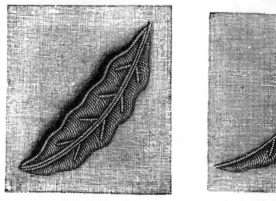

95.—Leaf Raised.   96.—Leaf Raised.

ILLUSTRATIONS 95 TO 97 (*Leaf in Raised Embroidery*).—This kind of embroidery is particularly beautiful, as it is worked separately and sewn on the material with an outline in very fine cotton ; this produces the shade seen in 95 (see also illustrations 98 and 113). For such leaves work first one half in overcast and satin stitch (illustration 96) ; the other half is worked on a

97.—Raised Leaf.

separate piece of material (see illustration 97) ; cut away the material along the overcast outline, and fasten it on the foundation material along the outline which forms the veining on illustration 96.

99.—Half of Leaf (98).

98.—Raised Embroidered Leaf.   100.—Centre of Leaf (98).

ILLUSTRATIONS 98 TO 100 show a similar leaf ; both halves are worked separately (see 99) ; the centre is worked in open lace stitch. The latter (see No. 100) is traced, then make ladder stitches across, work the outlines in overcast stitch, and cut away the material underneath the ladder stitch. The cross stitches are then worked in darning stitch with very fine cotton wherever two threads meet.

101.—Blossom in Satin Stitch.

ILLUSTRATION 101 (*Blossom in Satin Stitch*).—The eyelet is worked in overcast stitch, then work the upper part of the blossom all in one piece as far as the beginning of the veining, thence the blossom is worked in two halves.

102.—Blossom in Satin Stitch.   103.—Bead partly covered.

ILLUSTRATIONS 102 & 103 (*Blossom in Satin Stitch*).—The raised centre of this flower is formed by a bead, over which the embroidery is worked.   When the leaves have been worked one after the other, place a bead in the centre, left free in such a manner that one hole lies on the material, and work over the bead by inserting the needle into its upper hole, then underneath the material, drawing it out above the material close to the bead, and so on (see 103).

104.—Star in Satin Stitch.

ILLUSTRATION 104 (*Star Pattern in Satin Stitch*).—The centre, which forms a wheel, is worked first.   Draw the threads across *t*he circle marked by an outline ; in the centre they are wound round, always taking one thread *on the needle* and leaving the next thread *under the needle,* as can be seen in 122 on the half-finished pattern. The material underneath the wheel is only cut away when the rest of the pattern has been embroidered.

105.—Star in Point de Reprise.

ILLUSTRATIONS 105 & 106 (*Patterns in Back, Satin, and Ladder Stitches*).—The small star in the centre of No. 105 is worked in *point de reprise.*

106.—Star.

:07.—Flower in Satin Stitch.

ILLUSTRATION 107 (*Flower in Satin Stitch*). — The fine veinings are worked with fine black silk in *point russe,* which renders the effect of the flower very beautiful.

108.—Rose in Satin Stitch.

109.—Petal for Rose.

ILLUSTRATIONS 108 & 109 (*Rose in Satin Stitch*).—No. 109
shows one petal larger than full size. The outer circle only is
prepared with chain stitches underneath, so as to appear raised ;
the inner circles are worked flat. The centre of the rose is
embroidered in open work.

110.—Heartsease.

111.—Raised Flower.

ILLUSTRATION 110 (*Embroidered Heartsease*).—For the knotted
stitch see No. 75, for the *point croisé* see 71 and 72.

ILLUSTRATION 111 (*Flower in Raised Satin Stitch*).

112.—Ear of Corn.

ILLUSTRATION 112 (*An Ear of Corn in Point de Minute*).

113.—Bluebell.

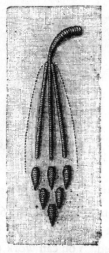

114.—Inner part of Bluebell.

ILLUSTRATIONS 113, 114, & 116 (*Bluebell in Raised Satin Stitch*).—This flower is worked partly in separate pieces, as has

been described.   Illustration 116 shows the raised part stretched
out flat.   When it is finished it is fastened down along the dotted
line on No. 114, which shows the inner part of the flower.

115.—Flower.

ILLUSTRATION 115 (*Flower in Point de Minute*).—This stitch
is here worked over a thick foundation of chain stitches.   For
raised patterns it looks very well.

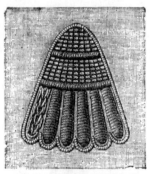

116.—Outer part of Bluebell.

117.—Flower appliquéd on Net.

ILLUSTRATIONS 116 & 117 (*Flower worked in Applique*).—To
work in appliqué, two materials, either similar or different, are
needed.   You can work either in appliqué of muslin on muslin, or
of muslin on net, or of net on net.   Muslin on Brussels net is the
prettiest way of working in appliqué ; we will therefore describe
it : the other materials are worked in the same manner.   Trace

the pattern on the muslin, fasten the latter on the net, and trace the outlines of the pattern with very small stitches work them in overcast stitch with very fine cotton, taking care not to pucker the material. The veinings are worked in overcast. When the pattern has been embroidered cut away the muslin round the outlines with sharp scissors, so that the net forms the grounding (see No. 117). The greatest care is required in cutting out the muslin to avoid touching the threads of the net.

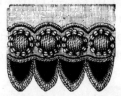

118.—Border.

ILLUSTRATIONS 118 & 119 (*Narrow Borders*).—It will be easy to work these borders from the above instructions. Observe only that on border 118 the outer row of scallops is worked first, then the button-hole stitch row, and the rest afterwards. The spots are edged all round in knotted stitch. The wheels in the

119.—Border.

centre of the eyelets of No. 119 are worked with very fine cotton in loose button-hole stitch; they are wound round with the cotton in a second row.

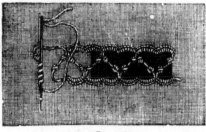

120.—Insertion.

ILLUSTRATIONS 120 TO 122.—Three strips of insertion, which
are worked nearly like the ladder stitch. For No. 120, in tracing
the outlines, make two small knots at short distances by winding
the cotton four times round the needle, as can be seen in illustra-

121.—Insertion.   122.—Insertion.

tion ; the windings are held down with the thumb of the left
hand, draw the needle through, and a knot is formed. The outlines are worked in button-hole stitch only when all the knots
have been made, and then the material is cut away underneath.
Illustration 121 is a variety of the slanting ladder stitch. Illustration 122.—The cross threads are worked in two rows in the
common herring-bone stitch, as can be seen by the black lines on
the illustration. The straight lines at the top and at the bottom
are worked in double overcast ; lastly, the wheels are worked in
a row as described for the star pattern, No. 104.

ILLUSTRATIONS 123 TO 129 (*Embroidered Initials*).—To learn to work initials the Roman characters are the easiest to begin with. They must be traced and prepared like other embroidery in satin stitch, only the chain stitches underneath must not be too thick : it would take away the shape of the letters. All depends on the fineness and regularity of the stitches ; they must be worked in overcast stitch. Work from left to right, and the letter

123.

124.

125.

126.

when completed must look rather like raised printing than like embroidery. Gothic letters are much more difficult to work on account of the many flourishes ; it requires great practice in needlework to embroider them well. Illustration 123.—The small black dots are worked in black silk on the thick parts of the letter : the fine strokes are covered with cross threads of black silk. Illustration 124.—The outlines of the letter and the fine strokes are worked in black silk. Illustration 125.—This

127.

128.

129.

letter is embroidered in raised satin stitch and *point de plume.*
Illustration 126.—This letter is worked in back stitches, over
which are worked at regular distances cross stitches of black
silk. Illustration 127.—Letter in satin and back stitch. Illustration 128 to be worked in overcast and double overcast. Illustration 129.—Letter G in *point russe* with black silk.

130.

ILLUSTRATION 130 (*Embroidered Figures*).—They are worked
like the letters in *point de plume* and overcast; the dots are worked
in knotted stitch

EMBROIDERY.

———◆———

[In working the following Embroidery Patterns it will be found advisable to trace the design clearly upon tracing-paper with a sharp-pointed lead pencil. The pattern thus traced must be perforated with a fine needle in a succession of tiny holes, at the rate of about twenty to the inch. Those ladies who possess a sewing-machine will find no difficulty in accomplishing this. Several thicknesses of paper can be perforated at the same time, if required, by any ordinary machine. To transfer the traced and perforated design to the fabric to be embroidered, it is only necessary to rub a small quantity of powder blue through the holes.]

———◆———

131.—*Insertion in Embroidery.*

Material: Messrs. Walter Evans and Co.'s embroidery cotton No. 16.

This insertion is worked in raised satin stitch and button-hole stitch. The outlines must first be traced and the space filled up with chain stitches. To work a leaf, begin at the point, working from right to left, making short stitches, and always inserting the needle close above the outline and drawing it out below. The holes left for the ribbon to pass through are worked in plain button-hole stitch, the dots are worked in raised satin stitch.

I

131.—Insertion in Embroidery.

132.—*Insertion in Embroidery and Stitching.*

Materials: Messrs. Walter Evans and Co.'s embroidery cotton Nos. 10 and 16.

The veinings of this pretty insertion must be worked in overcast stitch (No. 68, *Embroidery Instructions*), the leaves and flowers in raised satin stitch, the scallops in button-hole stitch, and the outer edge of the leaves in back stitch (No. 70, *Embroidery Instructions*) with No. 10 cotton.

132.—Insertion in Embroidery and Stitching.

133.—*Cravat End in Embroidery.*

Materials: Muslin, cambric, or linen; Messrs. Walter Evans and Co.'s embroidery cotton No. 24, or fine black China silk.

This graceful design is worked in raised satin stitch (see Nos. 76 and 77, *Embroidery Instructions*) and back stitching, or point Russe. Black silk may be introduced at will, and the deli-

133.—Embroidered Pattern for Cravat Ends, &c.

cate leaves may be stitched in fine black silk, and the flowers embroidered in white, with the stamens in black silk.

134.—*Basket Embroidered in Chenille.*

Materials: A basket of fine wicker-work; 1 skein of black chenille, and 3 of blue chenille.

This small round basket measures seven inches across; it has a cover and two handles. The wicker is very delicately plaited, and is ornamented with a pattern in chenille which is very easy to work. Upon the cover, work in point Russe one large star in blue chenille, with the centre and outer circle in black. All round, work small stars in blue chenille, with a

134.—Basket Embroidered in Chenille.

black stitch in the centre. The position of these stars is shown in our illustration. The basket requires no mounting; it is not even lined.

135.—*Pattern for Collars and Cuffs in Embroidery.*

Materials: Muslin, cambric or lawn; Messrs. Walter Evans and Co.'s
embroidery cotton perfectionné No. 40.

Work the outer circle in long even scallops (see page 90 of
Embroidery Instructions) in raised button-hole stitch ; the spray
of flowers is embroidered in raised satin stitch, the leaves in the
same, and the rosebud calyx in tiny eyelet-holes. The centres
of the roses are embroidered in open-work.

135.—Embroidery Pattern for Collars, Cuffs, &c.

136.—*Cravat End in Embroidery.*

Materials: Muslin, Brussels net; Messrs. Walter Evans and Co.'s
embroidery cotton No. 30.

Tack the traced muslin over the net and work the scallop
of the inner edge ; next the design in the centre must be
worked in raised satin stitch (see No. 77 in *Embroidery Instructions*).
The raised dots are also worked in satin stitch (see page 90 of
Embroidery Instructions). Lastly, work the outer edging of
round scallops and the lines of raised dots, and with a pair of
embroidery scissors carefully cut away the muslin from the outer
edge and from the leaves of the centre pattern.

136.—Cravat End in Embroidery.

137.—*Embroidery Pattern for Collars, Cuffs, &c.*

Materials : Linen ; Messrs. Walter Evans and Co.'s cotton perfectionné No. 40.

This pretty star should be worked in fine overcast stitch (see No. 68 in *Embroidery Instructions*). The centre is worked in raised satin stitch leaves round a circle of button-hole stitch, in the middle of which a wheel is worked thus :—Slip the cotton under the thick edge and fasten it, then cross it over and back

137.—Embroidery Pattern for Collars, Cuffs, &c.

so as to make 8 bars, then twist the cotton twice round 1 bar ; this will bring it to the centre ; work over and under each of the bars until a thick dot is formed ; fasten the cotton beneath this, and twist it twice round the bar opposite to the first one you worked, and finish off.

138.—*Embroidery Covering for a Quilted Counterpane.*

Materials : Cashmere, cambric muslin, or linen ; Messrs. Walter Evans and Co.'s embroidery cotton No. 4.

This is an embroidery pattern for a woollen or silk quilted counterpane. Such counterpanes generally have a lining which

15 . Embroidery Covering for a Quilted Counterpane.

is turned back on the right side, and buttoned down at the point of each scallop. The pattern is a quilted counterpane of scarlet cashmere; the lining is of fine linen. Before embroidering it, make the points for the corners. The embroidery is worked in button-hole stitch, overcast, satin, and ladder stitch. It can also be worked on fine cambric or muslin, and then the embroidered pattern sewn on the piece of linen which forms the cover on the wrong side. Make the button-holes as seen on illustration, and sew on mother-of-pearl or china buttons.

139.—Embroidery Pattern for Cravat Ends, &c.

139.—*Embroidery Pattern for Ornamenting Collars, Cuffs, &c.*

Materials: Muslin, cambric, or linen; Messrs. Walter Evans and Co. s embroidery cotton No. 40.

This pattern is worked in satin stitch, point Russe, and point d'or on muslin, cambric, or linen; it is suitable for collars, or cravat ends, or handkerchief corners.

140.—*Handkerchief in Embroidery*

Materials: French cambric; Messrs. Walter Evans and Co.'s embroidery
cotton No. 50.

Three rows of hem-stitching ornament this handkerchief; the
pattern forms an insertion within the outer rows, the flowers are

140.—Handkerchief in Embroidery.

worked in raised satin stitch, with eyelet-hole centres (see No. 87 of *Embroidery Instructions*); the tendrils are worked in overcast stitch ; three rows of raised dots, in groups of four, are worked on the inner side of the last row of hem-stitching. This pattern looks very handsome on a broad-hemmed handkerchief.

141.—*Convolvulus Leaf Insertion.*

Materials : Muslin ; Messrs. Walter Evans and Co.'s embroidery cotton No. 20.

141.—Convolvulus Leaf Insertion.

The convolvulus leaves are worked in raised satin stitch, the veinings and stems in overcast stitch, the eyelet-holes in slanting overcast stitch. (See No. 69 of *Embroidery Instructions*.)

142.—*Insertion.*

Materials : Muslin ; Messrs. Walter Evans and Co.'s embroidery cotton No. 20.

This simple insertion is worked in raised satin stitch, the stems alone excepted; these are embroidered in overcast stitch.

142.—Insertion.

143 and 144.—Two Patterns in Embroidery for Trimming Lingerie.

Materials: Messrs. Walter Evans and Co.'s embroidery cotton No. 20, and
Mecklenburg thread No. 50.

143 and 144.—Patterns for Trimming Lingerie.

These patterns are worked in point Russe and stitching; tne
spots in satin and knotted stitch. Illustration 143 is ornamented
in the centre with lace stitches.

145 *and* 146.—*Insertion.*

Materials: Muslin; Messrs. Walter Evans and Co.'s embroidery cotton No. 16.

The two insertions, Nos. 145 and 146, are worked partly in satin stitch, partly in open-work embroidery, and are edged on either side with an open-work hem.

145.—Insertion.

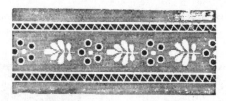

146.—Insertion.

147.—*Couvrette in Appliqué Embroidery*

Materials: Net, fine muslin; Messrs. Walter Evans and Co.'s embroidery cotton No. 16.

The pattern must be traced on the muslin, which should be tacked on the net. The outline of the design must be traced with very small stitches, and worked in overcast stitches, as are also the veinings ; the dots are worked in raised satin stitch ; the border is embroidered with satin stitch flowers and scallop button-hole stitch. To work appliqué on net, see No. 117 of *Embroidery Instructions.*

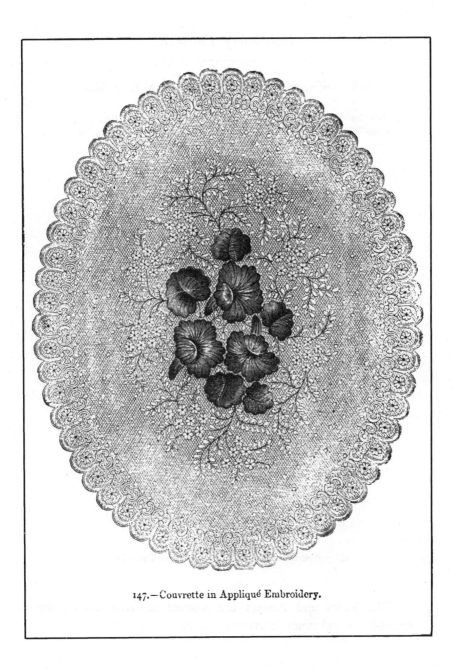

147.—Couvrette in Appliqué Embroidery.

148.—*Wreath for centre of Pincushion or Toilet Mat.*

Materials for Pincushion : Jaconet muslin ; Messrs. Walter Evans and Co.'s
embroidery cotton No. 16.   For toilet mat : White piqué ; cotton No. 12.

148.—Wreath for centre of Pincushion or Toilet Mat.

The leaves and flowers are worked in satin stitch ; the
eyelet-holes and stems in overcast stitch.

149.—*Corner for Handkerchief in Point Russe.*

Materials: French cambric, fine China black sewing-silk, or filoselle.

149.—Corner for Handkerchief in Point Russe.

Point Russe stitch is made by a succession of back stitches. These stitches carefully follow every line of the design, and are worked in black China sewing-silk or filoselle. The pattern should be repeated at each corner of the handkerchief.

K

150 *to* 152.—*Borders and Insertions.*—*White Embroidery.*

Materials: Lawn; Messrs. Walter Evans and Co.'s embroidery cotton No. 30, and Mecklenburg thread No. 50; fine black sewing-silk.

For the border No. 150, trace first the outlines of the scallop, then draw the threads which are to form the wheel in each scallop (take for this fine Mecklenburg thread, for the rest embroidery cotton), fasten them at the places where they cross each other, and work at these places small and large spots in satin stitch. Then work the scallops in button-hole stitch; edge

150.—Embroidered Border.

each larger spot with button-hole stitch all round, and make a row of button-hole stitches for the upper edge of the border, and above this a row of herring-bone stitches. The material is cut away underneath the wheels.

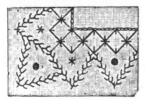
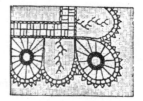

151.—Corner in Embroidery.   152.—Corner in Embroidery.

The corner borders, illustrations 151 and 152, are worked in point Russe, chain and satin stitch, with fine black sewing silk.

153.—Cravat End in Embroidery

153.—*Muslin Cravat.*

Materials: Muslin; Messrs. Walter Evans and Co.'s embroidery cotton
No. 50; No. 40 for the edges.

This cravat is worked on fine muslin, embroidered upon
both ends in raised satin stitch ; the scalloped edge is worked in
button-hole stitch ; the bouquet in the centre is worked in
appliqué satin stitch—that is, the leaves of the rose and the
foliage are worked separately on muslin; they are then cut out
and worked in appliqué (see Nos. 113 and 116, *Embroidery Instructions*) upon the cravat, as seen in the illustration.

154.—*Sandwich Case.*

Materials: Strip of grey kid; strip of oil silk; 1 skein black silk; 1 skein red
purse silk; 1 hank steel beads; steel button.

This case will be found very useful on the occasion of a
journey or picnic, as it can be carried in the pocket without any
inconvenience.

The case is made of a strip of grey kid, scalloped out at the
edges. The words " Bon appétit," or " Good appetite," at will,
are worked over it in overcast with black purse silk and steel
beads ; the scroll pattern in chain stitch with red silk. The
back and front of the case are formed of the same strip, which is
lined with oilskin, and to which narrow side-pieces are added to
form the pocket. These pieces are lined and scalloped out in
the same way as the back and front, and then the scallops of
both sides are joined together, and worked round in button-hole
stitch with purse silk.

The case is fastened down with a steel button.

If another colour is preferred, the sandwich case can be

made of brown kid. The scroll pattern should then be worked in rich blue purse silk, and gold beads used for the letters,

154.—Sandwich Case.

which should be embroidered as before in black silk. The edge may be worked in double overcast stitch in blue or black silk. A gold button must replace the steel when this alteration of colour is made.

155.—*Insertion.*

Materials: Muslin; Messrs. Walter Evans and Co.'s embroidery cotton No. 16.

This insertion is worked in raised satin stitch between two rows of hem-stitching ; a small eyelet-hole is worked in the centre of each flower.

155.—Insertion.

156.—*Cravat End in Raised Embroidery.*

Materials: Messrs. Walter Evans and Co.'s embroidery cotton Nos. 50 and 16.

This pattern is a muslin cravat 32 inches long. The greater part of the embroidered ends is worked in satin stitch; the leaves in the bouquet of the centre are worked in raised embroidery. (See Nos. 113 and 116, *Embroidery Instructions.*)

The dotted lines are raised by taking four threads of the muslin on the needle, draw it half out, wind the cotton twice round the point, holding it tightly under the thumb, draw the needle out and insert it at the place where the stitch was begun, and draw it out where the next stitch is to be worked.

156.—Cravat End in Raised Embroidery.

157.—*Lady's Purse.*

Materials: Russia leather; blue silk; black purse silk; blue silk soutache; fine
gold braid; and gold thread.

This purse is embroidered upon Russia leather; an oval-
shaped medallion is cut out in the centre; a piece of blue silk is
gummed on under the leather so as to show within the oval;
both leather and silk are then lined with calico and stretched

157.—Lady's Purse.

upon a small embroidery frame. The front and back of the
purse are made all of one piece, the centre of which is the
bottom; after the embroidery is completed a piece of leather is
added on each side to give the necessary fullness. Four flowrets
are worked over the blue silk, with black purse silk, in raised
satin stitch, with a dot in gold thread for the centre. The stems
are black and the leaflets gold. The inner border round the

oval medallion is worked in gold braid, and the outer one in blue soutache. The network upon the leather is formed of threads of black purse silk, fastened at every crossing with a stitch of gold thread; the outer border round this network is formed entirely of gold braid. On the opposite side of the purse initials may be worked in black and gold, over the blue silk oval medallion.

The purse is lined with brown watered silk, and mounted with a clasp of gilt steel.

158.—*Table-Napkin Ring.*

Materials: Crimson cashmere; *toile cirée*; 1 reel each of white, black, green, blue, and yellow Chinese silk.

158.—Table-Napkin Ring

Stretch a strip of cashmere of a bright shade of crimson over a piece of *toile cirée*, and work the pattern over it in point Russe with fine silk. The outer borders have white and black outlines, and leaflets of green silk. The stars have black and blue outlines, a yellow cross and dots. The figure between the stars is black and yellow.

159 *and* 160 —*Knife Basket.*

Materials: Grey American cloth; red cloth; black jet beads and bugles; red
worsted braid, three-quarters of an inch wide; some strong wire; a cigar-box.

This basket is meant for holding dessert knives. It consists
of a common cigar-box nine inches and two-fifths long, five

159.—Knife Basket.

inches and four-fifths wide, and two inches and one-fifth high,
covered inside and out with grey American cloth, which is ornamented with embroidery worked in appliqué. The seams are
made in overcast stitch. The feet consist of four pieces of
strong wire three inches and two-fifths long. These pieces of
wire are first covered with wool, and then with jet beads; they
are then bent into loops, and fastened on at the bottom of the
box by means of holes bored into it for that purpose. The feet

must be fastened before covering the inside of the box. The inside of the basket is ornamented with an embroidered pattern in appliqué, which must also be worked before covering the box. The leaves are made of red cloth, the stems and veinings of black bugles. No. 160 shows the pattern in full size ; the

160.—Knife Basket.

flowers and leaves are edged with light grey purse silk, over which small stitches in black silk are fastened at regular intervals. Inside the box fasten a deal board covered on both sides with American cloth, so as to divide the basket into two compartments, and fasten on to this board a handle consisting of a piece of wire seven inches long, wound round with beads. The basket is ornamented with ruches of red worsted braid ; between two box pleats of the ruche a black bugle is fastened.

161.—*Satin Stitch Embroidery.*

Materials: Purse silk of two colours, in 4 shades of green and 4 shades
of red or magenta for the flowers, gold twist.

161.—Fuchsia Spray.

This branch is embroidered with purse silk of the natural
colours of the flowers and leaves, or in different shades of one
colour, on silk canvas.   Fuchsia blossoms are here designed, and
should be worked in raised embroidery; the stamens to be
worked in gold twist.

162.—Acacia Spray in Raised Satin Stitch Embroidery.

Materials: Four shades of green purse silk for the leaves; 1 skein of brown silk; 3 shades of white or gold silk for the flowers.

162.—Acacia Spray.

This spray of acacia is worked in raised satin stitch embroidery; the flowers should be carefully shaded, and the veinings should be worked before the leaves are embroidered. The flowers may be worked gold colour, or imitate the white acacia blossom.

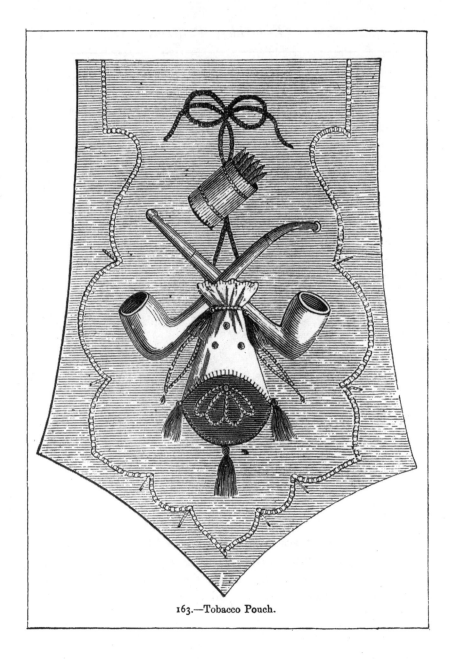

163.—Tobacco Pouch.

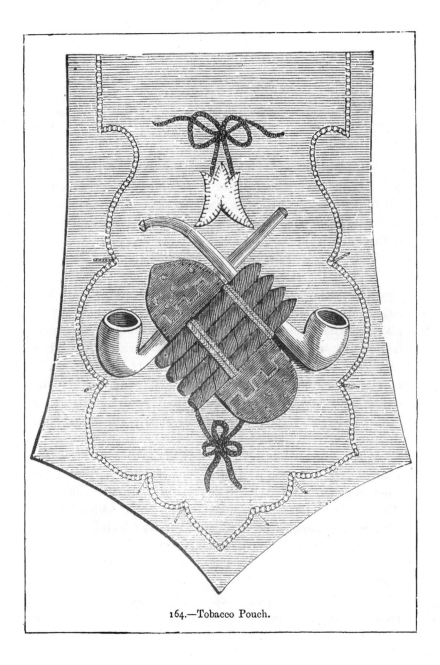

164.—Tobacco Pouch.

163 *and* 164.—*Tobacco Pouch.*

Materials: Fine crimson cloth; bits of coloured and white cloth for the
pattern; purse silk of various colours; white kid; brass rings; gimp cord;
and silk tassels.

This pouch is cut in four pieces, two of which are given in
full size ; the two others must be worked after the same patterns.
These patterns represent the attributes of a lover of tobacco ;
they are cut out of cloth and worked in appliqué over crimson
cloth.

In No. 163 the outer chain stitch border is green. The knot
from which the different articles are suspended is black, the
cigar-case yellow in cloth appliqué, the cigars brown in satin
stitch. The case is crossed by two rows of chain stitch in blue
silk, and edged all round with button-hole stitch, also blue.
The two pipes are of white cloth, edged round with yellow
silk ; the shade is imitated by long stitches of grey silk. The
upper part of the pouch is of blue cloth, with a white silk
edging and yellow dots ; the under part of brown cloth with a
black edging and a pattern worked in chain stitch with white ;
the three tassels are embroidered with black and yellow silk.

In No. 164 the outer border is yellow, the knots black, the
small pattern at the top is of blue cloth edged with yellow ; the
pipes of white cloth edged with blue and shaded with grey.
The bundle of cigars is of brown cloth, shaded with black silk
stitches, and fastened on with double rows of chain stitch in
yellow silk. The cigar-case is of light green cloth, edged with
white ; the Grecian pattern and dots are embroidered over it
with white silk also.

To make up the pouch, cut out the four pieces and join
them together by seams, which are hidden under yellow

soutache; cut out also and join in the same way four pieces of white kid for the lining, and fasten it on to the crimson cloth at the top only. Sew small brass rings round the top, and pass a double piece of crimson silk cord through them. Add silk tassels of various colours at the bottom of the pouch, and at each of its four corners.

165.—*Insertion*

Materials: Linen; Messrs. Walter Evans and Co.'s embroidery cotton No. 16.

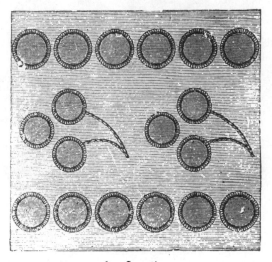

165.—Insertion.

This strong and simple insertion is useful for petticoat trimmings. It is worked in button-hole stitch; the stems in overcast stitch; the circles can be filled up with lace stitches or with wheels, or the pattern may be worked upon Brussels net and the linen cut away.

L

166.—*Embroidery Pattern for Ornamenting Needlebooks, Work-
baskets, &c.*

Materials : Coloured purse silk ; silk or cashmere ; glacé silk ; gold beads.

This pattern is worked in French embroidery and point
Russe, with coloured purse silk on silk or cashmere. The

166.— Pattern for Needlebook, &c.

thimble, cotton, and ribbon are worked in appliqué with glacé
silk. The colours are chosen according to personal taste. The
thimble is ornamented with small gold beads. A bead is placed
in the centre of each pair of scissors to imitate the screw.

167.—*Embroidery Pattern for Ornamenting Needlebooks, &c.*

Materials: Coloured purse silk; silk or cashmere; beads.

The shuttlecocks are worked in raised satin stitch; the feathers in point Russe; the battledores in very thickly raised

167.—Pattern for Needlebook, &c.

double overcast; the interior is filled with a netting worked in chain stitch or dotted stitch; the flowers are worked in satin stitch and beads; the ribbon is embroidered in appliqué, with a contrasting shade of silk ribbon.

168 *and* 169.—*Travelling Bag*

Materials: 20 inches of Java canvas; single Berlin wool of 2 shades of a pretty green; 2 shades of bronze colour and white; floss silk—white, brown, and 2 shades of yellow; purse silk—black, yellow, cerise, blue, and grey; steel beads; brown silk fancy braid.

This pattern is of the ordinary shape of travelling-bags, but it is very prettily worked. Besides the engraving showing

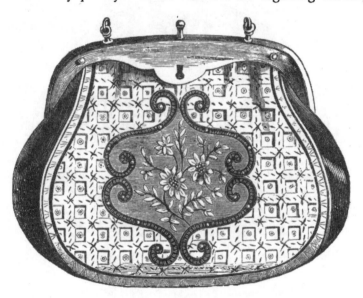

168.—Travelling Bag.

the bag when completed, the bouquet in the centre in full size is given. This bouquet is also worked upon the Java canvas. For each petal the white wool is passed several times from one stitch of the canvas to another till the required thickness is obtained, then 1 stitch is worked at the point with white silk. The centres are filled up in point d'or with 2 shades of yellow silk. The buds are made like the petals, but with 3 stitches of white silk at the point instead of 1. The leaves are

169. - Bouquet for Travelling Bag.

worked in 2 shades of green wool with 1 stitch of brown silk in the centre; the stems are embroidered in overcast with light brown wool. The scroll-pattern border round the bouquet is

made with brown fancy braid put on with steel beads. The
remaining space outside this border is worked in coloured purse
silk. The 1st outline of the squares is worked in black silk, by
inserting the needle in and out of the stitches of the canvas.
When you have worked all the square thus, 12 stitches one from
the other, work on either side, at one stitch's distance, the outlines of yellow silk, which are worked in back stitch, two strips
of the Java canvas being covered by each stitch. Next to the
inner yellow outline comes a border worked over two strips of
the canvas, in slanting stitches ; this border is alternately blue in
one square and grey in the other. A star is embroidered in point
Russe in the centre of each square ; it is grey in the blue squares
and blue in the grey ; a steel bead is placed in the middle of
each star. The small crosses between the squares are worked
in cerise. The outer border of the work is composed of a piece
of black soutache, edged with a tiny trefoil pattern in cerise silk.
The front and back pieces of the bag are worked in the same
manner. The side pieces are made of plain Java canvas. The
embroidered part measures 14 inches in its widest part, and is
11 inches deep. The bag is lined with light brown silk, and
made up with a steel clasp.

170.—*Embroidery Trimming for Muslin Bodices.*

Materials : Fine muslin; fine black silk; Messrs. Walter Evans and Co.'s
embroidery cotton No. 24.

This pattern is very easily worked, and looks very nice for a
trimming. It is worked on fine white muslin ; the border is
worked in button-hole stitch with white cotton ; these scallops
are covered with loose button-hole stitch in black silk. The

feather-like branches are worked likewise in black silk in herring-bone stitch. The white spots are worked in raised embroidery. The large oval openings through which a narrow ribbon velvet is drawn are worked round with button-hole stitches.

170.—Trimming for Bodices.

171, 172, *and* 173.—*Toilet Cushion Cover in White Embroidery.*

This handsome embroidery pattern is to be worked on fine muslin ; if lined with coloured silk or satin it is very effective. The patterns, which are covered white dots on illustration, are worked in point d'or ; the outlines of these patterns are worked in fine double overcast. The flower-leaves and wings of birds, which appear raised on illustration on account of the dark shadows, are worked separately and sewn on at the corresponding places. No. 172 shows the wing of a bird, No. 173 a rose-leaf somewhat increased in size ; the former is worked entirely in button-hole stitch, or trimmed with a ruche of coloured ribbon. This pattern may also be worked on glacé silk with purse silk.

172.—Wing of Bird.

171.—Toilet Cushion Cover

173.—Rose Leaf.

in White Embroidery.

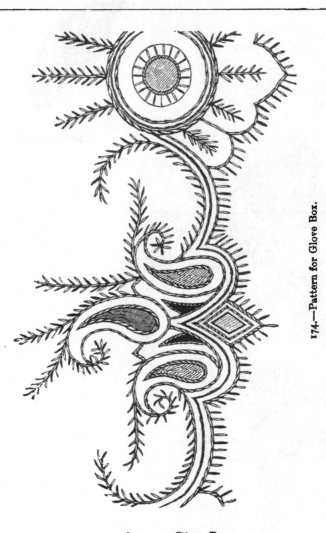

174.—Pattern for Glove Box.

174 *and* 175.—*Glove Box.*

Materials: 15 inches of French blue cashmere; silks of various colours.   A shape
in bamboo cane, painted brown and varnished.

The ornamentation of this box is both novel and tasteful. It is embroidered in coloured silks, upon light blue cashmere. Part of the embroidery pattern is given in full size. All the outlines are worked in overcast, the stitches being made rather long and slanting, and the small leaves are each composed of one stitch, as in point Russe. The leaves are alternately red and yellow upon a green stem; the scalloped outline which has no

175.—Glove Box.

leaves is red. The pine patterns are worked in satin stitch—the centre one is green, edged with red; the side ones are pink, edged with red; the small wing-like figures are black, edged with maize; the diamond, maize, edged with black, with an outer rim of maize. In the round pattern the centre is pink; the edge red, with red and yellow leaves; the 3 outer circles are successively white, green, and red ; at the top the centre branch is yellow, the leaves red and yellow, the side ones are green, with the leaves pink and green.

The strip of embroidered cashmere is lined with blue silk, slipped through the bamboo-canes of the mounting, and joined together at the side by a seam. The cover is lined with plain blue cashmere, upon which initials might be embroidered at discretion. The four corners are ornamented with pretty silk tassels, of colours to match with the embroidery. To fasten the box, sew on a blue ribbon to the cover, and one to the box.

176 *and* 177.—*Hanging Letter Case.*

Materials : Crimson velvet ; white satin beads ; gold soutache ; and fine gold bouillon.

No. 176 shows the letter case when completed in a reduced size, No. 177 the principal part of the embroidered pattern in full size.

The letter case is composed of two parts. The larger part is 11 inches long, 8 inches wide ; it is ornamented on the upper part with a pattern in gold soutache, and the word LETTERS or LETTRES embroidered in gold bouillon ; underneath there is a pattern embroidered in oval white satin beads, edged round with fine white chenille ; the scroll pattern is embroidered in gold bouillon.

The second part is placed over the lower part of the first, and forms the pocket which contains the letters. The centre flower is composed of 11 oval beads, edged round with white chenille ; another white bead is placed in the centre, and edged with gold bouillon. The other flowers are also composed of white satin beads, edged with gold bouillon.

176.--Hanging Letter Case.

177.—Pattern for Embroidered Letter Case.

178.—*Embroidered Edging.*

Materials: Muslin; Messrs. Walter Evans and Co.'s embroidery cotton No. 24.

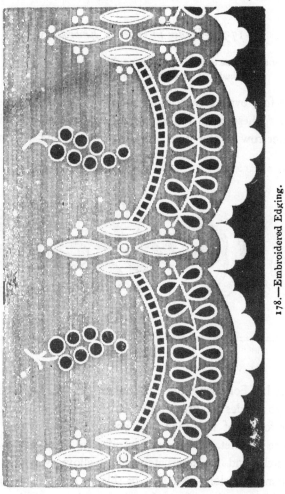

178.—Embroidered Edging.

This edging is worked in broderie Anglaise or overcast stitch; the edge in scallop button-hole stitch; the ovals and dots in raised satin stitch. The stems are worked in slanting overcast stitch (No. 122, *Embroidery Instructions*).

179.—*Border in Oriental Embroidery.*

Materials: Purse silk of the following shades:—dark red, bright red, 2 shades of green, 2 of blue, 2 of yellow violet.

The four ovals placed together are worked of four contrasting colours. These ovals are composed of two rows of chain stitch. The outer row of the first oval is dark red, and the inner one

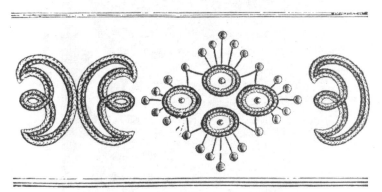

179.—Border in Oriental Embroidery.

bright red. Following the same arrangement, the second oval is of two shades of green ; the third of two shades of blue ; and the fourth of two shades of yellow. The knotted stitch in the centre is violet. The dots outside the ovals are worked in satin stitch, and are alternately red, yellow, violet, and blue. The stems are long stitches of black silk. The arabesque patterns between those formed of four ovals are worked in chain stitch with silk of two shades of brown. The colours of the ovals may be varied as much as you please, but the brown shades of the arabesque patterns should remain the same for the whole of the border.

180 *and* 181.—*Embroidery Stars.*

Materials : Fine linen; Messrs. Walter Evans and Co.'s embroidery
cotton No. 40.

These stars are designed for medallions, to be worked on linen collars and cuffs. No. 180 is worked in successive rows of

180.—Embroidery Star.

181.—Embroidery Star.

back-stitching, round an open wheel; ladder stitch (see No. 81, *Embroidery Instructions*) is worked round this, and a raised scallop in button-hole stitch forms the edge.

No. 181 is worked in raised satin stitch ; the interior of the star is filled with lace wheels.

182 *and* 183.—*Key Bag.*

Materials : Grey kid; grey silk; steel-coloured glacé silk; purse silk of 5 shades
of blue-green, 4 shades of brown, and silver-grey, scarlet, and white; grey
silk cord; grey glacé silk ribbon.

This bag is made of grey kid, and lined with grey silk. The embroidery imitates on one side a key formed of poppies, leaves, and stems, in the upper part of which sits an owl, " the

M

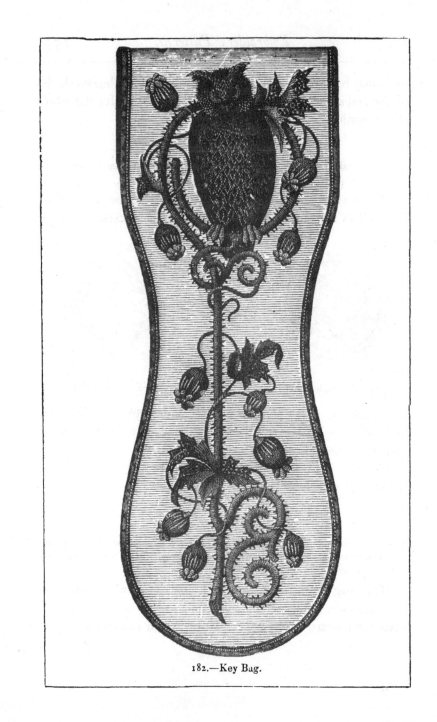

182.—Key Bag.

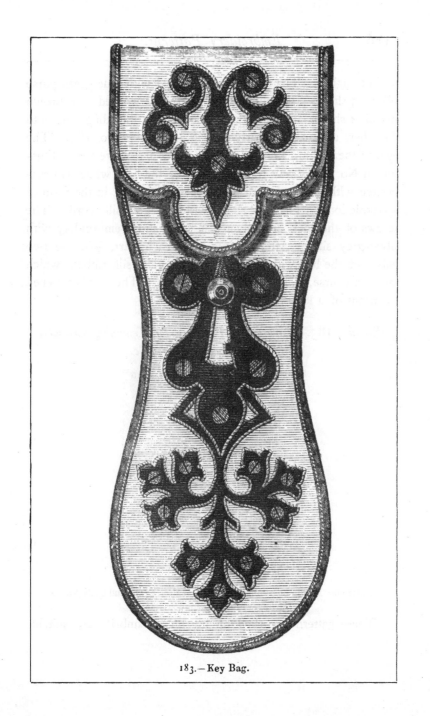

183.—Key Bag.

bird of night." The poppies are worked with blue-green purse silk in 5 shades ; the plumage of the owl is worked with brown silk of 4 shades in satin stitch, the colours blending one into the other, as can be clearly seen in illustration No. 182. The eyes of the owl are embroidered in scarlet and white silk. Illustration No. 183 shows the other side of the bag, which is ornamented with steel-coloured silk appliqué figures, in the form of a Gothic lock. They are edged with fine grey silk cord. The screws of the lock are imitated in satin stitch embroidery with silver-grey silk. After having lined each part, join the two halves of the bag with a border of grey glacé silk ribbon, which must, of course, continue round the revers. The bag is fastened by means of a loop and steel button.

184 *and* 185.—*Embroidery Patterns for Trimming Cravats, Bodices, Morning Caps, &c.*

184 —Embroidery Pattern for Cravats, &c.

Materials : Muslin or cambric ; Messrs. Walter Evans and Co.'s No. 24 for lingerie, No. 12 for couvrettes.

These patterns, worked on muslin or cambric, are suitable

for trimming various articles of lingerie; joined on to other squares they make pretty covers. They can also be embroidered with coloured silk, wool, or thread, on cloth, rep, or cashmere, for trimming couvrettes and toilet pincushions. The patterns should be embroidered in satin stitch and edged with chain stitch; they can also be worked in button-hole stitch. When the pattern is worked on woollen material this material must be cut away inside the leaves and spots.

185.—Embroidery Pattern for Cravats, &c.

186 and 187.—*Pen-Wiper in Cloth Appliqué.*

Materials: 4 circles of black cloth; 1 large white, 4 small white, and 4 red circles of cloth; 4 white and 4 red stars of cloth; small black beads; gold and black purse silk; small ivory handle or figure.

This pretty little pen-wiper is covered with small circles of cloth. No. 187 is one of these circles seen in full size. There are 4 white and 4 red ones, and they are pinked out round the edge. In the centre of each red circle place a white, and in the centre of each white circle a red star, and work a cross over it with

small round black beads.   The border, in herring-bone stitch,
is worked with gold-coloured purse silk on the red, and with
black on the white cloth.   The centre of the pen-wiper is
covered with a circle of white cloth larger than the side ones,

186.—Pen-wiper in Embroidery.

worked in point Russe and point Mexico in black silk.   When
all the circles are prepared, sew them neatly on to a round
piece of red cloth, placing alternately 1 white and 1 red, so as to
overlap one another, and between each a circle of black cloth,
also pinked out round the edge.   The work is then fastened
upon a round of cardboard lined with black glazed calico, and a

small handle of carved ivory, or an ivory figure, is fixed in the centre. The circles of black cloth are used to wipe the pens.

187.—Full-sized Circle for Pen-wiper.

188.—*Insertion.*

Materials: Fine muslin; Messrs. Walter Evans and Co.'s embroidery cotton No. 30.

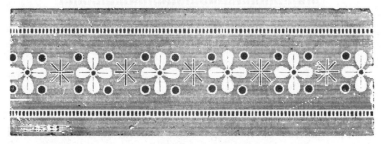

188.—Insertion.

The flowers of this insertion are embroidered in raised satin stitch round an open eyelet hole, worked in overcast stitch, the stars are worked in point Russe stitch; the four eyelet holes which surround each flower, in overcast stitch; and the edge is finished with a row of hem-stitching on each side.

189.—*Insertion.*

Materials: Fine muslin; Messrs. Walter Evans and Co.'s embroidery
cotton No. 24.

This insertion is entirely embroidered in raised satin stitch ;
the dots and stems should be worked first, and the leaves afterwards. It is edged on both sides with a row of hem-stitching.

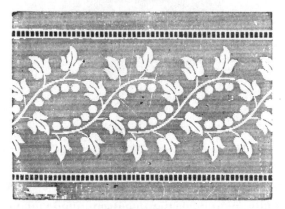

189.—Insertion.

190.—*Cigar Case.*

Materials: Russia leather; fine silk cord; black purse silk; gold thread.

The material of this cigar case should be finely-embossed
light brown Russia leather ; the centre pattern to be embroidered
in well-raised satin stitch with black purse silk. All the lighter
outlines shown in the illustration are worked in gold thread.
The border to be worked in fine silk cord of the same colour as
the leather, with a network of black purse silk, stitched with
gold at all the crossings. On the opposite side of the cigar case

190.—Cigar Case.

initials may be worked. The lining of light brown watered silk, or fine leather, and the mountings gilt or steel.

191.—*Wicker Waste Paper Basket.*

Materials : Basket and stand; coloured Berlin wools; cloth fringe; and glazed calico.

191.—Waste Paper Basket.

The basket may be of any size, but of the shape of the pattern. It rests upon two brass hooks fastened upon a stand. This stand can be made by any joiner, and should match the furniture of the room. The trimming consists of an embroidered border, lined with glazed calico, and put on round the edge; the lower part of the border is trimmed with a woollen fringe.

The shades selected should correspond with the prevailing colour of the room.

192.—Insertion.

192.—*Insertion.*

Materials: Messrs. Walter Evans and Co.'s embroidery cotton No. 16.

The edge of this insertion is worked in raised button-hole

stitch, and embroidered in sharply-pointed scallops ; the dotted line is worked in raised satin stitch, as are also the flowers which compose the centre wreath ; the eyelet holes are worked in overcast stitch.

193.—Embroidered Linen Collar.

193 *and* 194.—*Embroidered Linen Collars.*

Materials : Double linen ; Messrs. Walter Evans and Co.'s embroidery cotton No. 40.

These patterns are to be worked on linen taken double.

No. 194 is worked in button-hole, satin, and knotted stitch (see Nos. 81, 82, 76, and 73 of *Embroidery Instructions*), and point d'or with white cotton, and point Russe with black silk. No. 193 is

194.—Embroidered Linen Collar.

worked entirely with white cotton in button-hole, satin, knotted ladder, and overcast stitch. (See Nos. 82, 76, 73, 81, and 68 of *Embroidery Instructions*.)

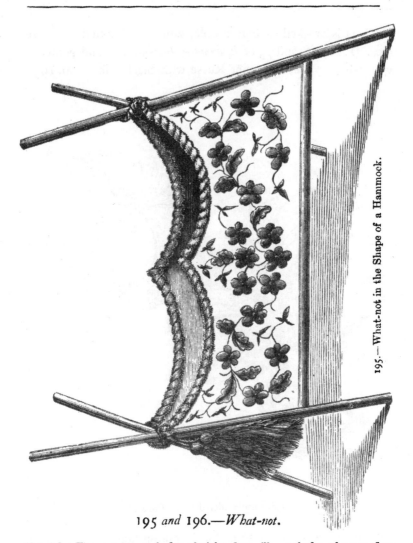

195.—What-not in the Shape of a Hammock.

195 and 196.—*What-not.*

Materials **:** Fine canvas; 3 shades of violet floss silk; 4 shades of green floss silk; sea-green wool, or floss silk; 1 skein of yellow floss silk; green chenille; cord and tassels.

196.—Pattern for What-not (full size).

This small what-not or jewel-stand is very elegant. It is meant to place upon the toilet-table. No. 195 shows the hammock when completed, No. 196 one-half of the embroidery pattern in full size; it is worked upon fine canvas. The violets are in floss silk of three shades of violet, with a raised spot worked in yellow silk in the centre, the leaves are worked in Berlin wool of various shades of green, and the stems in overcast of a light green shade. The pattern is grounded in tent stitch with sea-green silk. The hammock is composed of two sides and an under-piece cut out in cardboard, covered with the embroidered canvas outside, lined and quilted with plain green silk inside. It is edged round the top with green chenille. The mounting is composed of bamboo-canes ; the hammock is fastened on to it with green silk cord, finished off with tassels.

197.—*Embroidered Handkerchief.*

Materials: Grass lawn or French cambric; Messrs. Walter Evans and Co.'s embroidery cotton No. 40.

This embroidery pattern is worked between the borders of a handkerchief, which may be either of French cambric or grass lawn. The design is simple, but effective, and very easy to work. If worked on fine French cambric, the handkerchief should be lightly tacked upon *toile cirée*. The rows of raised dots should be worked first, and then the graceful branches of pointed leaves in satin stitch. The plain round dots might be worked in bright red marking cotton in either of the patterns. To produce a good effect, rather fine cotton must be selected, and No. 40 will be found very effective on either lawn or cambric. For mourning wear, this pattern should be embroidered with black filoselle, or the leaves can be worked in white cotton, and the dots in filoselle.

197.—Handkerchief Border.

198 *and* 199.—*Two Medallions for a Purse in Embroidery.*

Materials : Light brown russia leather ; black, scarlet, and gold silk ;
steel or gold clasp.

These medallions are intended to ornament a small purse,
but may be employed on a variety of articles.

198.—Medallion for a Purse in Embroidery.

199.—Medallion for a Purse in Embroidery.

The raised spots of No. 198 should be worked in black silk,

in satin stitch, the branched sprays in point Russe in scarlet and gold, the four largest being in scarlet and the intermediate sprays in gold silk. Medallion No. 199 is worked entirely in point Russe, and may be embroidered in one colour, or in alternate branches of scarlet and gold, or scarlet and black.

200.—*Work-Bag.*

Materials: Drab cloth; small pieces of cloth of different colours; embroidery silk of different colours; scarlet satin; red silk braid; red cord; cardboard; cotton wool; and a strap of light-coloured leather.

This work-bag is made in the shape of a rolled-up plaid.

200.—Work Bag.

The outside consists of drab cloth, trimmed with appliqué embroidery. The inside of the bag is slightly wadded and lined with red satin, which is quilted in diamonds. The seams are covered with red braid, and a leather strap completes the whole. Cut out a good pattern in paper, and then cut the satin and

wadding and the drab cloth which forms the outside. After
having traced the pattern on the cloth, work it with small pieces
of coloured cloth in appliqué embroidery. The different figures
are sewn over the centre partly in point Russe, partly in button-
hole stitches, with embroidery silk. The stems in the middle
are worked with silk in chain stitches. The colours may be
chosen according to taste. Cut a pattern in cardboard, and fasten
the drab cloth on it. The edge must be bordered with red
satin, and the satin lining must be sewed in. The ends of the
bag are likewise cut out of cardboard ; the inside is wadded and
lined with red satin ; the outside worked in appliqué embroidery
like the rest of the bag. All the seams are covered with red silk
cord. The straps are fastened with a few stitches, as seen in the
illustration.

201 *to* 203.—*Pattern for Braces.*

Materials : Java canvas; black silk; red wool; calico.

These braces are made of Java canvas lined with calico

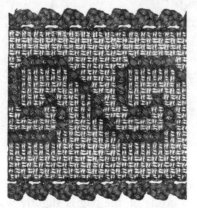

201.—Pattern for Braces (full size).

ornamented with embroidery in black silk and red wool, and
edged on either side with loose button-hole stitch and crochet

vandykes in red wool. Illustration 201 shows part of the embroidered braces, full size. Work first the embroidery of the braces, then line them with calico; work loose button-hole stitch and crochet vandykes on all the edges of the cross bands as well as at the top and bottom of these strips, and sew on the tabs for the braces between the lining and the canvas. The

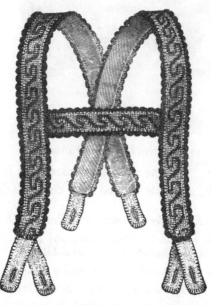

202.—Embroidered Braces.

latter a e then edged with button-hole stitch and crochet van-dykes. The vandykes are worked as follow—in one row: 1 double in 1 button-hole stitch, * 1 purl (3 chain, 1 double in the 1st), missing the next button-hole stitch under it; 1 double in the following button-hole stitch, repeat from *. The tabs are made of tape worked round with red button-hole stitch, with button-holes worked with red cotton. No. 203 shows another

way of working these braces on fine ribbed piqué. Work any
Berlin wool work pattern in the common cross stitch over the

203.—Pattern for Braces (Full size).

ribs of the piqué. For the vandyke border work in every other
button-hole stitch, 2 double divided by 3 chain stitches

204.—*Embroidery Border for a Reading-Desk.*

Materials : White silk rep; black velvet, rep, or cloth; gold and silver brocade;
gold and silver braid; silk cord and thread.

This pattern is embroidered on white silk rep with silver
and gold thread, and sewn on over a black velvet, rep, or cloth
centre. The dark patterns are worked in appliqué with black
velvet, the two other shades in gold and silver brocade. The
embroidery is worked in satin stitch with gold and silver braid,
silk and cord of the same material. The border can also be
worked upon the material for the centre if it is not intended to
contrast with it. The pattern can also be worked entirely in
silk with satin stitch. The size of the border may, of course, be
increased if desired, but the third pattern in the darkest shade
must, in any case, form the centre of it.

204.—Embroidery Border for a Reading Desk.

205.—Lappet or Sash End in Venetian Embroidery.

205.—*Lappet or Sash End in Venetian Embroidery.*

Materials : Messrs. Walter Evans and Co.'s embroidery cotton No. 6 and No. 12 ;
net and muslin.

The pattern must first be traced on muslin, which is then
tacked over net. The outlines are worked in button-hole stitch,
and the veinings are sewn over, using the coarse cotton for
tracing ; the muslin is then cut away all round the pattern.

206.—*Venetian Border.*

Materials : Messrs. Walter Evans and Co.'s embroidery cotton No. 12 and
No. 16 ; net and muslin.

206.—Venetian Border.

This design is elegant and effective, without there being a
great deal of work in it. It is useful for tuckers for evening
dresses or handkerchief borders. The muslin is laid over the
net, sewn neatly over, and then cut away between the pattern,
leaving the net for the groundwork.

207.—Lace Insertion.

207.—*Lace Insertion.*

Materials: Fine black sewing silk ; black Brussels net.

This lace insertion is first outlined in running stitch upon the net ; the leaves are then darned across the net holes ; the stems are worked in overcast stitch ; the dots are embroidered by darning across the circle previously outlined ; the lace stitches in the centre are formed by gently enlarging the net holes with a fine stiletto, and then sewn lightly round, the remaining holes being filled with lace stitches consisting of fine button-hole stitches, very evenly worked over the entire space surrounding the open holes.

To be effective the very finest black silk should be employed. This pattern may be worked in appliqué by placing muslin over net, sewing all the outlines in fine overcast stitch, and when finished, carefully cutting away the muslin.

208 and 209.—*Slipper on Java Canvas.*

Materials: Light brown Java canvas; green silk; green filoselle and purse silk ; green silk ribbon three-fifths of an inch wide ; some wadding; 2 cork soles

This slipper is very pretty, and easy to work.   It is made of

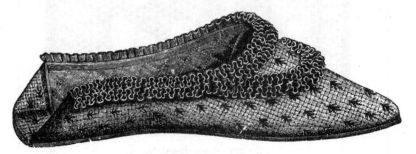

208.—Slipper on Java Canvas.

light brown Java canvas, and embroidered in point Russe with
green filoselle. It is lined with green silk, and slightly quilted
The soles are of cork. The slipper is trimmed all round with
a ruche of green silk ribbon three-fifths of an inch wide, pleated
in double box pleats. The heel is turned down inside. No. 209
shows the pattern of the point Russe stitch nearly full size.

209.—Point Russe Stitch for Slipper (No. 208)

210 and 211.—*Medallions in Point Russe.*

Materials : Coloured filoselle, cloth, velvet, cashmere, or silk.

These medallions can be alternated for ornamenting small
covers, cushions, borders, &c. They are worked with coloured
filoselle in point Russe, herring-bone stitch, coral stitch, and
knotted stitch, on cloth, velvet, cashmere, or silk. The middle
oval of both medallions contrasts with the colour of the ground,
and must therefore be worked in appliqué on the latter with
herring-bone stitch, before working the outer border. The
wreath on No. 211 is worked in coral stitch ; the knots, which
imitate small blossoms, in knotted stitch. The choice of colours
is left to the personal taste of the worker.

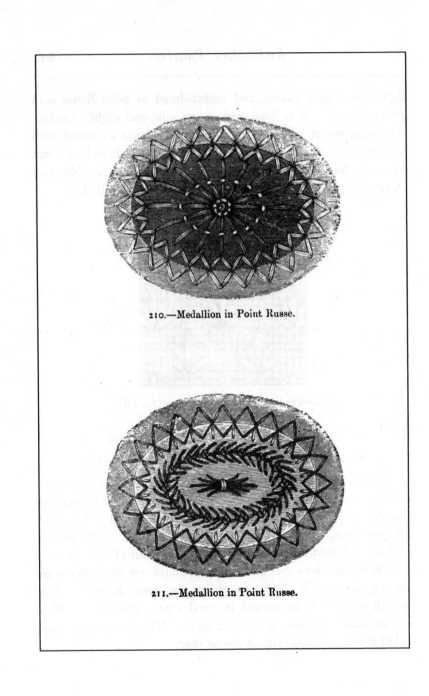

210.—Medallion in Point Russe.

211.—Medallion in Point Russe.

212.—*Butterfly for Handkerchief Corner.*

Materials: French lawn or cambric; fine black silk.

This butterfly is worked in the finest black silk procurable, in order more closely to imitate etching. It is worked in point Russe and scallop stitch ; the dark shaded scallops are worked in

212.—Butterfly for Handkerchief Corner.

buttonhole scallop stitch, the stitches being taken very closely together, but not raised by the usual method of placing chain stitches beneath the button-hole stitches. The outlines and flowers are worked in point Russe, the dot in knotted stitch (see No. 73, *Embroidery Instructions.*)

The initials are embroidered in raised slanting overcast stitch, and should be worked with great regularity.

213 to 215.—Pattern for a Couvrette in Appliqué.

(see pages 576-7.)

Materials: Messrs. Walter Evans and Co.'s embroidery cotton Nos. 24 and 30; cambric muslin; Brussels net; flesh-coloured silk; sewing silk of the same shade; 1 skein of a darker shade; blue silk; brown silk; gold thread.

This style of work is most effective for couvrettes or bed covers. It is worked in cambric muslin and silk, over Brussels net.

The arabesque patterns are worked in cambric muslin, the outlines are embroidered in overcast, and the material is cut away all round. The medallions are made of blue silk; the figures upon them are cut out of flesh-coloured silk, and are gummed first upon tissue-paper, then upon the blue silk; the figures are further fastened upon the medallions in overcast stitch with fine silk of a rather darker shade of flesh-colour. The scarfs are cut out of bright rose-coloured silk; the quiver and arrows and all the other attributes are worked in gold thread; the hair in fine brown silk. The edge of the blue silk medallions is worked round in button-hole stitch, but so as to be easily unripped when the couvrette has to be cleaned. A border in open ladder stitch is worked round them (see No. 81, *Embroidery Instructions*). The openings in the centre pattern are also filled in with lace stitches.

CROCHET

INSTRUCTIONS.

———◆———

COTTON or thread, wool or silk, with a crochet-needle, are the materials required for working crochet. The needle, whether it be steel or bone, must be smoothly polished. The long wooden and bone crochet-needles are used for wool; for cotton and silk work short steel needles screwed into a

bone handle are best. The beauty of the crochet-work depends upon the regularity of the stitches, as is the case with every other style of needlework. The stitches must be elastic, but if too loose they look as bad as if too tight. The size of the needle and that of the cotton or wool must correspond; work only with the point of the needle, and never move the stitch up and down the needle. The cotton with which you work must be of the very best quality; for borders, insertions, rosettes, imitation of guipure, use Evans's crochet cotton; for couvrettes, counterpanes, covers, &c., use knitting-cotton. All crochet-work

o

patterns are begun on a foundation chain ; there are three kinds of foundation chains—the plain foundation, the double foundation, and the purl foundation chain.

The plain foundation chain consists of chain stitches.

216.—Plain Foundation Chain.   217.—Double Foundation Chain.

ILLUSTRATION 216.—Form a loop with the cotton or other material with which you work, take it on the needle, and hold the cotton as for knitting on the forefinger and other fingers of the left hand. The crochet-needle is held in the right hand between the thumb and forefinger, as you hold a pen in writing ; hold the end of the cotton of the loop between the thumb and forefinger of the left hand, wind the cotton once round the needle by drawing the needle underneath the cotton from left to right, catch the cotton with the hook of the needle and draw it as a loop through the loop already on the needle, which is cast off the needle by this means and forms one chain stitch. The drawing the cotton through the loop is repeated until the foundation chain has acquired sufficient length. When enough chain stitches have been made, take the foundation chain between the thumb and forefinger of the left hand, so that these fingers are always close to and under the hook of the needle. Each stitch must be loose enough to let the hook of the needle pass easily through. All foundation chains are begun with a loop.

ILLUSTRATION 217 (*The Double Foundation Chain*).—Crochet 2 chain stitches, insert the needle downwards into the left side of the 1st chain stitch, throw the cotton forward, draw it out as a loop, wind the cotton again round the needle and draw it through the two loops on the needle, * draw the cotton as a loop through the left side of the last stitch (see illustration), wind the cotton round the needle, and draw it through both loops on the needle. Repeat from * till the foundation chain is long enough.

218 —Purl Foundation Chain.

ILLUSTRATION 218 (*Purl Foundation Chain*).—* Crochet 4 chain stitch, then 1 treble stitch—that is, wind the cotton round the needle, insert the needle downwards into the left side of the 1st of the 4 chain stitches, wind the cotton round the needle, draw it through the stitch, wind the cotton again round the needle, and at the same time draw the cotton through the last loop and through the stitch formed by winding the cotton round the needle. Wind the cotton once more round the needle, and draw it through the 2 remaining loops on the needle. The 4 chain stitches form a kind of scallop or purl. Repeat from *. The following crochet stitches require foundation chains like Nos. 216 and 217 ; they are all worked in separate rows excepting the two Nos. 222 and 234. Make a loop at the beginning of every row, as has been described (No. 216), and take it on the needle.

219.—Slip Stitch.

ILLUSTRATION 219 (*Slip Stitch*).—Draw the needle through the back part of a foundation chain stitch, or in the course of the work through the back part of a stitch of the preceding row, wind the cotton round the needle, and draw it through the stitch and loop on the needle. The illustration shows a number of slip stitches, the last of which is left quite loose ; the arrow marks the place where the needle is to be inserted for the next stitch.

220.—Double Stitch.

ILLUSTRATION 220 (*Double Stitch*).—These are worked nearly like the preceding ones. Draw the cotton as a loop through the back part of a stitch, wind the cotton round the needle, and draw it through the two loops on the needle.

221.—Double Stitch.

ILLUSTRATION 221.—These double stitches are worked nearly like the preceding ones; the 1st row is worked like that of No. 220; in the following ones insert the needle into the two upper sides of a stitch of the preceding row.

222.—Ribbed Stitch.

ILLUSTRATION 222 (*The Ribbed Stitch*). — This stitch is worked backwards and forwards—that is, the right and wrong sides are worked together, which forms the raised ribs. Insert the needle always into the back part of every stitch. Work 1 chain stitch at the end of every row, which is not worked, however, in the following row.

223.—Slanting Stitch.

ILLUSTRATION 223 (*Slanting Stitch, double stitch*).—This stitch is worked like that described in No. 220; the cotton is not wound round the needle the first time in the usual manner, but the needle is placed in the direction of the arrow, above the cotton. Draw the cotton through as a loop; the stitch is finished like the common double stitch.

224.—Cross Stitch.

ILLUSTRATION 224 (*Cross Stitch*).—This stitch is worked like No. 223 on a foundation like No. 217, only insert the needle through the two upper sides of a stitch.

225.—Long Double Stitch.

ILLUSTRATION 225 (*Long Double*).—For this stitch wind the cotton round the needle, insert it into the back part of a stitch, draw the cotton out as a loop, wind the cotton again round the needle, and cast off together the two loops and the loop formed by winding the cotton round the needle.

226.—Treble Stitch.

ILLUSTRATION 226 (*Treble Stitch*). — These stitches are worked as has been described for the purl foundation chain, No. 218. The treble stitches are worked on a foundation chain or in the stitches of the preceding row.

ILLUSTRATION 227 (*Long Treble*).—These are worked like treble stitches, only the cotton is wound twice round the needle ;

the double long treble (illustration 228) is worked by winding the cotton three times round the needle. The loops formed by winding the cotton round the needle are cast off one by one with

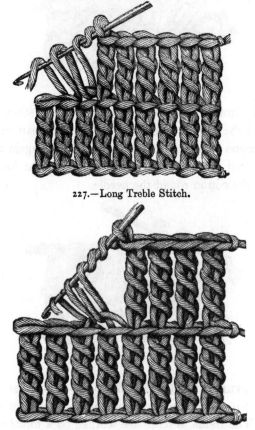

227.—Long Treble Stitch.

228.—Double Long Treble Stitch.

one of the loops on the needle. The two loops that remain at the end are cast off together after winding the cotton round the needle.

229.—Cross Treble Stitch.

ILLUSTRATIONS 229—231 (*Cross Treble*).—Illustration 229 shows this stitch completed ; illustrations 230 and 231 show them in the course of the work. Wind the cotton twice round the needle as for a long treble, insert the needle into the stitch in which the first half of the cross treble is to be worked, wind the cotton round the needle, draw the cotton through as a loop, wind the cotton again round the needle and cast off together with the same the loop on the needle and the loop formed by throwing the

230.—Cross Treble Stitch.

cotton forward ; you have now 3 loops left on the needle, 1 of which has been formed by winding the cotton round the needle ; missing these, wind the cotton again round the needle, miss the 2 next stitches of the foundation chain, and draw a loop through the third stitch. You have now 5 loops on the needle. Always cast off 2 loops at a time till only 1 loop remains on the needle. Work 2 chain stitches (if you wish to have the stitches more or

231.—Cross Treble Stitch.

less) slanting, work 1, 2, or 3 chain stitches, missing, of course, the same number of foundation chain, work 1 treble stitch, inserting the needle, as shown by the arrow on No. 231, into the 2 cross chain of the completed treble stitch.

232.—Raised Spots.

ILLUSTRATION 232 (*Raised Spots*).—The grounding on which these spots are worked consists of double crochet. They are worked across 3 rows of the ground, and formed of treble stitches, the spots of one row being placed between those of the preceding. Work first 2 rows of double stitch, in the 3rd row work first 2 double stitches and then 1 spot as follows :—1 treble, inserting the needle into both sides of 1 stitch of the first row (the preceding row is missed) ; the treble stitch is only completed so far that 2 loops remain on the needle ; then work

2 treble stitches in the same stitch as the first, which are also only completed as far as the first treble stitch, so that after the 2nd treble there remain 3 loops and after the 3rd 4 loops on the needle (see illustration). The 4 loops are cast off together by winding the cotton once more round the needle and drawing it through. Miss under the spot the next double stitch of the preceding row ; the spots are repeated at intervals of 5 stitches and in every other row.

233.—Hollow Spots.

ILLUSTRATION 233 (*Hollow Spots*).—The ground is worked in double crochet (illustration 220). These spots, which appear raised, consist of 5 treble stitches ; they are worked in every other row at intervals of 5 stitches. For working them leave 1 loop on the needle, insert the needle between the 2 long sides of the last-worked double stitch, and work 5 treble stitches, always inserting the needle into the front part of 1 stitch of the preceding row. The first 4 treble are completed entirely without taking up the loop which was on the needle ; with the fifth treble stitch only the 3 loops are cast off together by winding the cotton round the needle. Miss 1 stitch of the preceding row under the spot.

234.—Open-work Spots.

ILLUSTRATION 234 (*Open-work Spots*).— These spots are treble stitches divided by 2 chain ; miss 2 stitches under the latter ; for the rest, they are worked like the raised spots (illustration 232).

235.—Raised Treble Stitch.

ILLUSTRATION 235 (*Raised Treble Stitch*).—These stitches are long treble worked on a ribbed ground (illustration 222), and are thrown across 3 rows of the same. The raised treble are always worked on the same side of the work and in the long side of the corresponding stitch of the last row but two. After every row with treble stitch comes a row in ribbed stitch. At the beginning work 3 rows of ribbed stitch; the treble stitches begin only in the 4th row.

236.—Purl Stitch.

ILLUSTRATION 236 (*Purl Stitch*).—These purl stitches imitate a lace edging perfectly well. Work 1 double, draw out the loop to a certain length (this forms the purl), take the needle out of it, insert it in the front part of the last stitch which has been worked (see illustration), wind the cotton round the needle and draw it through as a loop; 1 double, 1 purl, and so on.

237.—Purl Stitch.

ILLUSTRATION 237 (*Purl Stitch turned upwards*).—Work 1 treble, then 7 chain stitch. Insert the needle into the 2nd of the 7 chain stitch downwards, so that the chain stitches form a scallop upwards (see illustration), wind the cotton round the needle and draw the cotton through ; work 1 chain stitch and 1 treble in the next stitch but 3, missing 3 stitches under it.

238.—Purl Stitch.

ILLUSTRATION 238 (*Purl Stitch turned downwards*).—The chain stitches form a scallop turned downwards. After having worked the 7 chain stitches take the needle out of the loop, insert it underneath the upper chain of the 2nd chain stitch, from right to left, and draw it through the loop in the direction of the arrow. Wind the cotton round the needle and cast all the loops off together. It is evident that the purl stitches may be worked at larger or smaller distances.

CROCHET PATTERNS.

239.—*Small Crochet Basket.*

Materials: 2 balls of closely-covered white and silver, and 1 ball of pink and silver twine; a crochet needle.

For the bottom : Make a chain of 4 stitches and unite it,

239.—Small Crochet Basket.

work 3 long, 3 chain, and repeat three times more.   2nd round : Work 3 long into the 1st 3 chain, make 3 chain, work 3 long into the next 3 chain, make 3 chain, work 3 long into the same place, make 3 chain, and repeat.   3rd round : 3 long, 3 chain, working twice into the 3 chain of last round.   4th round : 3 long, 3 chain, increasing in every other 3rd chain by working twice into it.   5th round : Increasing in every 3rd chain, repeat.   For the leaves : Make a chain of 32 stitches, then work a row of 1 long stitch and 1 chain stitch with the silver twine.   2nd round : Work 1 long stitch into each chain stitch in 1st row, make 1 chain stitch, repeat.   (At the point, make 4 long, with a chain stitch between each), repeat on the other side of the chain, 1 long stitch and 1 chain stitch alternately.   3rd round : With pink : Work over a wire in double crochet 1 stitch into each loop, work 15 more leaves in the same way, join each leaf half way, then sew it to the centre, work a row of double crochet 1 yard in length, and twist it for the handle.   This should also be crocheted over wire.

240 to 243.—*Couvrette in Crochet.*

Materials : Messrs. Walter Evans and Co.'s Boar's Head cotton No. 10, and steel crochet needle.

This very pretty pattern is composed of separate circles representing dahlias in raised work upon an open centre. No. 242 shows one of these large circles in full size, No. 241 one of the small circles placed in the spaces between the larger ones, No. 243 part of the border, and No. 240 the couvrette when completed, but in reduced size.

For each large circle make a chain of 20 stitches, and join it into a circle.   1st round : 30 stitches of double crochet over the circle of chain stitches.   2nd round : 36 stitches of double crochet.   3rd round : 1 double, 5 chain, miss 1.   4th round

240.—Couvrette in Crochet.

The same as the preceding—the 1 double always on the 3rd chain.   5th round : Close double crochet ; 3 stitches in 1 in the centre stitch of each loop.   6th to 12th round : The same as the 5th, close double crochet, increasing in the centre of each small scallop, which forms the 18 raised petals of the dahlia. 13th round : Here begins the open-work border round the dahlia.   Work 1 double between 2 petals, taking together the 2 centre stitches, 1 double in the next, 5 chain.   There will be

241.—Showing one of the small Circles
full size of No. 240.

18 loops of 5 chain in the round.   14th to 17th round : 1 double in centre of each loop, 5 chain between.   18th round : 1 double in centre of 1st loop, 4 chain, 1 treble in next loop ; in the top of this treble stitch work 3 double, with 3 chain between each ; make 4 chain.   Repeat the same all round, and the large circle is completed.   Six of these are required.

For each small circle make a chain of 10 stitches, and join it into a round.   1st round : 16 stitches of close double crochet. 2nd round : 1 treble, 3 chain, miss 1, 8 times.   3rd round : 9 treble over each loop of chain, 1 double between.   This completes 1 of the 6 small circles placed round the large ones in the centre of the couvrette. The 6 that are placed between the 5 other large circles have 1 more round, which is worked as

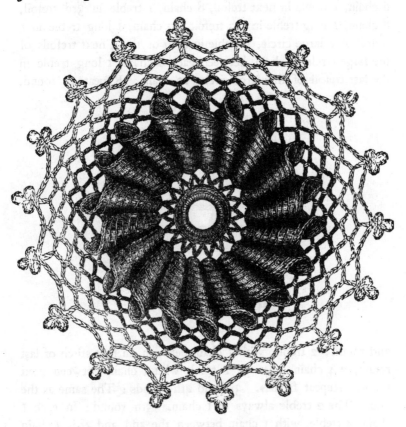

242.—Showing one of the large Circles full size of No. 240.

follows :—1 treble in the centre of 1 scallop in the top of this treble stitch, 3 double, with 3 chain between each, 6 chain Repeat the same all round.

When all the circles are completed, join them together, as seen in illustration 217, and work the border as follows : — 1st round : 1 treble in one of the trefoil branches of a small circle, 8 chain, 1 treble in next trefoil, 8 chain, 1 treble in 3rd trefoil, 8 chain, 1 long treble in 4th trefoil, 10 chain, 1 long treble in 1 trefoil of a large circle, 1 treble in each of the 4 next trefoils of the large circle, 8 chain between each 8 chain, 1 long treble in the last trefoil of the large circle, 10 chain. Repeat all round.

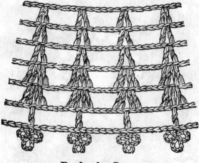

243.—Border for Couvrette.

2nd round : 2 treble, with 1 chain between, in first stitch of last round, * 4 chain, miss 5, 2 treble with 1 chain between next stitch. Repeat from *. 3rd and 4th rounds : The same as the 2nd. The 2 treble always in 1 chain. 5th round : In each 1 chain, 4 treble, with 1 chain between the 2nd and 3rd, 4 chain after the 4 treble. The same all round. 6th round : The same as the 5th. 7th round : 1 treble in 1 chain, 1 trefoil in the top of the treble, 6 chain. Repeat the same all round, which completes the couvrette.

244.—*Star in Crochet.*

Materials: Messrs. Walter Evans and Co.'s crochet cotton No. 80, or with No. 8 or 10 for couvrettes.

A number of these stars joined together will make very pretty strips of insertion. For this purpose they should be worked with fine cotton. They may also be used for trimming

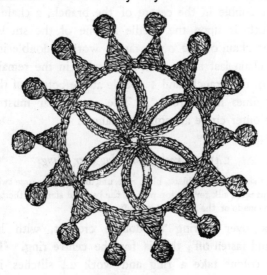

244.—Star in Crochet.

collars, cuffs, and cravats, the material being cut away underneath. If worked with crochet cotton No. 8 or 10, they will make nice couvrettes, bed-quilts, &c.

The star is begun by the outer circle. Make a chain of 70 stitches, and join it into a circle. * Make 10 chain, miss 3, work 1 extra long treble, 1 treble, and 1 double, inserting the needle under the chain, then 1 double worked as usual, 1 long double, 2 extra long double, miss 4, and work 1 double, in-

serting the needle *under* the 5th. Repeat 13 times from *
Fasten off, and for the centre of the star work as follows :—

1st round : * 10 chain, turn, miss 1 and work 1 double in
the next 7 chain, 1 double in the 1st of the 10 chain, thus
forming 1 loop. Repeat from * 5 times more.

2nd round : 12 double on the first loop of chain of the first
branch, 1 double in the centre of the branch, 2 chain ; slip the
stitch which is upon the needle in one of the stitches of the
foundation chain of the outer circle, work 1 double in the first
of the 2 chain last made, then 12 double in the remaining loop
of chain of the branch, and 1 double at the bottom of the branch.
Repeat 5 times more from *. The centre star must be joined
on to the outer circle at regular distances.

245.—*Crochet Silk Bag over Rings.*

Materials : 2 skeins each of black, blue, rose, and drab coarse purse twist ; 8 skeins
of the spangled silk for the top part of the bag and strings ; the tassel for the
bottom is made of the silks that are left ; rings.

Work over a ring in double crochet, with black, 48
stitches and fasten off; this is for the centre ring. Then with
the rose colour take a ring and work 24 stitches in double
crochet as before, take a second ring, and work 24 double
crochet over it without cutting off the silk, work over 4 more
rings in the same manner, then work on the other side of the
rings to correspond, join the first and last ring together, and sew
in the centre ring ; this completes the 1st circle. Work 12 more
rounds in the same way, 3 rose colour, with drab centre, 3 blue
with black, 3 drab with rose centre, 3 black with blue, join 6
circles of the alternate colours to the 1st circle, 1 to each ring,
then sew the second ring to the corresponding one of the next
circle, till the 6 are united ; join the other 6 circles in the fol-

lowing manner : join one ring to the second from the one that was sewed to the 1st circle, join the next ring to the correspond-

245.—Crochet Silk Bag.

ing one of the next circle (which will be the one opposite to the one sewed in the 1st circle, and repeat, joining the other 5 in the same way. For the small diamond make a chain of 5 stitches and unite it, work 4 long stitches into the circle, make 2 chain, work 1 single stitch to the centre of the ring missed in joining the last circle, make 2 chain, work 4 long into the circle, make 2 chain, and work a stitch of single crochet to the centre of the next ring, make 2 chain, work 4 long into the same place, make 5 chain, work 4 long into the same place, make 2 chain, and work a stitch of single crochet to the next ring, make 2 chain, and join it to the first of the long stitches; this completes the diamonds; work 5 more, joining them in the same way, then work over 12 rings, and join one on each side of every diamond; this completes the lower part of the bag. For the top part of the bag work 3 stitches of double crochet to the centre of each ring, make 5 chain, and repeat. 1st round : Work 1 long stitch, make 1 chain, miss 1 loop, and repeat. Work 12 more rounds in the same way, working the long stitch into the chain stitch of last row. Run some cord in the top of the bag to match one of the colours used, and make the tassel for the bottom from the silk that is remaining after working the crochet.

246.—*Crochet Sovereign Purse.*

Materials : 1 skein of black purse silk: 1 skein of coloured ditto ; a few steel beads; and a steel clasp.

The open portion of this purse is worked in coloured, and the raised rose and outer border in black, silk, the latter being dotted with steel beads. A few rows of plain double crochet are worked, increasing where necessary, to make the work lie flat; then 4 rows of loops of chain in coloured silk, and then 3 rows of thick double crochet, threading the beads first on the

246.—Crochet Sovereign Purse.

silk, and pushing them up to the stitches when required. The black silk must now be joined on to the centre, and the little raised piece worked in treble crochet, inserting the hook on the *upper* side of the stitches. Three rounds of treble are executed, and when both sides of the purse are finished they should be joined together (except where the clasp is put on) by a row of open treble, ornamented with beads. This purse is so easy to make, that it might be worked without the least difficulty from the illustration.

247.—*Stars in Crochet.*

Materials: Messrs. Walter Evans and Co.'s crochet cotton No. 8 or 20.

This pattern can be used for a couvrette or pincushion cover, according to the size of the cotton with which it is worked.

Each star is begun in the centre by a chain of 8 stitches. In the 1st stitch work 1 treble, * 4 chain, 1 treble in this same 1st stitch, repeat from * 3 times more, 4 chain, 1 slip stitch in the 4th of the 8 chain. You have thus formed 8 rays, joined to the 1st stitch. Now work (without cutting the cotton) the branches, which are begun from the centre.

1st branch.—1st round: 18 chain, 1 treble in the 13th, so as to form a purl with the last 5, 2 chain, 3 treble with 2 chain between, missing 2 stitches under the 2 chain, 2 chain, 1 slip stitch in the last of the 18 chain.

2nd round: 2 double over the 1st 2 chain, 2 double with 1 purl between over the next 2 chain, 2 double over the next 2 chain, 1 purl, 7 double over the next 5 chain; then, on the other side of the branch, 1 purl, 2 double, 1 purl, 2 double, 2 double with 1 purl between, 2 double on the last 2 chain of the branch, 1 slip stitch in the stitch from which the leaf was begun, 5 double over the 4 chain of the circle. Here begins the second branch.

1st round of the 2nd leaf : 22 chain, 1 double in the last so as to form a circle.

247.—Stars in Crochet.

2nd round : 1 double in each of the 10 first chain, in the next stitch work 1 double, 1 chain, 1 double to form the point,

1 double in each of the 10 remaining stitches, 1 slip stitch in the 1st stitch of the 1st round.

3rd round : 3 double, 1 purl, repeat from * twice more, then work in double crochet as far as the point, work 2 double with 1 chain between, then work the 2nd half of the branch the same as the 1st. Before beginning the next leaf, work 5 double on the chain stitches of the circle; work 6 branches, repeating alternately the 2 above explained ; cut the cotton and fasten it on again to the point of one of the branches, in order to join them together by the two following rounds :—

1st round : 1 double in the point of one of the leaves, * 4 chain, 1 purl under the chain ; thus make 5 chain, turn the chain with the crochet to the right, insert the needle downwards in the first chain, and make a slip stitch, 4 chain, 1 purl under, 4 chain, 1 purl under, 4 chain, 1 slip stitch in the point of the next leaf, repeat from * five times more.

2nd round : * 4 double over the nearest 4 chain ; 1 purl as usual—that is, above the chain—4 double over the next 4 chain Now work 1 trefoil (thus : 1 chain, 1 purl, 1 chain, 1 purl, 1 chain, 1 double in the 1 double coming just before the 3 purl). 1 double on each of the next 4 chain of last round, 1 purl, 5 double, 1 trefoil, repeat five times from *.

Join the stars by a few stitches, as seen in the illustration.

248.—*Crochet Purse over Rings.*

Materials : 67 rings ; 2 skeins each of cerise and black, and 1 of maize coarse purse silk.

Work in double crochet with maize over one ring 38 stitches ; this is the centre ring for the bottom of the purse.

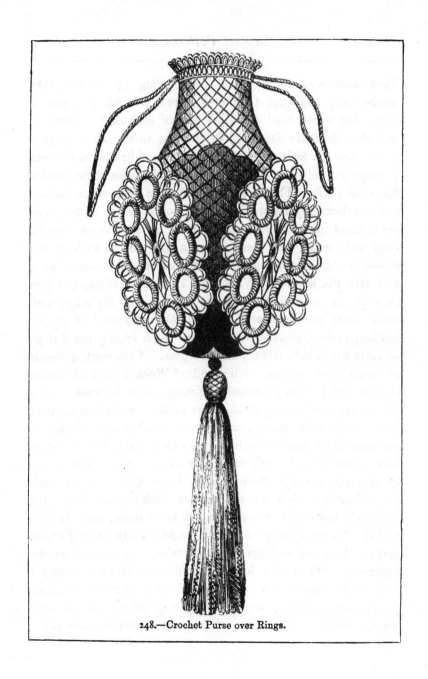

248.—Crochet Purse over Rings.

Then work with cerise colour over a ring 19 stitches, take another ring and work 19 stitches, repeat this till you have 6 rings, then work round the other half of each ring 19 stitches ; and when the 6 are finished, join the first to the last to make a circle ; sew the maize ring into the centre of it, then work over 12 rings with black in the same manner, and place them outside the cerise circle. Then work over 16 rings with maize colour, and join them beyond the black, but not to lie flat down ; they are to stand up to form the sides of the purse. Work over 16 rings with cerise, and these you can join one to each of the former rounds in working the second half of the crochet, as it will save the sewing. Work over 16 rings in black, and join them in the same manner to the cerise. For the edge, with cerise, work into the centre stitch of the ring a stitch of double crochet, make 5 chain, work into the stitch joining the 8 rings an extra long stitch, make 5 chain, repeat. Then work 4 rounds of single open crochet. 6th round : * Work a stitch of double crochet and 1 chain alternately, missing 1 loop between each 4 times, then work a long stitch, make 1 chain, work into the next loop 1 long stitch, make 2 chain, work another long stitch into the same place, make 1 chain, work a long stitch into the next loop, repeat from *. 7th round : Work into the 2 chain 1 long stitch, make 2 chain, work another long stitch into the same place, * make 1 chain, work a stitch of double crochet into the 1 chain in last round, repeat from * 3 times more, miss the next 1 chain, * work a stitch of double crochet into the next 1 chain, make 1 chain, repeat from * 3 times more, then repeat from the beginning. 8th round : Join the black, work into the 2 chain 1 long stitch, make 2 chain, work another long stitch into the same place, make 2 chain, work another long stitch into the same place, make 1 chain, work a 4th long stitch into the same place,

* make 1 chain, work a stitch of double crochet into the 1 chain, repeat from * 3 times more, miss the next 2 stitches of double crochet, * work a stitch of double crochet into the 1 chain, make 1 chain, repeat from * 3 times more, then repeat from the beginning. 9th round: Work into the 2 chain 1 long stitch, make 2 chain, work another long stitch into the same place, repeat the stitches of double crochet with 1 chain between, as in last round, then repeat from the beginning. 10th and 11th rounds the same as the 9th. Add a tassel at the bottom, and strings run into the last row of open crochet complete the purse.

249.—*Crochet Brioche Cushion.*

Materials: 10 skeins of 12-thread fleecy, of six shades of red (these should be most of the darker shades); 2 skeins of white ditto; 1 skein of white filoselle.

Make a chain of 196 stitches with the darkest shade of red

wool, and join it into a circle. Work 1 round of raised spots
thus :—Turn the wool 5 times round the needle, insert the
needle in 1 chain, and draw it through all the loops, then work
1 slip stitch, insert the needle in the next stitch, work 1 double,
and begin a fresh spot. Continue in the same way all round.
2nd round : Divide the round into 7 parts ; work 12 spots with
the 3rd shade of red, always working 1 double between each
spot, and taking care to place them between those of preceding
round : after 12 spots, work 1 double, then 12 more, and so
on. 3rd round : 3rd shade of red, 11 spots, 1 double. 4th
round : 4th shade, 10 spots, 3 double. 5th round : 5th shade,
9 spots, 5 double. 6th round : Same shade, 8 spots, 7 double.
7th round : 5th shade, 7 spots, 9 double. 8th round : Same
shade, 6 spots, 11 double. 9th round : Same shade, 5 spots,
13 double. 10th round : 6th shade, 4 spots, 15 double. 11th
round : Same shade, 3 spots, 17 double. 12th round : Same
shade, 2 spots, 19 double. 13th round : Same shade, 1 spot,
21 double. The pattern of raised spots being now completed,
continue to work with the lightest shade of red in double
stitches, decreasing once above each pattern, so as to close up
the circle gradually. The white flowers are worked over the
plain part of the cushion with white wool, and silk for the
petals, and a black dot in the centre. The cushion is stuffed
with horsehair and lined with glazed calico. A round of thick
pasteboard is stitched in at the bottom, to make it stand firmer.

250.—*Daisy Pattern for a Crochet Couvrette.*

Materials : For a large couvrette, Messrs. Walter Evans and Co.'s Boar's Head
cotton No. 8 ; for pincushion covers, mats, and such-like small articles, Boar's
Head cotton No. 16 or 20.

A pattern of this description is most useful, as it can be converted to so many purposes. Counterpanes, couvrettes of every description, mats, pincushions, and a thousand other things can all be arranged from the design.

250.—Daisy Pattern for a Crochet Couvrette.

Each circle is made separately, and joined to the others, **as** the last row is crocheted. Begin in the centre ; make 8 chain, insert the needle in the first, and make * a long treble stitch,

Q

then make 3 chain, repeat 4 times from •, always inserting the
needle in the 1st chain stitch, join the last chain to the 5th of the
1st 8 chain to close the round. 2nd round: Work 1 double
crochet, • 9 chain, turn, work a slip stitch in each of the 9
chain; work round the stem thus made in close crochet,
working 3 stitches in 1 to turn at the point; miss 1 stitch of
preceding row, work 2 double crochet, and repeat from • 5 times
móre, making 6 petals in all. 3rd round: Work at the back of
the last row, behind the petals; make 1 petal between each petal
in last row, 1 double crochet at the back of each, and cut the
cotton at the end of the round. 4th round: 2 double crochet
at the point of each of the 12 petals, 5 chain between each petal
5th round: 2 treble, 5 chain, repeat. 6th and last round: 1
double crochet in the centre of the 1st 5 chain, • 5 chain, 1
treble in the centre of the next 5 chain, 5 chain, 1 slip stitch in
the top of the treble stitch, 6 chain, 1 slip stitch in the same
place, 5 chain, a 3rd slip stitch in the same place, 5 chain, 1
double crochet in the centre of the next 5 chain, repeat from • to
the end of the round. There should be 12 trefóil patterns in
the round.

For the couvrette join the circles together, as shown in illustration, in working the last round. As many circles can be
added as may be required for the couvrette.

251.—*Crochet Lace.*

Materials: Messrs. Walter Evans and Co.'s crochet cotton No. 40 or 60.

This lace produces a very good effect when worked with
fine cotton. Make a sufficiently long foundation chain, and
work the 1st row entirely in double stitch. 2nd row: * 1 treble

in the next stitch, 1 chain, miss 1 stitch under it ; repeat from *.
3rd row : 1 long treble in the 3rd stitch of the preceding row,
* 3 purl (each consisting of 5 chain, 1 double, in the 1st of the
same), 1 long treble in the same stitch of the preceding row, 1
purl, miss 3, 3 double in the 3 following stitches, 1 purl, miss 3
stitches, 1 long treble in the 4th stitch ; repeat from *.　4th row:

251.—Crochet Lace.

* 3 double in the middle of the next 3 purl of the preceding
row, 1 purl, 2 long treble divided by 3 purl in the middle of the
3 next double in the preceding row, 1 purl ; repeat from *.　5th
row : * 2 long treble, divided by 3 purl in the middle of the
next 3 double of the preceding row, 1 purl, 3 double in the
middle of the next 3 purl of the preceding row, 1 purl ; repeat
from *.　Repeat the 4th and 5th rows alternately till the border
is wide enough.

252.—*Crochet Border.*

Material: Messrs. Walter Evans and Co.'s crochet cotton No. 12, 16, 24, or 40.

This border is suitable for a great variety of purposes, according to the size of the cotton employed; in coarse cotton it will make a trimming for couvrettes and berceaunette covers; with fine cotton it can be used for children's clothes, small curtains, &c. Make a sufficiently long foundation chain, and work the 1st row: * 2 treble divided by 3 chain in the 1st

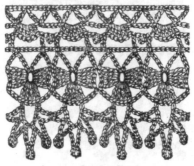

252.—Crochet Border.

foundation chain stitch, miss 3; repeat from *. 2nd row: * In the 1st scallop of the preceding row, 1 double, 5 treble, 1 double, then 1 chain, 1 purl (4 chain, 1 slip stitch in the 1st of the four), 1 chain, miss under these the next chain stitch scallop; repeat from *. 3rd row: 1 treble in the chain stitch on either side of the purl in the preceding row, 5 chain. 4th row: * 2 double divided by 7 chain in the two first treble of the preceding row (insert the needle underneath the upper parts of the stitch), 10 chain, 1 slip stitch in the 5th of these 10 stitches so as to form a loop, 4 chain , repeat from *. 5th row: * 1 slip in the middle stitch of the scallop formed by 7 chain in the preceding row, 4 treble, 3 chain, 5 treble, 3 chain, 4 treble, all these 13 stitches in the loop of the preceding row, so as to form a clover-leaf pattern ; repeat from *, but fasten the 4th treble with a slip stitch on the 10th treble of the preceding figure.   6th row: In the first and last stitch of the 5 middle treble of the clover-leaf 1 double, 7 chain between.   7th row : * 1 double in the 2nd chain stitch of the scallop which is above the 5 middle treble of the clover-leaf, 2 chain, 1 purl (5 chain, 1 slip stitch in the 1st),

253.—Crochet Border.

2 chain, 1 double in the next chain stitch of the same scallop, 2 chain, 1 purl, 2 chain, miss one chain of the scallop, 1 double, 2 chain, 1 purl, 2 chain, 1 double in the next chain stitch, 3 chain. 1 double in the middle stitch of the following scallop, 3 chain, repeat from *.

253 —*Crochet Border*

Materials : Messrs. Walter Evans and Co.'s crochet cotton No. 24, 40, or 60, according to the article for which it is required.

On a sufficiently long foundation chain work the 1st row :

1 double in each chain stitch. 2nd row: Alternately 1 double, 7 chain, miss under the latter 3 stitches of the preceding row. 3rd row: 1 treble in each double of the preceding row, 1 double in the middle stitch of each scallop, 2 chain between. 4th row: 1 double on each double of the preceding row, 1 treble on each treble, 3 chain between. 5th row: 1 double on each treble of the preceding row, 3 chain between. 6th row: 1 double in each stitch of the preceding row. 7th row: * 1 treble in the 1st stitch of the preceding row, 4 chain, miss 1, 3 treble in the following 3 stitches, miss 3 stitches, 3 treble in the following 3 stitches, 4 chain, miss 1 stitch, 1 treble, 3 chain, miss 4; repeat from *. 8th row: Repeat regularly 8 treble in the scallop formed of 4 chain in the preceding row, 1 double in the middle of the following 3 chain. 9th row: * 1 double in the 4th treble of the preceding row, 2 treble, 1 long treble in next treble but 2, 2 long treble in each of the 2 following treble, 1 long treble, 2 treble in the next treble, 1 double in the next treble but 2, 3 chain, 1 purl (4 chain, 1 slip), 3 chain stitch; repeat from *. 10th row: * 1 double in the 4th treble of the preceding row, 2 chain, 1 purl, 2 chain, miss 2 under them, 1 double, 2 chain, 1 purl, 2 chain, 1 double in the next chain but 1 of the next scallop, 2 chain, 1 purl, 2 chain, 1 double in the 2 chain stitch after the purl of the preceding row, 2 chain, 1 purl, 2 chain; repeat from *. 11th row: In each scallop of the preceding row 2 double (they must meet on either side of the purl); they are divided alternately by 5 chain, and by a scallop formed of 2 chain, 1 purl, and 2 chain, only in the chain stitch scallops which join the two treble figures work no double, but 2 chain, 1 purl, 2 chain.

254 *to* 257.—*Wicker Arm Chair, covered with Crochet.*

Material : Berlin wool in two colours.

The seat and back of this arm-chair are covered with two round couvrettes, worked in crochet with Berlin wool of two

254.—Wicker Arm Chair, covered with Crochet.

colours. They are fastened on the chair with woollen braid, finishing off with tassels of the same colour. Begin each couvrette in the centre with a foundation chain of 6 stitches, with the lightest wool ; join them into a circle, and work the 1st round in the following manner :—12 double. 2nd round : * 3 chain, 1 double, in the next stitch of the 1st round, inserting the needle in the upper part of the stitch ; repeat from * 11 times more ; at the end of this round work 1 slip stitch in the 1st chain of this round. We shall not repeat any more the repetitions from * to the end of the round. 3rd round : * 4 chain, 1

255.—Pattern for Arm Chair Border.

double, in the next scallop of the preceding round ; at the end of the round 4 chain. 4th round : 4 double in each scallop of the preceding round. 5th round : Begin to work with the darker wool and crochet slip stitch, inserting the needle in the front chain of the stitches of the 4th round. The 6th round is worked once more with light wool, and consists entirely of

256.—Border for Arm Chair (254).

double stitch, worked by inserting the needle at the back of the stitches of the 4th round, so that the slip stitches appear raised on the right side of the work, and form a round of chain stitches. The middle part of the couvrette is then finished. Illustration

257 shows it in full size. 7th round : * 2 chain, missing 1 stitch of the preceding round under them, 1 double. 8th round : * 3 chain, 1 double, in the next scallop of the preceding round. 9th round : 3 double in each scallop. 10th round, like the 5th ; 11th round, like the 6th ; 12th, 13th, 14th, 15th, and 16th

257.—Couvrette for Arm Chair (254).

rounds, like the 7th—11th ; 17th—19th rounds like the 7th— 9th. 20th round : Alternately 1 treble with the light wool, 1 treble with the dark ; but every treble stitch must be cast off with the wool of the colour of the next stitch ; that is, a light treble stitch with the dark wool, and a dark treble stitch with the light wool. Now and then crochet 2 treble stitches in one stitch of the preceding round, so that the couvrette remains

perfectly flat. 21st round : 1 double in every stitch. The
22nd—31st rounds consist of a double repetition of the 7th—
11th rounds. The 32nd and 33rd rounds are made in open
work like the 7th and 8th rounds. The 34th round is worked
in treble stitches like the 20th round. Then work the outer
border. It consists of chain stitch scallops which are worked
alternately with dark and light wool. Illustration No. 256 shows
a part of the border with the treble round in full size. Work
from it with the light wool 1 double on 1 light treble stitch of
the preceding round, 5 chain, 1 double, on the next light treble,
throw the wool off the needle and let it hang over the right side
of the work ; crochet with the dark wool 1 double on the treble
stitch between the 2 double of this round, leave the wool on the
right side of the work ; 5 chain, 1 double, on the next dark
treble. Take the needle again out of the loop, draw the wool
on to the right side, and work the next chain stitch scallop again
with the light wool.

Instead of this border, pattern No. 255 may be worked. It
consists of 3 rounds to be worked after the 34th round of the
couvrette. 1st round of the border : With dark wool, * 1
double in 1 stitch of the 34th round ; 1 double, 3 treble, 1
double, in the next stitch ; repeat from *. 2nd round : With
the light wool, * 1 treble, inserting the needle in the next treble
stitch of the 34th round, thus working over the double stitch
between the spots of the preceding round ; 1 chain. 3rd round
* 3 double in each chain stitch of the preceding round. To
work the 2nd of these 3 double, insert the needle at the same
time in the upper part of the middle treble of the 1st round.
4th round : Dark wool, * 1 double in each double of the preceding round, miss 1, and work 3 treble in the next stitch but
one ; the last of these 3 treble is cast off with light wool, miss 1,

and continue to work with the light wool 1 double in the next stitch but one, miss 1, 3 treble in the next stitch, cast off the last with the dark wool, miss 1 ; repeat from *.

258 *to* 260.—*Crochet Insertions.*

Material : Messrs. Walter Evans and Co.'s crochet cotton No. 30, 40, or 60.

These insertions are worked with crochet cotton of sizes which depend upon the use you wish to make of them. The

258.—Crochet Insertion.

insertion seen in illustration 258 is worked the long way in 8 rows. Make a sufficiently long foundation chain, and work the 1st row as follows :—1 slip stitch in the 1st stitch of the foun-

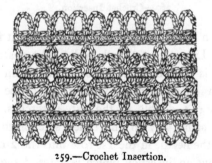

259.—Crochet Insertion.

dation, * 5 chain, miss 3, 1 double in the next stitch but 3, repeat from *. 2nd row : 1 slip stitch in the middle of the 1st 5 chain, * 3 chain, 1 slip stitch in the middle stitch of the next 5

chain, repeat from *.   3rd row : 1 treble in the 1st stitch, * 1 leaf
worked as follows : 6 chain, then without noticing the loop left
on the needle 1 long treble in the 2nd and 1 in the 1st of the 6
chain ; these stitches are not cast off separately, but together
with the loop left on the needle.   Then 5 chain, miss 7, 1 treble
in the 8th stitch, repeat from *.   4th row : 1 double in the 1st
of the 5 chain, * 8 chain, 1 double in the 1st of the next 5
chain, repeat from *.   5th row : * 1 leaf as in the 3rd row, 1
double in the double stitch of the preceding row, 5 chain, repeat
from *.   6th row : 1 treble in the point of the 1st leaf, * 7

260.—Crochet Insertion.

chain, 1 treble in the point of the next leaf, repeat from *.   7th
and 8th rows : Like the 1st and 2nd. The insertion seen in
illustration 259 is worked in 6 rows, and is begun in the centre
on a foundation chain sufficiently long not to be worked too
tight.   1st row : 4 double in the 1st 4 stitches, * 4 double
divided in the same way on the other side of the foundation
chain, inserting the needle in the 1st row into the 2 chain.   Illustration 260 shows an insertion which imitates darned netting ; it
is worked on a grounding imitating netting with raised figures.
The grounding consists of 9 rows. Work on a sufficiently long
foundation chain the 1st row as follows : 1 cross treble in the

1st and 3rd stitch, * 2 chain, missing 2 stitches under them, 1 cross treble in the 6th and 8th stitch, repeat from *. 2nd row . 1 double in the 1st stitch, * 9 chain, miss 4 under them, 1 double in the 5th stitch, repeat from *. 3rd to 8th rows: 1 double in the middle stitch of every chain stitch scallop, 4 chain between. 9th row: Like the 1st. Work from illustration square patterns on this grounding, consisting each of 4 leaves; for these leaves carry on the cotton taken double in double windings from 1 double stitch to another, so as to have 4 threads lying close to each other; darn these as can be seen in illustration, with single cotton.

261.—*Crochet Lace.*

Material: Messrs. Walter Evans and Co.'s crochet cotton No. 30.

A particular kind of purl makes this border look very like guipure lace. Begin with a foundation chain worked in the

261.—Crochet Lace.

following manner:—* 3 chain, the last of them forms 1 purl; this is made by drawing out a long loop on the needle, taking the needle out of the loop, inserting it in the chain stitch before the last one, drawing the cotton through it, and continuing to work so that the loop out of which the needle has been drawn forms 1 purl. All the purl must be equally long; to do this more easily the loop may be kept on the needle till a chain stitch has been worked in that which comes just before the purl, continue the foundation chain, and repeat from *. 1st row: 1 long double in the 1st stitch of the foundation, * 1 chain, 1 slip stitch in the nearest purl of the foundation chain; repeat from *. 2nd row: 1 double in the 1st stitch, * 1 purl, 1 chain, missing 1 stitch under it; 1 slip stitch in the slip stitch of the preceding row; repeat from *. 3rd row: Like the 1st. 4th row: 1 double in the 1st stitch, * 1 purl, 5 chain, 1 purl, 1 chain, missing 5 stitches under them; 1 double in the 6th stitch; repeat from *. 5th row: 1 long double in the 1st stitch, 3 chain, 1 purl, 1 chain, * 1 double in the middle of the next 5 chain of the preceding row, 1 purl, 5 chain, 1 purl, 1 chain; repeat from *. 6th to 9th rows: Alternately like the 4th and 5th rows. 10th row: 1 double in the 1st stitch, * 6 chain, 1 double long treble (throw the cotton 3 times round the needle) in the 1st of these chain stitches; the stitch is only completed so far as still to leave 2 loops on the needle; 1 double long treble in the same chain stitch. This stitch is cast off so as to leave in all 3 loops, and the cotton over the needle; these loops are cast off together by drawing the cotton once through them. This forms 1 leaf, or one-half of the bell-shaped patterns. 3 purl, 1 chain, 1 leaf like the preceding one, 1 slip stitch in the 1st of the first 6 chain stitches; the other half of the pattern is then completed; 1 purl, 5 chain, 1 purl, 1 chain, 1 double in the middle stitch of the next scallop of the preceding row, 1 purl, 5 chain, 1 purl, 1 chain, 1 double in the middle stitch of the following scallop

11th row : 1 slip stitch in the next purl of the preceding row, 1 purl, 2 chain, 1 slip stitch in the next purl of the preceding row, 1 purl, 2 chain, 1 slip stitch in the following purl, 1 purl (the 3 purl which are worked on the 3 purl of the bell-shaped pattern are made in this row and in the following one as follows : —Crochet 1 chain after the slip stitch, leave it for 1 purl, and work the next chain stitch in the slip stitch), 1 purl, 5 chain, 1 purl, 1 chain, 1 double in the middle stitch of the following scallop, 1 purl, 3 chain, 1 purl, 1 chain. 12th row : 3 purl on the next 3 purl of the preceding row, 3 chain between, 1 purl, 3 chain, 1 purl, 1 chain, 1 double in the middle stitch of the next 5 chain stitches, 1 bell-shaped pattern like those of the 10th row, 1 purl, 3 chain, 1 purl, 1 chain.

CROCHET D'OYLEYS IN IMITATION OF POINT LACE.

262.—*D'Oyley No.* 1.

Material : Messrs. Walter Evans and Co.'s Boar's Head cotton No. 20.

Pattern No. 1.—Make a chain of 8 stitches, unite it. Round 1 : * 1 double crochet, 9 chain, repeat from * 7 times more, 1 double crochet, unite it to the 1st stitch. Round 2 : 3 single crochet up the 3 1st of the chain in last row, *, 5 long into the loop of 9 chain, 1 chain, repeat from *. Round 3 : 1 long into the 1 chain in last round, 9 chain, repeat. Round 4 : 11 double crochet into the 9 chain in last round, repeat. Round 5 : 1 double crochet, 5 chain, miss 1 loop, repeat. Round 6 : 1 double crochet into the 5 chain, 5 chain, repeat. Round 7· The same as 6th.

No. 2.—Make a chain of 6 stitches, and unite it. Round

1 : * 1 double crochet, 4 chain, repeat from * 5 times more. Round 2 : Into the 4 chain 1 double crochet, 4 long, and 1 double crochet, repeat. Round 3 : 1 double crochet over the double crochet in 1st round, 6 chain, repeat. Round 4 : Into the 6 chain in last round 1 double crochet, 6 long, 1 double crochet, repeat. Round 5 : 1 double crochet over the one in 3rd round, 8 chain, repeat. Round 6 : Into the 8 chain 1 double crochet, 8 long, 1 double crochet, repeat. Round 7 : 1 double crochet over the 1 in 5th round, 10 chain, repeat. Round 8 : Into the 10 chain 1 double crochet, 10 long, 1 double crochet, repeat. Round 9 : 1 double crochet over the 1 in 7th round, 12 chain, repeat. Round 10 : Into the 12 chain 1 double crochet, 12 long, 1 double crochet, repeat. Round 11 : 1 double crochet over the 1 in 9th round, 14 chain, repeat. Round 12 : Into the 14 chain 1 double crochet, 14 long, 1 double crochet, repeat. Round 13 : 1 double crochet over the 1 in 11th round, 14 chain, repeat Work 3 patterns of No. 2 for this d'oyley.

No. 3.—Make a chain of 12 stitches, and unite it. Into the circle 1 double crochet, *, 2 long, 3 chain, repeat from * twice more, 2 double long, 4 chain, 2 double long, * 3 chain, 2 long, repeat from * twice more, 1 double crochet, 7 chain. Repeat from the beginning. In working the 2nd pattern, join it to the 1st with the 2nd 3 chain, work 3 leaves in this manner, then make only 3 chain, and work a 4th leaf without joining it to the 3rd, make 3 chain after 4th leaf, and work a stitch of double crochet into last 7 chain, make 3 chain. Work a 5th leaf, and join it to the 4th as before, 3 chain, 1 double crochet into the next 7 chain, 3 chain. Work a 6th leaf in the same way, and join it ; but make no chain stitch after the 6th leaf. Work 3 patterns of No. 3 for this d'oyley.

No. 4.—The same as No. 3, only work 4 leaves instead of 6, 2 on each side. Work 3 patterns of No. 4 for this d'oyley.

No. 5.—Work the 3 1st leaves of No. 3. This is not repeated in this d'oyley.

No. 6.—Make a chain of 15 stitches, and unite it. Work into the circle 1 double crochet, 7 long, 6 double, 6 long, 5 chain, 6 double long, 7 long, 1 double crochet, 7 chain, joining the 7th long stitch to the corresponding stitch in 1st leaf, 3 chain. Work the 3rd leaf the same as the 1st without joining it to the 2nd, 3 chain, 1 double crochet into the 7 chain, 3 chain,

work a 4th leaf, and join it to the 3rd, 3 chain, and join it to the 1st stitch of double crochet at the beginning of the 1st leaf. This pattern is not repeated in this d'oyley.

No. 7.—Tie a round of cotton about this size O. Round 1 : 20 double crochet into the round. Round 2 : 2 double crochet into successive loops, work 2 into 3rd loop, repeat. Round 3 : 1 double crochet into every loop. Round 4 : 1 double crochet, 5 chain, miss 2 loops, repeat. Round 5 : Into the 5 chain in last round 2 long, 5 chain, 2 more long stitches into the same place, 2 chain, repeat. Round 6 : Into the 5 chain 1 double crochet, 6 long, 1 double crochet, 5 chain, repeat. This pattern is not repeated in this d'oyley.

No. 8.—Make a chain of 10 stitches, and unite it. Round 1 : 28 double long into the circle. Round 2 : 2 double crochet between each long in last round. Round 3 : 1 long, 2 chain, miss 1 loop, repeat. Round 4 : 3 long into the 2 chain, 1 chain, repeat. Round 5 : 1 double crochet into the 1 chain in last round, 5 chain, repeat. This pattern is not repeated in this d'oyley.

No. 9.—1st row : Make a chain of 30 stitches, work 1 long stitch into the 6th, *, 3 chain stitches, miss 3 loops, 1 long into the next, repeat from * to the end of the row. 2nd row : 11 chain, *, 1 double crochet on the other side of the chain into the centre one of the 3 between the long stitch, 1 chain, turn, and work into the 11 chain 3 double crochet and 9 long, 11 chain, repeat from * 7 times more, work into the chain stitches at the end 3 loops of 11 chain with the double crochet and long stitch as before, then work the other half of the pattern to correspond. 3rd row : Into the space between the long stitches 5 double crochet, 2 chain, repeat. This pattern is not repeated in this d'oyley.

No. 10.—Make a chain of 8 stitches, and unite it. Round
1 : Into the circle 24 double long, with 1 chain between each.
Round 2 : 2 double crochet into the 1 chain in last round,
repeat. Round 3 : 1 long, 2 chain, miss 1 loop, repeat. Round
4: 1 double crochet into the 2 chain in last round, 5 chain,
repeat. This pattern is not repeated in this d'oyley.

No. 11.—Make a chain of 7 stitches, and unite it. Round
1 : 20 long into the circle. Round 2 : 1 double crochet into
every loop. Round 3 : 1 double crochet, 6 chain, miss 2 loops,
repeat. Round 4: 1 double crochet into the 6 chain, 7 chain,
repeat. Round 5 : 10 double crochet into the 7 chain, repeat.
Round 6 : 1 long, 2 long into the next loop, repeat. Round 7 :
1 double crochet, 5 chain, miss 3 loops, repeat. This pattern is
not repeated in this d'oyley.

No. 12.—Make a chain of 21 stitches, and unite it. Round
1 : 30 double crochet into the circle. Round 2 : *, 21 chain,
join it to the 18th, work into the circle 1 double crochet, 2 long,
3 chain, 2 long, 5 chain, 2 long, 7 chain, 2 long, 5 chain, 2
long, 3 chain, 2 long and 1 double crochet, 1 single crochet into
the 1st double crochet, 3 chain, 4 double crochet into the 3
chain, 2 chain, 6 double crochet into the 5 chain, 2 chain, 4
double crochet into the 7 chain, 3 chain, 4 double crochet into
the same place, 2 chain, 6 double crochet into the 5 chain,
2 chain, 4 double crochet into the 3 chain, 3 chain, 1 single
crochet into the stitches of double crochet at the end, 3 single
crochet down the 3 for the stem, 9 single crochet into successive
loops round the circle, repeat from * twice more. This pattern
is not repeated in this d'oyley.

No. 13.—*, make 9 chain stitches, turn, 1 double crochet into
each loop, repeat from * twice more, then work round both sides
of these 3 points 1 double crochet, 3 chain, miss 1 loop at the

top of each point, work twice into the same loop, then 5 chain, 1 double crochet into each end, unite the 5th to the last of the centre point of 9.   This pattern is not repeated in this d'oyley.

No. 14.—Round 1 : * make a chain of 13 stitches, and unite it, repeat from * 4 more times.   Round 2 : 1 double crochet into 6 successive loops, 3 stitches into the 7th, 1 into each of the next 6 loops, repeat.   Round 3 : 1 double crochet, 7 chain, 1 double crochet into the centre 1 of the 3 in last, 7 chain, miss 6, repeat.   Round 4 : 1 double crochet, 3 chain, miss 1 loop, repeat.   This pattern is not repeated.

No. 15.—*, make a chain of 19 stitches, unite it, 3 long into successive loops, 3 double long, 2 long, 1 double crochet, 5 chain, 1 double crochet into the next loop, 7 chain, 1 double crochet into the same place, 5 chain, work into successive loops 1 double crochet, 2 long, 3 double long, 3 long, unite the last to the first, 9 chain, repeat from * once more, then 5 double crochet into the 5 1st of the 9 chain, 7 chain, 1 double crochet into each, and 1 into each of the 4 remaining of the 9 chain.   This pattern is not repeated in this d'oyley.

No. 16.—Make a chain of 11 stitches, *, work into successive loops 2 double crochet, 7 long, 2 double crochet, 2 more double crochet into the same loop as the last, repeat from * once, make a chain of 24 stitches, unite to the 20th, work into the circle, *, 1 long, 3 chain, 1 long, repeat from * 12 times, work into the 3 chain 1 long, 3 chain, work another long into the same place, repeat, join the last with 1 single crochet to the last of the 24 chain, 2 double crochet over the 2 of the leaf, 7 long into successive loops, 4 double long into successive loops, 4 long into the next loop, and 1 long into the next.   This pattern is not repeated.   When all these pieces are done, join them as shown in the engraving, sewing them firmly together with the same cotton, then work an edging round in the following manner :—1st row : 1 double long into the 4 chain at the point of the leaf of No. 4 pattern, 7 chain, 1 double long into the 2nd 3 chain in the same leaf, 8 chain, 1 double long into the 1st 3 chain of the 2nd leaf of the same pattern, 15 chain, 1 long into the 4 chain of No. 6 pattern, 15 chain, 1 long into the 4 chain of the next leaf in the same pattern, 12 chain, 1 long into the 3rd 5 chain from the join of the 11th pattern, 6 chain, 1 single crochet into the 2nd 5 chain from the long stitch, 9 chain, 1 single crochet into the 3rd 5 chain from the last, 6 chain, 1 long into the 2nd 5 chain from the last, 12 chain, work into the 2nd 5 chain from the join of the 7th pattern 1 long, 8 chain, 1 double crochet into the next 5 chain, 9 chain, 1 long into the next 5 chain, 8 chain, 1 double crochet in the 1st 3 chain from the join of 4th pattern, 11 chain, 1 double crochet into the 1st 3 chain of the 2nd leaf of the same pattern, 6 chain, 1 double crochet into the last 3 chain of the same leaf, 4 chain, 1 double crochet into the 3 chain of No. 5 pattern, 6 chain, 1 long into the 7 chain between the leaves of the same pattern, 10 chain, 1 long into the next 7 chain, 6 chain, 1 long into the 1st 3 chain of the 3rd leaf of the same pattern, 12 chain, 1 single crochet into the 3rd 5 of double crochet from the join of 9th pattern, 8 chain, 1 single crochet into the centre of the 2nd 5 double crochet from the last, 11 chain, 1 single crochet into the 2nd 5 of double crochet from the last, 12 chain, 1 double crochet into the 7 chain of 15th pattern, 7 chain, 1 double crochet into the 6th long stitch of the same leaf, 11 chain, 1 double crochet into the end of the stem of 15th pattern, 8 chain, 1 double long into the 1st 3 chain of the 4th pattern, 4 chain, 1 double long into the last 3 chain of the same leaf, 9 chain, 1 double long into the

2nd 3 chain of the 2nd leaf, 12 chain, 1 long into the 3rd 3
chain of No. 16 pattern, 8 chain, 1 long into the 2nd 3 chain of
the same pattern from the last, 12 chain, 1 long into the 3rd 5
chain from the join of the 10th pattern, 10 chain, 1 long into the
3rd 5 chain from the last, 12 chain, 1 double crochet into the
centre of the 7 of double crochet in 12th pattern, 12 chain, 1 long
into the 5 double crochet of same pattern, 8 chain, 1 double crochet
into the 3 chain in centre of same leaf, 9 chain, 1 long into the
3rd 5 chain from the join of the 8th pattern, 8 chain, 1 single
crochet into the 3rd 5 chain from the last, 10 chain, 1 double
long into the 3rd 5 chain from the stitch of single, 13 chain,
and join it to the double long stitch at the beginning of the row.
2nd row : *, 12 chain, and unite it, 1 chain to cross, and on the
other side into the circle 1 double crochet, 2 long, 3 chain, 2
long, 3 chain, 2 double long, 4 chain, then work down the other
side to correspond, 8 double crochet into successive loops of the
foundation, repeat from *, joining the leaves in the 1st 3 chain.

263.—*D'Oyley No. 2.*

Material : Messrs. Walter Evans and Co.'s Boar's Head cotton No. 20.

Pattern No. 1.—Make a chain of 4 stitches, and unite it.
Round 1 : 2 double crochet into each loop.   Round 2 : 2
double crochet into each loop.   Round 3 : 1 double crochet, 2
double crochet into the next loop, repeat.   Round 4 : 1 double
crochet into each loop.   Round 5 : 1 double crochet, 5 chain,
miss 2 loops, repeat.   Round 6 : 9 double crochet into the 5
chain, repeat.   Round 7 : 9 double crochet into successive loops,
beginning on the 5th of the 9 in last round, 5 chain, 1 single

crochet into the last double crochet, and repeat. Round 8 : 1 double crochet into the centre one of the 9 in last round, 11 chain, repeat. Round 9 : 15 double crochet into the 11 chain in last round, repeat. Round 10 : 15 double crochet into suc-

263.—D'Oyley No. 2.

cessive loops, beginning on the 8th of the 15 in last round, 5 chain, 1 single crochet into the last double crochet, repeat. Round 11 : 1 double crochet into the centre one of the 15 in last round, 17 chain, repeat. Round 12 : 21 double crochet into the 17 chain in last round.

No. 2.—Make a chain of 7 stitches, and unite it. Round 1:
*, 7 chain, 1 double crochet into the circle, repeat from * twice
more. Round 2 : 12 long into the 7 chain, repeat. Round 3 :
2 long into each loop. Round 4 : 1 long, 2 chain, miss 2 loops,
repeat. Round 5 : 2 long into the 2 chain in last round, 1
chain, repeat. Round 6 : 1 double crochet into the 1 chain, 5
chain, repeat.

No. 3.—Make a chain of 14 stitches, and unite it. Round 1 :
Into the circle 1 double crochet, 7 long, 6 double long, 4 chain,
6 double long, 7 long, 1 double crochet. Round 2 : 1 double
crochet into every loop. Round 3 : 2 chain, miss 1 loop, 1
long and repeat, 4 long at the point, finish with a single stitch, 3
chain, and repeat this once more.

No. 4.—Make a chain of 13 stitches, and unite it, chain of
15 and unite it, chain of 13 and unite it, work 6 double crochet
into successive loops, beginning on the 1st of the 1st loop of 13,
3 into the next loop, and 1 into each of the 6 next, 1 double
crochet into each of the 1st 7 of the loop of 15, 3 into the next,
1 into each of the next 7, 1 double crochet into each of the 6
1st of the next loop of 13, 3 into the next, 1 into each of the
next 6. 2nd row : 1 double crochet, 3 chain, miss 1 loop,
repeat.

No. 5.—Make a chain of 13 stitches, and unite it. Round
1 : Into the circle 3 double crochet, 3 long, 3 double long, 5
treble long, 3 double long, 3 long, 3 double crochet. Round 2 :
1 double crochet into each of the 9 1st loops, 2 into each of the
2 next, and 3 into the next, 2 into each of the 2 next, and 1 into
each of the 9 next. Round 3 : 1 long, *, 3 chain, 1 long into
the next loop, repeat from * at the end, unite the last to the 1st
stitch, 9 chain, repeat from the beginning ; in uniting the last
stitch of the 2nd leaf, take up the centre stitch of the 9 chain

with it, make 5 chain, and work a 3rd leaf in the same manner; in uniting the last stitch of the 3rd leaf, take up the last of the 5 chain with it, make 9 chain, turn, and work 1 double crochet into each, join the last to the last of the 5 and 9 chain stitch.

No. 6.—Make a chain of 6 stitches, and unite it. Round 1: 1 double crochet into 1 loop, 5 chain, repeat 5 times more. Round 2: Into the 5 chain 1 double crochet, 3 long, 1 double crochet, repeat. Round 3: 1 double crochet over the 1st double crochet in last round, 7 chain, repeat. Round 4: Into the 7 chain in last round 2 double crochet, 7 long, 2 double crochet, and repeat. Round 5: 1 double crochet into the 1st double crochet in last round, 11 chain, repeat. Round 6: Into the 11 chain in last round 3 double crochet, 9 long, 3 more double crochet, repeat.

No. 7.—1st row: Make a chain of 20 stitches. 1 long into the 15th, *, 2 chain, miss 2 loops, 1 long into the next, repeat from * to the end of the row. 2nd row: Turn, into the 2 chain 1 double crochet, 2 long, 1 double crochet, repeat this to the end, then into the 5 chain 1 double crochet, 2 long, 1 double long, 2 long, 1 double crochet, work the other side to correspond. 3rd row: 1 double crochet into the 1st double crochet in last row, 7 chain, and repeat to the point, 7 chain, 1 double crochet into the double long, work the other side to correspond. 4th row: Into the 7 chain 4 double crochet, 3 chain, 1 single into the last double crochet, 4 more double crochet into the same place, repeat.

No. 8.—1st row: 1 chain of 7 stitches, 1 double crochet into each of the 6 1st, 3 stitches into the 7th, work on the other side of the chain to correspond. 2nd row: 1 double crochet, 3 chain, miss 1 loop, repeat. 3rd row: 5 double crochet into the 3 chain, repeat.

No. 9.—The same as No. 3 in the 1st d'oyley, only 5 leaves instead of 6, 2 on each side, and 1 at the end ; 2 of these will be required for this d'oyley.

No. 10.—Work the 2 1st leaves of No. 4 in the 1st d'oyley ; 3 of these will be required for this d'oyley.

No. 11.—Work only 1 leaf of No. 4 in the 1st d'oyley. This is not to be repeated in this d'oyley.

No. 12.—The same as No. 4 in 1st d'oyley.

No. 13.—The same as No. 5.

No. 14.—The same as No. 8 in 1st d'oyley.

No. 15.—The same as No. 10.

No. 16.—The same as No. 11 in the 1st d'oyley.

No. 17.—The same as No. 2 in 1st d'oyley ; 2 of these will be required.

No. 18.—The same as No 6 in 1st d'oyley ; 2 of these will be required. When all these pieces are done, sew them firmly together, and work the edging round in the following manner :—
1 double crochet into the 1st 4 chain of 9th pattern, 9 chain, 1 double crochet into the last 3 chain of same leaf, 4 chain, 1 double crochet into the 1st 3 chain of 2nd leaf, 10 chain, 1 double crochet in the 4 chain of same leaf, 8 chain, 1 long into the 4th of the 5 chain, from the joining of 15th pattern, 4 chain, 1 double crochet into the 2nd 5 chain, 4 chain, 1 long into the 2nd 5 chain from the last, 12 chain, 1 long into the last 3 chain of 10th pattern, 3 chain, 1 double crochet into the 4 chain of same leaf, 9 chain, 1 double crochet into the 4 chain of 2nd leaf, 12 chain, 1 long into the 1st double crochet from the join of No. 6 pattern, 9 chain, 1 long into the next stitch of double crochet after the long stitch, 16 chain, 1 long into the 3rd 5 chain from the join of 14th pattern, 8 chain, 1 double crochet into the 3rd 5 chain from the long stitch, 9 chain, 1 long into the 3rd 5 chain

from the stitch of double crochet, 9 chain, 1 long into the 1st 3 chain of 10th pattern, 8 chain, 1 double crochet into the 4 chain of same leaf, 12 chain, 1 double crochet into the 4 chain of 15th pattern, 8 chain, 1 double crochet into the last 3 chain of same leaf, 9 chain, 1 long into the 1st 14 chain from the join of 17th pattern, 10 chain, 1 long into the next 14 chain of same pattern, 14 chain, 1 long into the 4th 5 chain from the join of 16th pattern, 6 chain, 1 double crochet into the 2nd 5 chain from last, 6 chain, 1 long into the 2nd 5 chain from last, 12 chain, 1 double crochet into the 1st 4 chain of 9th pattern, 8 chain, 1 double crochet into the last 3 chain of same leaf, 4 chain, 1 double crochet into the 1st 3 chain of 2nd leaf, 5 chain, 1 double crochet into the last 3 chain of 2nd leaf, 6 chain, 1 double crochet into the last 3 chain of 10th pattern, 8 chain, 1 double crochet into the 7 chain of same pattern, 6 chain, 1 double crochet into the 1st 3 chain of 2nd leaf, 11 chain, 1 double crochet into the 4 chain of 11th pattern, 9 chain, 1 double crochet into the last 3 chain of same pattern, 8 chain, 1 long into the centre 3 chain of 1st leaf of 12th pattern, 7 chain, 1 double crochet into the 1st 3 chain of 2nd leaf same pattern, 7 chain, 1 double crochet into the 4 chain of same leaf, 10 chain, 1 long into the 5th 3 chain from the join of the 3rd pattern, 4 chain, 1 double crochet into the 2nd 3 chain, 4 chain, 1 long into the 2nd 3 chain of same pattern, 8 chain, 1 long into the 1st 14 chain from join of 17th pattern, 12 chain, 1 long into the next 14 chain of same pattern, 10 chain, and unite. 2nd row: The same edging as to 1st d'oyley.

264.—*D'Oyley No. 3.*

Material : Messrs. Walter Evans and Co.'s Boar's Head cotton No. 20.

Work 2 patterns from No. 2 in 1st d'oyley, 2 patterns from No. 3 in same d'oyley, 1 pattern from No. 4 in same d'oyley, and 1 pattern from No. 5, 2 patterns from No. 6 in same d'oyley, 1 pattern from No. 7, 1 pattern from No. 8, and 1 from No. 10 in same d'oyley, 2 patterns from No. 11 in 1st d'oyley, 1 pattern from No. 2 in 2nd d'oyley, 1 pattern from No. 3 in same d'oyley, 1 pattern from No. 9 in same d'oyley, and 2 from No. 10. Then 1 pattern in the following manner :—Round 1 : Make a chain stitch of 12 stitches, 1 double crochet, 10 long into successive loops, 1 double crochet, 1 double crochet at the point, and work down the other side to correspond.   Round 2 : 2 long into each loop.   Round 3 : 4 chain, miss 2 loops, 1 double crochet into the next, repeat.   Round 4 : 1 double crochet into the 1st 4 chain of 3rd round, 5 chain, repeat.   Work 1 pattern in this way, 1 chain of 14, 1 double crochet into each, 5 chain, 1 double crochet into the last double crochet, turn, 6 double crochet into the circle, with 3 chain between each, into each 3 chain, 5 long, turn, 1 double crochet between each of the 5 long, with 6 chain between each double crochet, turn, into the 1st double crochet 1 long, 2 chain, 1 double long, 2 chain, 1 treble long, 2 chain, 1 double long, 2 chain, 1 long all into the same place, 1 double crochet into the 6 chain.   Repeat this 5 times more, then work down the 7 of 14, 7 long, and 7 of single crochet.   The edging to be the same as in the former d'oyleys. The 1st round of the edging takes up so much space to write, that we think it better to leave it to the judgment of the worker.

It will be seen by the engraving when it is necessary to work a double long or long stitch, or a stitch of single or double crochet, and the number of chain stitches between must be just sufficient

264.—D'Oyley No. 3.

to make the circle perfect. The best way is to cut a round of blue paper and place them on it from the engraving, then sew them together, and tack them to the paper, and work the 1st row of the edging before removing the paper.

265.—*D'Oyley No. 4.*

Material: Messrs. Walter Evans and Co.'s Boar's Head cotton No. 20.

Work 3 patterns from No. 2 in 1st d'oyley, and 2 from
No. 3, 1 pattern from No. 4, 1 pattern from No. 5 in 1st d'oyley,
2 patterns from No. 6, and 1 from No. 8 in same d'oyley, 1
pattern from No. 2 in 2nd d'oyley, and 1 leaf from No. 3 in
2nd d'oyley, 1 pattern from No. 11 in 2nd d'oyley, and the
following pattern.

No. 1.—Make a chain of 30 stitches, turn, miss 1 loop, 29
double crochet into successive loops, turn, 1 double crochet, 1
long, 2 double long, 8 treble long into 4 loops, 8 double long,
9 long, 4 double crochet, 3 chain, work down the other side to
correspond, then 1 double crochet, 3 chain, miss 1 loop, repeat
all round.

No. 2.—Make a chain of 20 stitches, turn, miss 1 loop, 2
double crochet into successive loops, * 2 chain, miss two loops,
1 long into the next, repeat from * 3 times more, 2 chain, miss
2 loops, 3 double crochet into successive loops, 1 double crochet
into every loop on both sides. Next round : * 5 chain, turn,
miss 1 loop, 1 double crochet, 3 long, miss 2 loops of the
foundation, 1 double crochet, repeat from * at the point, miss
only 1 loop, work 2 patterns of this number.

No. 3.—Make a chain of 36 stitches, turn, miss 2 loops, 2
long, *, 1 chain, 3 long, repeat from * 3 times, 1 double crochet,
turn, *, 4 chain, 1 double crochet into the 1st chain stitch,
repeat from * 3 times, at the point make 5 chain instead of 4,
work down the other side to correspond, turn, and into each of
the 4 chain 1 double crochet, 7 long, and 1 double crochet, at
the point 10 long instead of 7, 2 double crochet down the stem,

1 chain of 28, turn, miss 12 loops, 1 single crochet, then into the circle 20 long, turn, 1 double crochet, 5 chain, miss 1 loop, repeat, turn, 1 double crochet into the 5 chain in last row, 5 chain, repeat, turn, into the 5 chain 1 double crochet, 7 chain,

265.—D'Oyley No. 4.

repeat, turn, into the 7 chain 1 double crochet, 1 long, 7 double long, 1 long, 1 double crochet, repeat, work down the stem, 1 double crochet, 1 long, 4 double long, 1 long, 4 double crochet, 1 chain of 14, turn, miss 3 loops, 10 long, 1 double crochet, 1 double crochet, turn, 1 double crochet, 3 chain, miss 1 loop, repeat, turn, into the 3 chain 1 double crochet, 5 long, 1 double crochet, repeat, work down the stem in double crochet.

No. 4.—Make a chain of 6 stitches, and unite it. Round 1: Into the circle 16 long. Round 2 : 1 double crochet into each loop, 3 chain after each. Round 3 : 1 double crochet into the 3 chain, 3 chain, repeat. Round 4 : 4 long into the 3 chain, repeat. Round 5 : 1 double crochet, make 3 chain, miss 1 loop, repeat. *, for the leaves, 1 chain of 22, turn, 4 double crochet, 1 long, 9 double long, 1 long, 1 double crochet, 1 chain to cross the stem, on the other side 1 double crochet, 1 long, 9 double long, 1 long, 4 double crochet, 2 double crochet at the point, work down the other side to correspond, 2 double crochet down the stem, 1 chain of 8, repeat from *, 1 chain of 12, and unite it to the 3 chain of the round, turn, 12 double crochet down the stem, work another leaf in the same manner, then work a stem of 8, and make another leaf the same as before, finish with a stem of 8.

No. 5.—Round 1 : Make a chain of 12 stitches, and unite it, 1 double crochet, miss 3 loops, 12 chain, repeat twice more. Round 2 : Into the 12 chain 2 double crochet, 13 long, 2 double crochet, repeat. Round 3 : 2 double crochet into successive loops, 13 long into successive loops, 2 double crochet into successive loops, repeat. Round 4 : 1 long, 5 chain, miss 3 loops, repeat. Round 5 : Into the 5 chain 2 double crochet, 5 long, 2 double crochet, repeat.

No. 6.—Make a chain of 11 stitches, and unite it. Round 1: 2 double crochet into each loop. Round 2 : 1 double crochet into each loop. Round 3 : 2 double crochet into 1 loop, 1 into the next, repeat. Round 4 : 1 long, 5 chain, miss 2 loops, repeat. Round 5 : Into the 5 chain 3 double crochet, 3 chain, 1 single crochet into the last double crochet, 3 more of double crochet into the same place, 4 chain, repeat. Round 6 : 1 long into the 4 chain, 7 chain, repeat. Round 7 : Into the 7 chain 4 double crochet, 3 chain, 1 single crochet into the last double crochet, 4 more double crochet into the same place, 4 chain, repeat. When all these pieces are done sew them together, as shown in the engraving, and work the edging to correspond with the other d'oyleys.

266.—*D'Oyley No. 5.*

Materials : Messrs. Walter Evans and Co.'s Boar's Head cotton No. 20 ; and 1 skein of fine embroidery cotton, by the same makers.

Pattern No. 1.—Make a chain of 8 stitches, and unite it. Round 1 : 1 double crochet, 7 chain, miss 1 loop, repeat 5 times more. Round 2 : Into the 7 chain 11 stitches of double crochet, repeat. Round 3 : 1 double crochet into the 1st of the 11, 9 chain, miss 5 loops, 1 double crochet into the next, 9 chain, repeat. Round 4 : Into the 9 chain 13 double crochet, repeat. Round 5 : 1 double crochet into the 1st of the 13, 7·chain, miss 3 loops, repeat. Round 6 : 5 double crochet into the 7 chain, and repeat.

No. 2.—Make a chain of 8 stitches, and unite it. Round 1 : 1 double crochet, 5 chain, repeat 7 times more. Round 2 : 6 chain, miss the 1st, then work into successive loops 2 double crochet and 3 long, 1 double crochet into the 1 double crochet in 1st round, repeat. Round 3 : 1 double crochet into the 1 in 1st round, 5 chain, and repeat. Round 4 : 7 chain, miss the 1st, and work into successive loops 2 double crochet, 3 long, 1 double long, 1 double crochet into the 5 chain, repeat. Round 5 : 1 double crochet into the 1 in the 3rd round, 5 chain, repeat Round 6 : Same as 4th. Round 7 : 1 double crochet into the

I in 5th round, 6 chain, repeat. Round 8 : 8 chain, miss the 1st, and work into successive loops 2 double crochet, 3 long, 2 double long. Round 9 : Same as 7th. Round 10 : Same as 8th. Two of these patterns will be required for this d'oyley.

266.—D'Oyley No. 5.

No. 3.—Make a chain of 16, and unite it. Round I : 2 double crochet into I loop, I double crochet into the next, repeat. Round 2 : 6 double crochet into successive loops, 5 chain, I single crochet into the last double crochet, repeat.

Round 3 : 1 double crochet into the 3rd of the 6, 13 chain. repeat. Round 4 : 17 double crochet into the 13 chain, repeat. Round 5 : 1 long and 1 chain alternately, missing 1 loop between each. Round 6: 1 double crochet into the 1 chain, 1 chain, 1 double crochet into the next chain, 5 chain, work another double crochet into the same place, 1 chain, repeat.

No. 4.—Make a chain of 14 stitches, and unite it. Round 1. 1 double crochet, 7 chain, miss 1 loop, repeat 6 times more. Round 2 : 5 double crochet into the 7 chain, repeat. Round 3 : 8 chain, miss the 1st, and work into successive loops 2 double crochet, 3 long, and 2 double long, 1 double crochet into the last of the 5 double crochet, repeat. Round 4: 1 double crochet at the top of the point, 4 chain, miss 1 loop, 1 double crochet into the next, 4 chain, miss 2 loops, 1 double crochet into the next, 4 chain, 1 double crochet into the 1 in last round. Work the other side of the point to correspond. Two of these patterns will be required for this d'oyley.

No. 5.—Make a chain of 8 stitches, and unite it. Round 1: 2 double crochet into each loop. Round 2: 2 double crochet into 1 loop, 1 into the next, repeat. Round 3 : 8 chain, miss the 1st, and work into successive loops, 5 double crochet and 2 long, miss 1 of the last round, work 4 double crochet into successive loops, repeat 3 times more, at the end of the round work 4 more double crochet. Round 4: 1 double crochet, 3 chain, miss 1 loop, repeat all round the 4 points and 2 stitches beyond the 4th, 7 chain, 1 double crochet into each of the 7, finish the round with 3 chain and 1 double crochet as before.

No. 6.—Make a chain of 5 stitches, and unite it. Round 1: 1 double crochet, 5 chain, repeat 4 times more. Round 2 : Into the 5 chain 1 double crochet, 3 chain, repeat till 5 double crochet are done, repeat. Round 3 : 1 double crochet into the 1 in 1st round, 7 chain, repeat. Round 4: Same as 2nd. Round 5 : 1 double crochet into the 1 in 3rd round, 7 chain, repeat. Round 6 : Same as 2nd. Round 7 : Same as 5th. Round 8 : Same as 2nd, only 4 chain instead of 3. Round 9 : 1 double crochet into the 1 in 7th round, 8 chain, repeat. Round 10 : The same as 8th, only making 5 chain instead of 4. Four of these patterns will be required for this d'oyley.

No. 7.—Make a chain of 6 stitches, and unite it. Round 1 : 1 double crochet, 7 chain, miss 1 loop, repeat twice more. Round 2 : Into the 7 chain 2 double crochet, 7 long, 2 double crochet, repeat. Round 3 : 1 double crochet, 3 chain, miss 1 loop, repeat, 11 chain, work 2 more leaves in the same way, 1 double crochet into the 3 chain, 4 chain, repeat round 2 sides of the leaf, 3 chain, repeat the stitch of double crochet and 4 chain round 2 sides of each leaf, joining them with 3 chain. Two of these patterns will be required for this d'oyley.

No. 8.—1st row : Make a chain of 14 stitches, miss the 1st, and work into successive loops 5 double crochet, 5 long, 3 double long, turn. 2nd row : 2 double long into each of the 3, 9 long into successive loops, 5 long into the double crochet at the point of the leaf, 9 long into successive loops, 6 double long into the next 2 loops, 9 double long into the end of the 1st row, unite the last to the first double long in 2nd row. 3rd row : 1 double crochet, 3 chain, miss 1 loop, repeat. No loop to be missed at the point, then work with the embroidery cotton a smaller leaf on it in satin stitch, raising it first with the cotton.

No. 9.—Make a chain of 10 stitches, and unite it. Round 1 : 20 long into the circle. Round 2 : 1 double crochet, taking both sides of the loop, 9 chain, miss 1 loop, repeat. Round 3 : Double crochet into the centre of the 9 chain, 7 chain, repeat. Round 4 : Into the 7 chain of last row 1 double crochet, 1 **long,**

3 double long, 1 long, 1 double crochet, repeat, then work 2 patterns from No. 2 in 1st d'oyley, 1 pattern from No. 3, 2 patterns with 3 leaves from No. 3 in 1st d'oyley, 2 patterns with 2 leaves, and 1 pattern with 1 leaf, work 3 patterns from No. 6 in 1st d'oyley.

When all these patterns are done join them as shown in the engraving, and work the edging as directed in the former d'oyleys.

267.—*D'Oyley No. 6.*

Material: Messrs. Walter Evans and Co.'s Boar s Head cotton No. 20.

Pattern No. 1.—Make a chain of 7 stitches, and unite it. Round 1 : 2 double crochet into each loop. Round 2 : 2 double crochet into 1 loop, and 1 into the next, repeat. Round 3 : Increase to 30 double crochet. Round 4 : 4 chain, 1 single crochet into the 1st chain, 5 double crochet, and repeat 5 times more. Round 5 : 1 double crochet into the centre one of the 5 in last round, 11 chain, repeat. Round 6 : 1 double crochet into every loop. Round 7 : 5 chain, 1 single crochet into the 1st, 12 double crochet, and repeat. Round 8 : 1 double crochet into the 6th of the 12, 15 chain, repeat. Round 9 : 1 double crochet into every loop. Round 10 : 7 chain, miss the 1st, and work into successive loops 1 double crochet, 2 long, and 3 double long, miss 5 loops of the last round, work 1 double crochet, repeat. Round 11 : 1 double crochet over the 1 in last round, miss 1 loop, 1 double crochet into the next, *, 3 chain, miss 1 loop, repeat from * 4 times more, repeat from the beginning of the row.

No. 2.—Make a chain of 20 stitches, and unite it. Round 1; 30 double crochet into the circle. Round 2 ; 1 double crochet, 13 chain, miss 5 loops. repeat. Round 3 ; 17 double crochet into the 13 chain, repeat. Round 4; 1 long, 5 chain, 1 single crochet into the 2nd of the 5 chain, miss 1 loop, repeat. Four patterns of this number will be required for this d'oyley.

No. 3.—Make a chain of 8 stitches, and unite it. Round 1;

267.—D'Oyley No. 6.

1 double crochet, 11 chain, miss 1 loop, repeat 3 times more. Round 2; Into the 11 chain, *, 3 double crochet, 5 chain, 1 single crochet into the 1st chain, repeat from * twice more, 3 more double crochet, repeat from the beginning of the row.

No. 4.—Make a chain of 6, and unite it. Round 1; 1 long,

4 chain, repeat 5 times more. Round 2 ; Into the 4 chain in last row 1 long, 4 chain, work another long into the same place, 2 chain, repeat. Round 3 ; Into the 2 chain 3 double crochet, into the 4 chain 1 double crochet, 11 chain, work another double crochet into the same place, repeat. Round 4 ; Into the 11 chain 3 double crochet, 5 chain, 1 single crochet into the 1st of the 5 chain, 3 double crochet, 7 chain, 1 single crochet into the 1st of the 7, 3 double crochet, 5 chain, 1 single crochet into the 1st of the 5 chain, 3 double crochet, 2 chain, 1 double crochet into the centre one of the 3 in last round, 2 chain, repeat ; then work 2 patterns from No. 2 in 1st d'oyley, 1 pattern from No. 3, 2 patterns from No. 4, 3 from No. 6, and 1 each from Nos. 11, 13, and 14 in 1st d'oyley, 1 pattern from each of Nos. 3 and 4 in 2nd d'oyley, 2 patterns from No. 2 in 5th d'oyley, and 1 pattern each from Nos. 4 and 6 in the 5th d'oyley. Sew these pieces firmly together as shown in the engraving, and add the edging as before.

268.—*D'Oyley No.* 7.

Materials : Messrs. Walter Evans and Co.'s Boar's Head cotton No. 20 ; and 1 skein of their fine embroidery cotton.

Pattern No. 1.—Make a chain of 16 stitches and unite it. 1st round ; 2 double crochet into each loop. 2nd round ; 1 double crochet into each loop. 3rd round ; 1 double crochet, 9 chain, miss 3 loops, repeat. 4th round ; Into the 9 chain 11 double crochet. 5th round ; 1 long, 2 chain, miss 2 loops, repeat. 6th round ; Into the 2 chain 1 double crochet, 3 chain, 1 single crochet into the one double crochet, work another double crochet into the 2 chain, 2 double crochet into the next 2 chain, repeat. 7th round ; 1 double crochet into the 1st of the

2 in last round, 13 chain, repeat. 8th round; Into the 13 chain
11 double crochet, repeat.

No. 2.—Make a chain of 13 stitches, work 1 double crochet
into each, make a chain of 15 stitches, work 1 double crochet
into each, make a chain of 13 stitches, 1 double crochet into
each. 2nd row; 1 double crochet into the end of each of these
points, then work round *both* sides of these points in double
crochet, working twice into the end of each point. 3rd row; 3
double crochet over the 3 at the beginning of last row, *, 4
chain, single crochet into the 1st of the 4 chain, miss 1 loop,
work a long stitch into the next, repeat from * all round, at the
beginning and end of the 3rd point miss 2 loops instead of 1,
then work a stitch of double crochet into the 1st of the 3, 6
chain, miss the 1st, work into successive loops 2 long and 3
double crochet, 1 double crochet into the last of the 3. This
completes the pattern.

No. 3.—Make a chain of 8 stitches, and unite it. 1st round ;
2 double crochet into each loop. 2nd round ; 1 double crochet
into 1 loop, 2 double crochet into the next, repeat. 3rd round ;
2 double crochet into successive loops, 2 double crochet into the
next, repeat. 4th round ; 11 double crochet into successive
loops, *, 9 chain, miss 2 loops, 1 double crochet into the next,
repeat from *. 5th round ; 11 double crochet over the 11 in
last round, work into the 9 chain 5 double crochet, 5 chain, 1
single crochet into the 1st of the chain, 5 more double crochet
into the same place, repeat. 6th round ; 13 double crochet over
the 11 in last round, *, 15 chain, 1 double crochet over the 1st
of the 5 in last round, repeat from *. 7th round ; 13 double
crochet over the 13 in last round, *, work into the 15 chain 8
double crochet, 5 chain, work a stitch of single crochet into the
1st of the 5, 8 double crochet into the same place, repeat from *.

This completes the pattern. Then work a circle in satin stitch on the plain part of the pattern with the Fine Embroidery Cotton. Two of these patterns will be required for this d'oyley.

No. 4.—Make a chain of 16 stitches, and unite it. * make

268.—D'Oyley No. 7.

a chain of 10 stitches, miss the 1st, and work into successive loops 3 double crochet, 3 long, and 3 double long, unite the last double long to the 4th of the 16 chain in the circle, repeat from * 3 times more, *, work in single crochet to the top of the point and down 6 stitches of the other side, then make a chain of 8 stitches, miss the 1st, work into successive loops 3 stitches of double crochet, 2 long, and 2 double long, unite the last to the 3rd of the next point, and repeat from * 3 times more. Three of these patterns will be reqaired for this d'oyley. Work 2 patterns from No. 2 in the 1st d'oyley, work 2 patterns from No. 3 in the same d'oyley, work 1 pattern from No. 5, and 1 from No. 6 in 1st d'oyley, work 2 patterns with 1 leaf from No. 3 in 1st d'oyley, and 1 pattern with 2 leaves, work 2 patterns from No. 3 in the 5th d'oyley, and 1 pattern from No. 4 in the same d'oyley, and 1 from No. 6, work 6 patterns from No. 3 in the 6th d'oyley, and 1 pattern from No. 4 in the same d'oyley, work 1 pattern from No. 2 in 6th d'oyley. Join these pieces as before, and add the same edging.

269.—*D'Oyley No.* 8

Materials: Messrs. Walter Evans and Co.'s Boar's Head cotton No. 20; and 1 skein of their fine embroidery cotton.

Pattern No. 1.—Make a chain of 9 stitches, work a stitch of double crochet into each of the 8 1st, work 2 into the 9th, work down the other side of the chain to correspond, and unite it. 2nd round: *, Work 1 long, make 4 chain, 1 single crochet into the 1st of the 4 chain, miss 1 loop, and repeat from *. No loop to be missed at the point. When this round is finished, make 10 chain, miss the 1st, and work into successive loops 2 long, and 7 of double crochet, then make 15 chain, unite to the 7th, and work into the circle 1 double crochet, make 5 chain, repeat 5 times more. 2nd round: Work into the 5 chain 1 double crochet, 3 long, and 1 of double crochet, repeat. 3rd round: Work 1 double crochet, make 3 chain, miss 1 loop, and repeat. Three of these patterns are required for this d'oyley.

No. 2.—Make a chain of 6 stitches. 1st round: Work 2 double crochet into each loop. 2nd round: Work 1 double crochet, make 9 chain, miss 1 loop, repeat. 3rd round: Work into the 9 chain 1 long, make 1 chain, work another 1 long into

269.—D'Oyley No. 3.

the same place, make 1 chain, work a third 1 long into the same place, make 7 chain, and repeat. 4th round: Work into the centre of 3 long 2 long, make 5 chain, work 2 more long into the same place, make 5 chain, work into the centre of the 7 chain 1 double crochet, make 3 chain, work another of double crochet into the same place, make 5 chain, and repeat. Two of these patterns will be required for this d'oyley. Work 1 pattern from No. 2 in 1st d'oyley, work 1 pattern from Nos. 3, 4, and 6, work 1 pattern with 3 leaves from No. 3 in 1st d'oyley, and 2 with only 1 leaf, work 1 pattern from each of Nos. 13 and 14 in 1st d'oyley, work 1 pattern from 2 in 5th d'oyley, and 1 from No. 4 in the same d'oyley, work 2 patterns from No. 6 in 5th d'oyley, work 3 patterns from No. 3 in 6th d'oyley, and 2 from No. 4 in the same d'oyley, work 1 pattern from No. 1 in 7th d'oyley, work 2 patterns from No. 3, and 1 pattern from No. 4 in 7th d'oyley, then sew them together as before.

270.—*D'Oyley No. 9.*

Material: Messrs. Walter Evans and Co.'s Boar's Head cotton No. 20.

Pattern No. 1 —Make a chain of 10 stitches, and unite it. 1st round: Work into the circle 1 long, make 3 chain, repeat 11 times more. 2nd round : Work 1 double crochet into every loop. 3rd round : *, Make 11 chain, turn, miss 1 loop, work 10 double crochet down the chain, miss 1 loop, work 7 double crochet and repeat from * 5 times more. 4th round : Work 1 double crochet, beginning on the 1st of the 10, make 5 chain, miss 3 loops,•work 1 double crochet, make 5 chain, miss 3 loops, work 1 double crochet, make 5 chain, work 1 double crochet into the point, work down the other side to correspond, make 2 chain, miss 3 loops, work 1 double crochet, make 2 chain, miss 3 loops, and repeat. 5th round : Work into each of the 5 chain 1 double crochet, 5 long stitches, and 1 double crochet.

No. 2.—Make a chain of 20 stitches, and unite it. 1st round : Work a stitch of double crochet into 1 loop, work 2 double crochet into the next, repeat. 2nd round: * Work 3 double crochet, make 5 chain, work 1 single crochet into the 1st of the 5 chain, repeat from * 9 times more, work 2 double crochet. 3rd round: * Make 21 chain stitches, work 1 double

270 —D'Oyley No. 9.

crochet in the centre one of the 3, turn, work 7 double crochet into the 21 chain, make 5 chain, work 1 single crochet into the 1st of the 5 chain, work 7 double crochet into the 21 chain, repeat from * 8 times more. 4th round: Work 15 double crochet into each loop of 21 chain, above the last 7 work 20 double crochet into the last loop of 21, make 5 chain, turn, work 1 single crochet into the last of the 5 chain, 7 double crochet, make 4 chain. 5th round : Work 19 double crochet, beginning on the 1st of the 7 in the 1st loop of 21 chain, * make 6 chain, turn, miss 1 loop, work into successive loops a stitch of double, 3 long, 1 double long, then miss 4 double crochet stitches, work 5 double crochet into successive loops, make 5 chain, 1 single crochet into the 1st of the 5 chain, miss 1 loop, 5 double crochet into successive loops, repeat from * 8 times more, then work 12 double crochet. Two of these patterns will be required for this d'oyley.

No. 3.—Make a chain of 8 stitches, and unite it. 1st round : Work into the circle 1 long, make 3 chain, repeat 9 times more. 2nd round : Work into the 3 chain 1 double crochet, make 17 chain, work another stitch of double crochet into the same place, make 1 chain, work 1 double crochet into the next 3 chain, make 1 chain, and repeat. 3rd round : Work into the 17 chain 20 double crochet, work 1 double crochet into the 1 chain, make 1 chain, work 1 double crochet into the next 1 chain, and repeat. 4th round : Work a stitch of double crochet into the 1 chain in last round, * work 5 double crochet into successive loops, beginning on the 1st of the 20, make 5 chain, work 1 single crochet into the 1st of the 5, repeat from * twice more, then work 5 double crochet into successive loops, and repeat from the beginning of the round. Two of these patterns will be required for this d'oyley.

No. 4.—Make 21 chain and unite it, make a chain of 27 and unite it, make a chain of 21 and unite it. 1st round : Work in the 21 chain 25 stitches of double crochet, work into the 27 chain 31 double crochet, work into the 21 chain 25 double crochet. 2nd round : Work 3 stitches of double crochet into successive loops, make 5 chain, work 1 single crochet into the 1st of the 5 chain, repeat this 6 times more, then work 3 double crochet and repeat from the beginning in the centre loop, repeat this 9 times instead of 7. Two of these are required for this d'oyley.

No. 5.—Make a chain of 44 stitches, work 1 double crochet into each, turn, make 21 chain, work 1 double crochet into the 4th chain on the other side, * make 21 chain, miss 3 loops, work 1 double crochet into the next, repeat from * 9 times more, work 1 single crochet into the end loop, work 44 double crochet into successive loops, work 15 double into the 1st loop of 21, work 4 double crochet into each loop of 21, and 15 into the end one, then * work 2 double crochet, make 3 chain, work 1 single crochet into the 1st of the 3, repeat from * all round.

Work 2 patterns from No. 2 in 1st d'oyley, 1 from No. 3, 2 with 3 leaves, and 2 with 2 leaves, from No. 3 in 1st d'oyley, 2 patterns from No. 6 in same d'oyley, and 3 patterns from No. 3 in 6th d'oyley, sew them together as shown in the engraving, and add the edging as before.

271.—*D'Oyley No.* 10.

Material: Messrs. Walter Evans and Co.'s Boar's Head cotton No. 20.

Pattern No. 1.—Make a chain of 19 stitches, turn, miss 5 loops, work 10 double crochet, make 3 chain, miss 3 loops. work 1 long, make 3 chain stitches, miss 3 loops, work 1 long stitch, make 3 chain stitches, work a stitch of double crochet into the last loop, then work into the 1st 3 chain on the other side, 1 double crochet, 5 long, work into the next 3 chain 4 long stitches, work 4 long stitches into the next 3 chain stitches, then work into the 5 chain at the point 8 long stitches, then work down the other side to correspond, * make 3 chain, miss 1 loop, work 1 long, make 1 chain, work 1 long stitch into the same place, make 1 chain, work another long stitch into the same place, miss 1 loop, work 1 double crochet, repeat from * 7 times more, then work into the 1st 3 chain 1 double crochet,

271.—D'Oyley No. 10.

make 1 chain, work 1 long stitch, * make 1, work 1 double long stitch, repeat from * twice more, make 1 chain, work 1 long ; all these stitches are worked into the same 3 chain, then work 1 double crochet into the chain stitch between the 2nd and

3rd long stitches, repeat this 7 times more; this finishes the leaf; then make 16 chain, and work a second leaf the same as 1st, then work 2 double crochet down, then make 12 chain, and work a third leaf the same as 1st, work 14 stitches down the stem, and work a 4th leaf the same as 1st, work 8 double crochet down the stem, work a 5th leaf the same as 1st, make a chain of 40 stitches, turn, and work back in double crochet.

No. 2.—Make a chain of 10 stitches, and unite it, *, work a stitch of double crochet into the circle, make 13 chain, and repeat from * five times more, then work 17 stitches into each of the 13 chain, then work 2 stitches of double crochet, beginning on the second of the 13, *, make 5 chain stitches, and work a stitch of single crochet into the 1st of the 5 chain, then work 2 stitches of double crochet, and repeat from * 5 times more; for the stem make a chain of 30 stitches, turn, * work 5 stitches of double crochet, make 5 chain, turn, and work a stitch of single crochet into the 1st, repeat from * 4 times more, then work down the other side to correspond; then work 1 pattern from No. 2 in 1st d'oyley, and 2 from No. 3, 2 with only two leaves, and 2 from No. 6 in the same d oyley; work 1 pattern from No. 6 in 5th d'oyley, and 3 from No. 3 in 6th d'oyley; work 1 pattern from No. 2 in 9th d'oyley, and 1 from No. 3 ; work 3 patterns from No. 4 in the same d'oyley, sew the pieces together as before, and work the edging.

272 and 273.—*Work-Basket in Straw and Silk Crochet-Work.*

Materials : Straw ; brown floss silk ; brown ribbon, 1¼ inch wide ; small glass beads ; a piece of bamboo cane.

This basket has a cover formed of two pieces. It can be employed for many things, and is formed entirely of crochet-

T

work with brown silk over straw. A ruche trimmed with beads
and bows of brown silk ribbon form the trimming of the basket.
The straws over which you crochet must be damp, so as not to
be stiff. They should be of unequal length, and when you
join the two ends of two straws together, try to hide the
beginning with the other straws. Begin the basket in the centre
of the bottom part with 46 stitches; then work 9 rounds on
either side of this first row, working alternately 1 double stitch,
1 or 2 chain stitches, the double stitch in the chain stitch of the
preceding round, the last round over wire.

It is necessary to increase regularly in all the rounds to keep

273.—Bottom of Work Basket (272).

the work flat. When you have finished the bottom begin the
border of the basket, which is worked of the same piece with it,
and consists of 11 rou:ds.

It is worked in the same way as the bottom, the first 2
rounds without increasing the number of stitches, but in the
following 9 rounds increase 2 double stitches at both ends, in
order that the edge may be a little wider in the upper part. In
the last round add a piece of wire to the straws.

The cover of the basket is formed of two pieces. Begin in
the middle with 28 stitches; crochet each half in rows forming a
half circle, working backwards and forwards; at the beginning

272.—Work Basket in Straw and Crochet.

of each row turn the straws, and take care that the rows which are finished form a straight line. Each half of the cover requires 9 rows; the last one is worked over wire. The two halves are united at the straight sides by a brown silk ribbon 1¼ inch wide, which is sewed on underneath, and which forms a sort of hinge; sew on also a piece of wire covered with brown silk, so as to make the hinge stronger. Form the handle with a piece of bamboo cane 23 inches long, and covered with straws; work over it in long stitches of brown silk, and let it go down to the bottom of the basket; then sew the cover on the handle with the brown ribbon, which forms the two parts. Trim the basket with a ruche of double box pleats, ornamented with glass beads and with bows of brown silk ribbon.

274 *and* 275.—*Two Crochet Borders.*

Materials: Messrs. Walter Evans and Co.'s crochet cotton Nos. 30 and 80.

No. 274.—Crochet cotton of two sizes is used for this border (No. 30 and No. 80); it is begun in the centre by a chain of stitches of the length required.

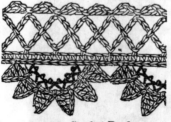

274.—Crochet Border.

1st row: 1 double in each stitch of the chain.

2nd row: Turn and work on the opposite side of the chain, * 1 double, 11 chain, miss 7. Repeat from *.

3rd row : * 1 double on the 1st loop of chain, 2 chain, 1 double in the centre of the 7 stitches which are under the 1st loop of chain, 2 chain, 1 double on the same loop, 5 chain. Repeat from *.

4th row : * 1 double in the centre of the 1st loop of chain, 3 chain, 1 treble in the 1st, but before you complete the treble stitch make 1 chain. Repeat from *. This row completes the upper half of the border. The lower half is worked over the 1st row of plain double crochet.

5th row : 1 double in each of the first 5 stitches, 15 chain,

275.—Crochet Border.

miss 9, 1 double, come back over the loop of chain and work 1 double in each stitch, come back again and work 6 small points, each made thus : 5 chain, 1 double in the 4th, and 1 treble in each of the 3 others, 1 double over the round scallop. When you have worked the 6 small points repeat from *, but always join the 1st point of 'one scallop to the last point of the next scallop. The pattern inside the scallops is worked in 2 rows with fine cotton. (See illustration.)

No. 275.—The border is begun above the pointed scallops, filled up with lace stitches, by making alternately 3 chain, 1 purl (*i.e.*, 5 chain and 1 slip stitch in the 1st). When the chain is long enough, turn and work the 1st row : Alternately 7 chain, 1 double in the centre stitch between the 2 purl.

2nd row : Turn, work 1 double in the centre of the 1st loop of 7 chain, 1 chain, 1 purl, 1 chain, 1 double in the centre of next loop, and so on.

The 3rd row (which is the last) is worked on the opposite side of the chain with purl. * In each of the 8 first stitches work 1 double, make 12 chain, miss the 4 last of the 8 double just worked, and work 1 double in the 5th, come back over the loop of chain, and work 7 small points over it. For each point make 3 chain, work 1 double in the 2nd, 1 treble in the 1st of the 3 chain, 1 double upon the loop of chain. Repeat from * 6 times more.

In the following scallops always fasten the first point of one scallop to the last point of the preceding scallop. When this row is completed fill up the inner part of each scallop with a network of fine thread, joining the threads at all the places where they cross each other by 2 or 3 stitches with a sewing needle.

276.—*Crochet Antimacassar.*

Materials: 18 reels of Messrs. Walter Evans and Co.'s Boar's Head
cotton No. 10.

This pattern can be adapted for a round couvrette or a square one, and is also pretty done in silk for a sofa cushion. Make a chain of 4 stitches, and unite it. 1st round : Work into 1 loop a long stitch, make 1 chain stitch, work another long stitch into the same place, make 1 chain, repeat. 2nd round : 3 long stitches into 1 loop, make 2 chain stitches, miss 1 loop, and repeat. 3rd round : 1 double crochet into the 2 chain in last

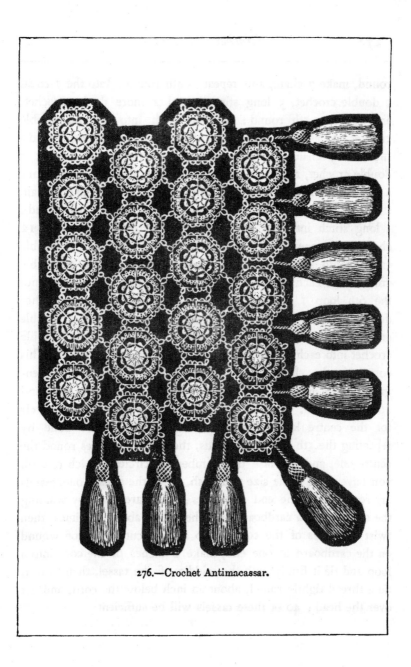

276.—Crochet Antimacassar.

round, make 7 chain, and repeat. 4th round : Into the 7 chain 2 double crochet, 5 long stitches, and 2 more double crochet, and repeat. 5th round : 1 long stitch into the 1st double crochet in last round, make 9 chain, and repeat. 6th round : Into the 9 chain 2 double crochet, * make 4 chain, work 2 double crochet, repeat from * 3 times more, make 5 chain, work a stitch of single crochet into the 2nd of the 5, make 1 chain stitch, and repeat from the beginning of the round. 7th round : 1 long stitch into the loop formed with the 5 chain, make 12 chain, and repeat. 8th round : Into the 12 chain 2 double crochet into successive loops, make 4 chain, work 1 double crochet into each of the 2 next loops, make 1 chain, work into the 6th loop 1 double crochet, 5 long stitches, and another double crochet, make 1 chain, miss 1 loop, work 2 double crochet into successive loops, make 4 chain, work 1. double crochet into each of the 2 next, make 5 chain, and repeat. This completes the circle. 120 circles sewn together like the engraving will make a good-sized couvrette, 12 in the length, and 10 in the width. If a round couvrette is wished, work 1 circle for the centre larger than the others ; this can be done by repeating the 5th and 6th rounds, then sew 8 circles round the centre one, and increase the number of circles in each row till you have made it the size you wish. For the square one, tassels are required for the end and sides ; these are made by winding the cotton over a cardboard 4 inches. deep about 80 times, then twist 8 threads of the cotton into a cord, cut the cotton wound on the cardboard at one end, make 2 inches of the cord into a loop and tie it firmly with the middle of the tassel, then turn it, tie a thread tightly round, about an inch below the cord, and net over the head ; 40 of these tassels will be sufficient.

277.—*Crochet Insertion.*

Material: Messrs. Walter Evans and Co.'s crochet cotton No. 40.

The patterns of this insertion are worked in a row, and always two opposite circles at a time. Make a foundation chain of 16 stitches, join them into a circle, then work a 2nd circle consisting again of 16 chain stitches. Work round this circle 24 double stitches, and 24 double round the 1st circle; after the last stitch begin again at the 2nd circle, and work 10 chain

277.—Crochet Insertion.

scallops as follows :—3 double in the next 3 stitches, * 5 chain, 2 double in the next 2 stitches, repeat 8 times more, 3 double in the last 3 stitches ; work in the same manner round the other circle. To get to the next pattern, work 4 slip stitches between the 2 circles in the middle of the just-completed pattern, leaving the cotton under the work and drawing it through the stitch upwards through the loop on the needle ; 7 chain stitches, and then 2 circles like those just described, and so on.

278 and 279.—*Tobacco Pouch in Crochet Work.*

Materials: Black purse silk ; crimson ditto ; gold thread.

The pouch is begun at the bottom, in the centre of the star. With crimson silk make a chain of 3 stitches, and join it into a circle. Work 4 rounds of double crochet, 2 stitches in each stitch.

5th round : 2 crimson stitches, 1 gold stitch, and so on.

6th round : All gold stitches.

7th round : 2 crimson stitches, 2 gold, and so on.

8th round : All crimson stitches.

9th round : 3 crimson stitches, 2 gold, &c.

10th round : Similar to the preceding

278.—Star for Tobacco Pouch, No. 279.

11th round : 4 gold stitches, 3 crimson, &c.

12th round : 4 gold stitches, 2 black stitches over the 2 centre gold stitches of preceding round, &c.

13th round : 3 gold stitches, 4 black stitches, &c.

14th round : 1 gold stitch, 6 black stitches, &c.

15th round : 3 gold stitches, 4 black stitches, &c.

16th round : 4 gold stitches, 2 black stitches, &c.

17th round : 4 gold stitches, 2 over the black stitches of preceding round, and 1 on either side, 4 crimson stitches, &c.

18th round : 2 gold stitches over the centre ones of preceding round, 7 crimson stitches, &c.

Now work 4 plain crimson rounds, and begin the pattern from No. 279. The centre is crimson, and the pattern is black and gold. The border round the top is of the same colours.

279.—Tobacco Pouch.

Complete the work by 2 rounds of open treble crochet, and 1 round of gold scallops.

In the open rounds pass a double cord of black silk, finished off with small balls of black silk gimp and gold ; and on either side of the pouch fasten one of these same balls with two tassels, one crimson and one black.   The pouch is lined with white kid.

280 *and* 281.— *Crochet Rosettes.*

Material: Messrs. Walter Evans and Co.'s crochet cotton No. 4, 24, or 40.

These rosettes are suitable for trimming cuffs, collars, and bodices, or for making couvrettes, according to the size of the cotton with which they are worked.

280.—Crochet Rosette.

280.—Make a foundation chain of 22 chain ; join them into a circle and work the 1st round ; 44 double.   2nd round : * 7 chain, missing 3 stitches of the preceding round under them, 1 double ; repeat 10 times more from *.   3rd round : 1 slip stitch in the first 4 stitches of the next scallop, * 5 chain, miss the last and work back on the other 4, 1 double, 1 treble, 1 long treble,

1 double long treble (throw the cotton 3 times round the needle),
1 slip stitch in the middle stitch of the next scallop; repeat 10
times more from *. Work a wheel in the centre of the rosette,
which is ornamented with a circle of chain stitch, as can be seen
in illustration; take up one thread of the wheel with every other
chain stitch.

281.—Begin the rosette with a leaf-like pattern in the centre,
and work the 1st row: * 11 chain, miss the last, work back

281.—Crochet Rosette.

over the following 8 stitches, 1 double, 1 treble, 2 long treble,
1 double long treble, 2 long treble, 1 treble, 1 double in the upper
part of the chain stitch before the last, 1 slip stitch in the lower
part of the same stitch. The first leaf of the middle pattern is
then completed; repeat 6 times more from *. Join the first and
last leaves together by working 1 slip stitch in the 1st of the 11
chain stitch. 2nd round: (Fasten on the cotton afresh), 1 slip
stitch in the point of each leaf, 12 chain between. 3rd round:
24 double in each scallop. The rosette is then completed.

282.—*Crochet Trimming, with Embroidered Flowers worked in Appliqué and Velvet Ribbon.*

This trimming consists of 2 strips of crochet insertion, ornamented with embroidery patterns worked in appliqué, and velvet

282.—Crochet Trimming, with Embroidered Flowers worked in Appliqué and Velvet Ribbon.

ribbon drawn through. They are worked the long way with fine crochet cotton. Begin on a sufficiently long foundation chain of stitches which can be divided by 20, and work the 1st row : 1 chain, * 5 double, on the first 5 stitches of the foundation, 1 leaf, as follows :—10 chain, without reckoning the loop left on the needle, 1 extra long treble (for which the cotton is wound 5 times round the needle) in the second of the 10 chain, a similar treble in the first, then cast off the 2 treble stitches together, wind the cotton once round the needle, and cast off the last loop with the loop left on the needle. Miss under the leaf 15 stitches of the foundation, and repeat from *. 2nd row : 5 double on the 5 double of the preceding row, inserting the needle in the whole stitches, 15 chain stitches between. 3rd row : * 5 double in the first 5 double of the preceding row, 7 chain, 1 slip stitch in every other stitch of the next scallop of the preceding row, 7 chain between, 7 chain stitches ; repeat from *. 4th row : * 1 double in the middle of the 5 double of the preceding row, 3 chain, 1 slip stitch in the middle stitch of each of the 8 scallops, consisting of 7 chain in the preceding row, 3 chain between, 3 chain ; repeat from *. These 2 last rows (the third and fourth) are repeated on the other side of the foundation chain.

When the 2 strips of insertion are completed, sew them together so that 2 opposite scallops meet, and ornament them with the embroidery patterns and velvet ribbon.

283.—*Crochet Insertion.*

This pretty insertion is very suitable for cerceaunette covers or pillowcases, and should be worked with middle-sized cotton. If the insertion is used for anything but a pillowcase, omit the lower border on which the button-holes are made. Begin the insertion in the middle of one of the star-like figures, with a foundation chain of 9 stitches ; join them into a circle by making

1 slip stitch, and crochet thus :—* 10 chain, 1 slip stitch in the 5th of these chain ; this forms 1 purl ; 4 chain, 1 slip stitch in the circle, repeat from * 5 times more. Work 4 slip stitches in the next 4 chain, then crochet * in the next purl ; 5 double divided by 5 chain, 4 chain, repeat 5 times from *. Fasten the thread after having fastened the last 4 chain stitches with a slip stitch to the 1st double stitch of this round. This completes the star-like figure. Work on one side of these figures the following rows :—

1st row : * 1 treble in the 2nd scallop of the four placed together, 3 chain, 1 double in the next scallop, 3 chain, 1 treble in the last of the 4 scallops, 3 chain, 1 treble in the 1st scallop of the following 4 placed together, 3 chain, 1 double in the next 2nd scallop, 3 chain, 1 treble in the 3rd scallop, 3 chain. Repeat from *.

2nd row : 3 treble in the 1st stitch of the preceding row, * miss 3 stitches, 3 treble in the 4th following stitch. Repeat from *.

3rd row : * 3 treble cast off together as one stitch on the next 3 stitches of the preceding row, 2 chain. Repeat from *.

4th row : 1 double on the next stitch of the preceding row, * 4 chain, 1 slip stitch in the 3 double ; this forms 1 purl ; 3 double on the next 3 stitches of the preceding row. Repeat from *. After having worked these four rows likewise on the other side of the star figures, work over the last the following 5 rows for the button-holes :—

1st row : 1 double in the next purl, * 2 chain, 1 double in the next purl. Repeat from *.

2nd row : 1 double in each stitch of the preceding row.

3rd row : Alternately 11 double, 7 chain, under which miss 7 stitches.

4th row : Like the 2nd row.

5th row : * 3 double on the next 3 double of the preceding

283.—Crochet Insertion.

row, 1 purl (4 chain, 1 slip stitch in the last double stitch). Repeat from *.

284.—*Crochet Insertion.*

Material: Messrs. Walter Evans and Co.'s crochet cotton No. 30.

This insertion is worked in our pattern with fine crochet cotton on a double foundation chain. For the outer edge work a row of purl stitches as follows :—1 double in the 1st stitch, * 1 chain, 1 purl, consisting of 5 chain, 1 slip stitch in the 1st 2 chain, 1 double in the next stitch but 2 ; repeat from *. The open-work centre consists of 6 rows of scallops ; the 1st of these rows is worked on the other side of the foundation chain ; 1 double in the middle stitch of every scallop, 5 chain between, then 1 row of slip stitches, and finally a row of purl stitches like the

U

1st row of the insertion. For the raised flowers, which are fastened over the grounding at unequal distances, * make a foundation chain of 10 stitches, fasten it on over the grounding from illustration by taking the needle out of the loop, inserting it into the 1 chain of the grounding, and drawing the loop through ; miss the last of the 10 chain, and work back over the others ; 1 slip stitch, 1 double, 1 long double, 3 treble, 1 long double, 1 double, 1 slip stitch, then 1 slip stitch in the 1st stitch, * 9 chain, missing 5 stitches under them, 1 double in the 6th stitch ;

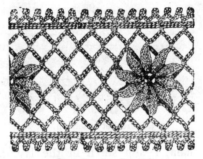

284.—Crochet Insertion.

repeat from *. Each following row consists of 1 double in the middle stitch of every scallop of the preceding row, 9 chain between. Then work the 1st row of the border on the other side of the insertion ; 1 double in the 1st stitch of the foundation, inserting the needle into the back part of the stitch ; repeat 8 times more from *, and the flower is completed.

285.—*Crochet Garter.*

Materials : Grey thread of medium size ; fine red wool ; fine round white elastic cord ; a pearl button.

This garter is worked in close double crochet, over fine

elastic cord ; the border and pattern in red wool, the centre in grey thread.

Begin in the middle by a chain of 98 stitches, with red wool ; take the elastic cord, which must always be stretched out a little, and work over it. Work on both sides of the foundation chain ; the pattern is completed in the course of the two first rounds ; the button-hole is made at the beginning of the first

285.—Crochet Garter.

round ; make a loop of 21 stitches, and, when you come to it, work over this loop instead of over the foundation chain. Increase the number of stitches at either end of the garter, to round it off. When the second round is completed work two plain grey rounds, then a plain red one. The last round (grey thread) is composed of alternately 1 double, 1 purl formed of 3 chain, 1 slip stitch in the first, missing 1 stitch under the 1 purl. Sew on a pearl button to correspond with the button-hole. The garter would be both more elegant and more elastic if worked entirely in silk.

286.—*Crochet Trimming for a Lady's Chemise.*

Materials : Messrs. Walter Evans and Co.'s crochet cotton, and a needle to match.

This pattern, as can be seen in illustration, is an imitation of old guipure lace ; it is worked all in one piece for the bosom and sleeves, and is part of one of the shoulder-pieces in full size. Both strips of rosettes join at that place, and one is continued for the part round the bosom and the other for the sleeve. In the pattern there are 42 rosettes round the bosom, and 14 round each sleeve. These rosettes are fastened one to another in the course of the work. They are made in the following manner :—
Make a chain of 6 stitches, and join it into a ring. 1st round :
8 chain, 1 slip stitch in the 4th chain, which forms a purl (the 3 first chain are reckoned as 1 treble), 1 chain, 1 treble in the ring, * 5 chain, 1 slip stitch in the 1st to form a purl, 1 chain, 1 treble in the ring. Repeat 6 times from *. Instead of the last treble, work a slip stitch to fasten the end of the round to the 3 chain of the beginning, which thus form 1 treble. 2nd round :
9 chain (the 3 first to be reckoned as 1 treble), * 1 treble on the 1st treble of last round, 6 chain. Repeat 6 times from *. 1 slip stitch in the treble at the beginning. 3rd round : On each scallop of preceding round work 2 double, 1 purl, 2 double, 1 purl, 2 double, 1 purl, 2 double. This completes the rosette. Each rosette is fastened to the last by joining the 2 middle purl of both. In the illustration, which is full-size, the purl that are to be joined to those of another rosette are marked by a cross. The joining between the part round the bosom and the sleeve is made in the same manner. The space left between 4 rosettes is filled up with a star formed of chain stitches, marked in our illustration with an asterisk. For this star make a chain of 5 stitches, the 1st of which forms the centre ; slip the loop

you have on the needle through one of the 8 purl that are free, make 5 chain, 1 double in the centre stitch. Repeat 7 times

286.—Crochet Trimming for a Lady's Chemise.

from * ; then tie the two ends tightly, or sew them together 3 of these stars are required for each shoulder

For the Border.—It is worked at the same time both round the bosom and sleeves. 1st round : * 1 double in the centre purl of the 1st scallop of the rosette, which we will call the *first rosette;* 5 chain, 1 double in the centre purl of the 2nd scallop of the same rosette, 4 chain ; then work the kind of cross which comes between each rosette (see illustration). To make this cross throw the cotton 3 times round the needle, work 1 double treble in the last purl left free of the 1st rosette, keep the last loop on the needle, throw the cotton twice round it, and work a double treble in the 1st purl left free in the 2nd rosette, throw the thread twice round the needle, work 1 treble with the loop left on the needle, make 2 chain, and work 1 treble in the last double treble, which completes the cross ; make 4 chain. Repeat from * at each slit on the shoulders ; after the last cross make 6 chain, 1 slip stitch in the 2 purl at the end of the slit, 6 chain to come to the next space, where a cross is to be made. 2nd round : Work alternately 1 treble, 2 chain, miss 2 ; at the slit on the shoulders work 6 double over the 6 chain. The two rounds just explained are also worked round the upper edge, and finished round the sleeves by the following round :—1 double in one of the spaces in last round, * 6 chain, 1 double in the 2nd of the 6 chain, which forms a purl, 1 chain, 1 double on the next but one of the last round, 6 chain, 1 double in the 2nd of the 6 chain, 1 chain, 1 double in the next space. Repeat from *. On the upper edge of the bosom, between the 1st and 2nd rounds of the border, work 1 round of crosses, but throwing the cotton twice only round the needle, so that the treble stitches are not double ; make 3 chain between each cross.

KNITTING.

KNITTING.

287.—KNITTING, though considered to be an old-fashioned art, is by no means so ancient as lacemaking. Knitting has never entirely quitted the hands of English and German ladies ; indeed, among all good housewives of any civilised country, it is reckoned an indispensable accomplishment. Knitting schools have been established of late years both in Ireland and Scotland, and Her Majesty the Queen has herself set an example of this industry, as well as largely patronised the industrial knitters of Scotland. Of the rudiments of this useful art many ladies are at present ignorant ; it is in the hope of being useful to these that the following instructions are offered.

To knit, two, three, four, or five needles, and either thread, cotton, silk, or wool are required.

Knitting needles are made of steel, of ivory, or of wood ; the size to be used depends entirely upon the material employed, whether thread, cotton, silk, single or double wool, for knitting. As the size of the needles depends upon that of the cotton, a knitting gauge is used (see No. 287). The gauge (page 290) is the exact size of Messrs. H. Walker and Co.'s knitting gauge. Our readers will remark that English and foreign gauges differ very essentially ; the finest size of German needles, for example, is

No. I, which is the size of the coarsest English wooden or ivory
needle. Straight knitting is usually done with two needles only
for round knitting for socks, stockings, &c., three, four, and five
needles are employed.

288.—*Casting On.*

This term is used for placing the first row or round of
knitting stitches on the needles—" casting them on "—and is
done in two ways — by "knitting on" the stitches, or as
follows :—

Hold the thread between the first and second finger of the

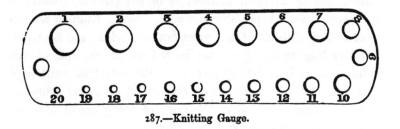

287.—Knitting Gauge.

left hand, throw it over the thumb and first finger so as to form
a loop, and pass the needle in the loop ; throw the thread lightly
round the needle, pass it through the loop, and draw up the
thread ; this forms the first stitch (see No. 288).

289.—*To Knit On.*

Take the needle on which the stitches are cast in the left
hand, and another needle in the right hand—observe the position
of the hands (No. 289). Hold the left-hand needle between the

thumb and third finger, leaving the first finger free to move the points of the needles. (The wonderful sense of touch in the first or index finger is so delicate, that an experienced knitter can

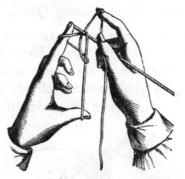

288.—Casting On.

work without ever looking at her fingers, by the help of this touch only—in fact, knitting becomes a purely mechanical labour,

289.—Knitting On.

and as such is most useful.) Insert the point of the right-hand needle in the loop or stitch formed on the left-hand needle, bring the thread once round, turning the point of the needle in front under the stitch, bringing up the thread thrown over, which in its turn becomes a stitch, and is placed on the left-hand needle.

290.—*Simple Knitting (plain).*

Pass the right-hand needle into the 1st stitch of the left-hand needle, at the back throw the thread forward, and with the first finger pass the point of the needle under the stitch in forming a fresh stitch with the thread already thrown over, as in "knitting on," only, instead of placing the newly-formed

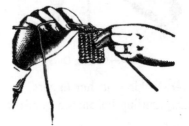

290.—Plain Knitting.

stitch on the left-hand needle, leave it on the right-hand needle, and let the stitch drop off the point of the left-hand needle. Continue thus until all the stitches are taken from the left to the right-hand needle, and the row is then complete.

291.—*To Purl, Pearl, or Seam.*

Seaming or purling a stitch is done by taking up the stitch *in front* instead of at the back, throwing the thread over and knitting the stitch as in plain knitting ; but before beginning to purl, the thread must be brought in front of the needle, and if a plain stitch follows, the thread is passed back after the purl stitch is made (see No. 291).

292.—*To Increase.*

Increasing or making a stitch is done by throwing the thread once round the needle and in the next row knitting it as an ordinary stitch.

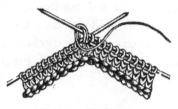

291.—Purling.

293.—*To Decrease.*

This is done in two ways : *firstly*, taking up two stitches and knitting them together as one ; *secondly*, by taking up a stitch

292.—Increasing.

without knitting it, called slipping, then by knitting the following stitch in the usual way, and then slipping the 1st (unknitted) over the 2nd (knitted) (see No. 293). When it is necessary to decrease two stitches at once, proceed thus :—Slip one, knit two stitches together, then slip the unknitted stitch over the two knitted together.

294.—*Round Knitting.*

To knit a round four or five needles are used; it is thus that stockings, socks, cuffs, mittens, &c., are made. To knit with four needles, cast on, say, 32 stitches upon one needle, insert a second needle in the last stitch of the first, and cast on

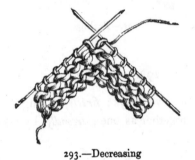

293.—Decreasing

30 stitches; proceed in a similar way with a third needle, but casting on 28 only; when this is done, knit the two extra stitches on the first needle on to the last; this makes 30 stitches upon each needle, and completes the round.

295.—*Casting Off.*

Knit two stitches, and with the left-hand needle slip the first stitch over the second; continue this to the end of the row. *Note.*—The last knitted row, before casting off, should be knitted loosely.

296.—*To Pick up a Stitch.*

This is done by taking up the thread between two stitches and forming a stitch with it.

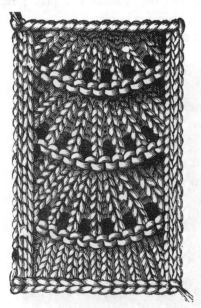

297.—Peacock's Tail Pattern.

The following Designs of New Stitches can be used for a variety of work :—

297.—*Peacock's Tail Pattern.*

Needles, wood or ivory ; Messrs. Walter Evans and Co.'s knitting cotton.

Cast on a number of stitches divisible by nine, as it takes nine stitches for each pattern, and two for each border ; the border, which is in plain knitting, will not be mentioned after the first row.

1st Row.—2 plain for border; 2 plain *, make 1, 1 plain, repeat this four times from *, make 1, 2 plain; repeat from the beginning—then 2 plain for border.

2nd Row.—2 purl, 11 plain, 2 purl; repeat.

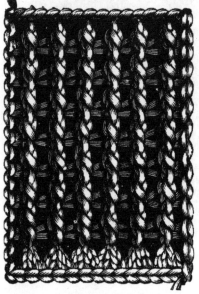

298.—Spiral Stitch.

3rd Row.—Take 2 together, 11 plain, take 2 together; repeat.

4th Row.—Purl 2 together, purl 9, purl 2 together; repeat.

5th Row.—Take 2 together, 7 plain, take 2 together.

Begin from the 1st row.

Thirteen stitches are large enough for a stripe for a sofa-cover. These stripes should be sewn together after all are finished.

298.—*Spiral Stitch.*

Materials : Needles, thick steel or bone; double wool.

This stitch is far more effective worked in thick wool than in cotton. It is done in stripes alternately wide and narrow.

299.—Knotted Stitch.

For wide stripes cast on twenty-one stitches, for narrow fifteen ; this without counting the first and last stitch, the first being slipped, the last always plainly knitted.

1*st Row.*—Purl 3 together to end of row.

2*nd Row.*—Make 1, * 1 plain, make 2, repeat from * end by making the last stitch before the plain knitted one at end of row.

X

299.—*Knotted Stitch.*

Materials : Needles, wood or ivory ; double wool.

Cast on 11 stitches.

1st Row.—All plain, throwing the wool twice round the needle before each stitch.

2nd Row.—Each stitch on the needle is now composed of 3 threads of wool : knit the first plain, the second purl, the third plain ; cast off the second over the third, and the first over the second ; this leaves but one stitch ; repeat from first row until a sufficient length is obtained. This pattern makes very pretty borders.

300.—*Knitted Moss Borders.*

Materials : Steel needles ; *moss* wool of several shades of green.

Cast on enough stitches for double the width required, say twenty, and knit very tightly in plain knitting, row by row, until a sufficient length has been obtained. Cut off and place the strip on a sieve over a basin of boiling water, and cover it over. When it has absorbed the steam, and while wet, iron it with a box-iron. Then cut the strip down the centre, and unravel the wool on each side. The threads of wool all curling, resemble moss. They are held firmly by the selvedge of the knitting.

301.—*German Brioche Stitch*

Materials : Wood or ivory needles ; wool.

Cast on an even number of stitches.

All the rows are knitted as follows :—Slip 1, taken as **for** purling, make 1, take 2 together. In the following rows the made stitch must always be slipped, the decreased stitch and the slipped stitch of the previous row knitted together.

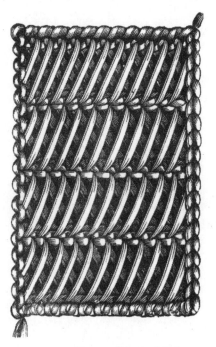

301.—German Brioche Stitch.

Ordinary Brioche Stitch is made by casting on an even number of stitches, and working the rows as follows :—

Make 1, slip 1, take 2 together ; repeat. *Note.*—The made stitch and the slipped stitch of the previous row must always be knitted together, and the decreased stitch of that row slipped.

NETTING.

———◆———

302.—NETTING is one of the prettiest and one of the easiest accomplishments of a lady. The materials are simple, while the effects produced by good netting are most elegant and of great durability. One great advantage of netting is that each stitch is finished and independent of the next, so that if an accident happens to one stitch it does not, as in crochet or knitting, spoil the whole work.

Netting, so easy to do, is most difficult to describe. The materials required are—a netting-needle and mesh (see illustration No. 302). These are made of bone, of wood, of ivory, and most commonly of steel. The wood, bone, and ivory are only used for netting wool, the steel for silk, cotton, &c.

The needle is filled by passing the end of the thread through the little hole at the left-hand point, and tying it; then the thread is wound on the needle as on a tatting shuttle. The needles are numbered from 12 to 24; these last are extremely fine. The meshes correspond to the sizes of the needles, and are made of the same materials. The larger the size of the stitch required the thicker the mesh must be selected; indeed, large flat meshes are often used for some patterns. A stirrup to slip over the foot to which the foundation is attached is required by those who do not use a netting cushion, placed before them on the table and heavily weighted ; to this the foundation is fastened.

The stirrup is made of a loop of ribbon, to which the foundation is tied. Some ladies work a pretty stirrup of the exact shape of a horseman's stirrup ; a loop of ribbon is passed through this, and the foundation fixed as before.

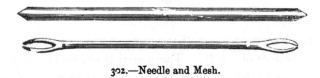

302.—Needle and Mesh.

303.—*To Net.*

Place the mesh under the thread, between the thumb and finger of the left hand ; it must rest on the middle of the finger and be held only by the thumb (see illustration No. 303). Take the needle in the right hand, pass the thread over the middle and ring finger and over the mesh, pass the needle upwards and behind the mesh in the large loop which forms the thread round the fingers, and at the same time through the first stitch or loop of the foundation. Draw the needle out, retaining the loops on the fingers and dropping them off, the little finger being the last to release the thread. As the thread tightens and the knot is firm, the loop on the little finger should be drawn up quickly and smartly. The next stitches are precisely similar, and row upon row is formed in the same manner.

Having learnt the stitch, the next task is to make a foundation. Tie a large loop of strong thread on the stirrup ribbon, and net fifty stitches into this loop, then net four or five rows, and the foundation is ready.

303.—Netting.

Simple netting as above explained forms diamonds or lozenges. When a piece of netting is finished it is cut off the foundation, and the little ends of thread that held the stitches are drawn out.

304.—*Square Netting*

Is done precisely in the same manner as plain netting, only begin from one stitch, then net two stitches into this first, and increase by making two in the last loop of every row. As soon as the right number of stitches is complete diminish exactly in the same way by netting two stitches as one at the end of each row until one stitch alone remains. These squares are used for guipure d'art and for darning on.

305 —*Round Netting*

Is nearly similar to plain netting.　A little difference exists in the way of passing the needle through the stitch ; this is shown in No. 305.　After having passed the needle through the stitch it is drawn out and passed from above into the loop just made.　This stitch is very effective for purses.

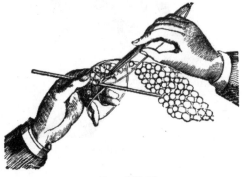

305.—Round Netting.

306.—*Diamond Netting*

Is often called " pointed netting," and is made by netting from one stitch, increasing one stitch at the end of each row, and decreasing in the same way, as described at page 303.

307.—*To Net Rounds.*

To form a circle, as for a purse, the needle must pass through the first stitch, keeping the last three or four on the mesh and removing this when required by the work.

308.—" *English" Netting*

Is made as follows :—Net a row of plain netting, begin the second row by netting the second stitch, then net the first ; repeat, always passing by one stitch and taking it up.

3rd Row.—Plain.

4th Row.—Begin by a plain stitch, then continue as in the 2nd row.

5th Row.—Plain.

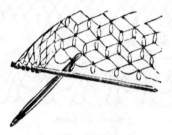

308.—" English" Netting.

309.—*Lace Edging.*

Begin by one stitch and net two in one at the end of each row until as many stitches are required for the narrowest part of the edge. * Increase one then in the two loops until the point of the edge or scallop is reached ; at the next row leave the squares which form the point, and begin from *.

310.—*Open Lace.*

This kind of edging is made with two meshes of different sizes and extremely fine crochet cotton.

Tie the thread to the foundation, net 3 rows with the small mesh of the required length.

4th Row.—On the large mesh, one stitch in each stitch.

5th Row.—On the *small* mesh take 3 stitches together to form 1 loop ; repeat to end of row.

6th Row.—On the large mesh make 5 loops in each stitch ; repeat to end of row.

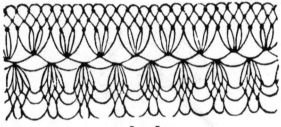

310.—Open Lace.

7th Row.—On the small mesh, one loop in each of the 4 first stitches, pass over the 5th, repeat to end.

8th Row.—On the small mesh make a loop in each of the two first stitches, pass over the 4th ; repeat.

9th Row.—On the small mesh make a loop in each of the two first stitches, pass over the 3rd ; repeat.

This lace is often used in fine wool of two colours to trim opera-caps, children's hoods, &c.

311.—*Shell Border.*

This border is intended as an edging for square netting for couvrettes, d'oyleys, &c. The mesh must be three times as long as that employed for the square netting.

Make 12 stitches in the first stitch of the edge, pass over 8, make 12 in the ninth, and repeat. Then take the mesh used for the square netting, and net one stitch in each stitch, take a still smaller mesh, and complete by adding another row of one stitch in each stitch.

This border forms a very appropriate edging for all articles in square netting, as couvrettes, mats, also for trimming guipure d'art work, and should be netted in the row of holes edging the work ; two sets of shells must be worked at the corners when a little fulness is required.

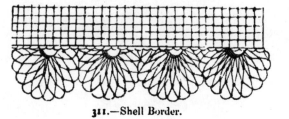

311.—Shell Border.

KNITTING AND NETTING PATTERNS

312.—*Knitted Sock for a Child.*

Ma'erials for 1 pair: 1 ounce of single Berlin wool; 1 yard of narrow pink or blue ribbon; 2 fine steel pins.

This sock fits well, and is easy to make. It is knitted upon two pins, backwards and forwards. Cast on 22 stitches and knit 22 rows, but increase once at the end of every other row on the right side of the work, so that there are 33 stitches in the 22nd row. Now cast off 28 stitches and knit 12 rows, increasing 1 stitch at the end of every other row. Now 12 more rows, decreasing 1 stitch at the end of every other row; this forms the toe. Cast on 28 stitches on the same needle, and knit 22 rows, decreasing 1 stitch at the end of every other row, and cast off. Pick up the 68 stitches on the upper part of shoe, and knit 20 rows, alternately 2 plain and 2 purl rows, decreasing 1 stitch on each side of the 12 stitches in every other row, which forms the toe and front of sock. Knit 14 rows of 2 plain, 2 purl stitches alternately, then 3 open rows with 1 plain row between. The open rows are worked as follows :—* Purl 2 together, purl 1, make 1, repeat *, 3 plain rows, 1 open row, 1 plain row, and cast off. The sock is sewn together down the back of leg, centre of sole, and the point joined like a gusset to form the toe.

312.—Knitted Sock.

313.—*Knitted Pattern for Counterpanes, Berceaunette Covers, Couvrettes, Antimacassars, &c.*

Materials : Messrs. Walter Evans and Co.'s knitting cotton; 5 steel knitting-needles of a corresponding size.

According to the size of the cotton employed, this beautiful square makes different articles, such as counterpanes, couvrettes, &c. &c.

If worked with Evans's cotton No. 10, it will be suitable for the

313.—Knitted Pattern for Counterpanes, Berceaunette Covers, &c.

first-mentioned purpose. Begin the square in the centre, cast on
8 stitches, 2 on each needle; join them into a circle, and knit

plain the 1st round. 2nd round: * Knit 1, throw the cotton forward, knit 1; repeat 3 times more from *. 3rd round: Plain knitting. This knitted round is repeated after every pattern round. We shall not mention this again, nor the repetition from *. 4th round: * Knit 1, throw the cotton forward, knit 1, throw the cotton forward, knit 1. 6th round : * Knit 1, throw the cotton forward, knit 3, throw the cotton forward, knit 1. 8th round: * Knit 1, throw the cotton forward, knit 5, throw the cotton forward, knit 1. The 9th to 18th rounds are knitted in the same manner, only in every other round the number of stitches between the 2 stitches formed by throwing the cotton forward increases by 2, so that in the 18th round 15 stitches are knitted between. 20th round : * Knit 1, throw the cotton forward, knit 1, throw the cotton forward, knit 5, slip 1, knit 1, draw the slipped over the knitted stitch, knit 1, knit 2 together, knit 5, throw the cotton forward, knit 1, throw the cotton forward, knit 1. 22nd round : * Knit 1, throw the cotton forward, knit 1, throw the cotton forward, slip 1, knit 1, draw the slipped over the knitted stitch, throw the cotton forward, knit 4, slip 1, knit 1, draw the slipped over the knitted stitch, knit 1, knit 2 together, knit 4, throw the cotton forward, knit 2 together, throw the cotton forward, knit 1, throw the cotton forward, knit 1. 24th round: * Knit 1, throw the cotton forward, knit 1, throw the cotton forward, slip 1, knit 1, draw the slipped over the knitted stitch ; throw the cotton forward, slip 1, knit 1, draw the slipped over the knitted stitch, throw the cotton forward, knit 3, slip 1, knit 1, draw the slipped over the knitted stitch, knit 1, knit 2 together, knit 3, throw the cotton forward, knit 2 together, throw the cotton forward, knit 2 together, throw the cotton forward, knit 1, throw the cotton forward, knit 1. 26th round: * Knit 1, throw the cotton forward, knit 1, throw the cotton forward 3 times alternately, slip 1, knit 1, draw the first over the last, throw the cotton forward; knit 2, slip 1, knit 1, draw the first over the last, knit 1, knit 2 together, knit 2, three times alternately, throw the cotton forward, knit 2 together, throw the cotton forward, knit 1, throw the cotton forward, knit 1. 28th round: * Knit 1, throw the cotton forward, knit 1, four times alternately, throw the cotton forward, slip 1, knit 1, draw the slipped over the knitted stitch; throw the cotton forward, knit 1, slip 1, knit 1, draw the slipped over the knitted stitch; knit 1, knit 2 together, knit 1, four times alternately throw the cotton forward, knit 2 together, throw the cotton forward, knit 1, throw the cotton forward, knit 1. 30th round: * Knit 1, throw the cotton forward, knit 1, six times alternately throw the cotton forward, slip 1, knit 1, draw the slipped over the knitted stitch, knit 1 six times alternately, knit 2 together, throw the cotton forward, knit 1, throw the cotton forward, knit 1. 32nd round: Knit 1, throw the cotton forward, knit 1, 6 times alternately throw the cotton forward, slip 1, knit 1, draw the slipped over the knitted stitch, throw the cotton forward, knit 3 stitches together, 6 times alternately throw the cotton forward, knit 2 together, throw the cotton forward, knit 1, throw the cotton forward, knit 1. 34th round: * Knit 1, throw the cotton forward, knit 1, 7 times alternately throw the cotton forward, slip 1, knit 1, draw the slipped over the knitted stitch, knit 1, 7 times alternately knit 2 together, throw the cotton forward, knit 1, throw the cotton forward, knit 1. 36th round: * Knit 1, throw the cotton forward, knit 1, 7 times alternately throw the cotton forward, slip 1, knit 1, draw the slipped over the knitted stitch, throw the cotton forward, knit 4 stitches together, 7 times alternately throw the cotton forward, knit 2 together, throw the cotton

forward, knit 1, throw the cotton forward, knit 1. 38th round:
* Knit 1, throw the cotton forward, knit 1, 8 times alternately
throw the cotton forward, slip 1, knit 1, draw the slipped
over the knitted stitch, 8 times alternately knit 2 together,
throw the cotton forward, knit 1, throw the cotton forward,
knit 1. 40th round : * Knit 1, throw the cotton forward, knit
1, 8 times alternately throw the cotton forward, slip 1, knit 1,
draw the slipped over the knitted stitch, throw the cotton
forward, knit 3 stitches together as 1 stitch, 8 times alternately
throw the cotton forward, knit 2 together, throw the cotton
forward, knit 1, throw the cotton forward, knit 1. You now
have 41 stitches on each needle ; knit 1 round, and cast off.
When completed, the squares are joined together on the wrong
side.

314.—*Knitted Sleeping Sock.*

Materials for one pair : 4 ounces white fleecy, 3 ply ; 2 ounces light blue
fleecy.

These socks are knitted with white and blue wool in a
diamond pattern, and in rounds like a stocking. Begin at the
upper part of the sock ; cast on 103 stitches with blue wool on
pretty thick steel knitting-needles, and knit 20 rounds of the
diamond pattern as follows :—1st round : Quite plain. 2nd
round : Purled ; both these rounds are worked with blue wool
3rd to 6th rounds : Knitted plain with white wool. 7th round :
With blue wool ; knit 3, draw the wool through the next stitch
of the 2nd round worked with blue wool, draw it out as a loop,
keep it on the needle, knit again 3 stitches, and so on. 8th
round : With blue wool ; the loop which has been taken up on
the preceding round is purled off together with the preceding
stitch. Repeat the 3rd and 8th rounds twice more ; the loop-

of one round must be placed between those of the preceding one. Then knit with white wool 31 rounds, alternately 2 stitches knitted, 2 stitches purled, then work the foot in the diamond pattern in the same way as usual for a stocking. The heel is formed by leaving 23 stitches on each side the seam

314.—Knitted Sleeping Sock.

stitch, and knitted backwards and forwards in the diamond pattern. At the toe decrease so that the decreasings form a seam on both sides of the toe. This is obtained by knitting the 3rd and 4th stitches of the 1st needle together ; on the 2nd needle slip the 4th stitch before the last, knit the next stitch and draw the slipped stitch over the knitted one ; decrease in the same manner on the other 2 needles of this round. Repeat these decreasings exactly in the same direction and at the same places, so that there are always 4 stitches between the 2 decreasings at the end and at the beginning of 2 needles ; they always take place after 3 or 2 plain rounds, and at last after 1 plain round. The remaining stitches are knitted off 2 and 2 together. To complete the sock, the outline of the sole is marked by working slip stitches with blue wool in crochet all round it ; work also slip stitches on the selvedge stitch of the heel. The stocking is finished off at the top with a double round of loops in blue wool, worked over a mesh four-fifths of an inch wide.

315 and 316.—*Netted Fichu or Cape.*

Material : Fine wool, or white and blue silk; netting needle and meshes.

This fichu or cape is made either with fine wool or with silk used three or four times double. It may be worn as an evening wrap, either over a cap or on the hair, or as a necktie. The ground in our pattern is white, the border blue. The illustration of the ground and of the border, in full size, will serve as a guide for the size of the meshes to be used. For the ground cast on the first mesh, with white silk, 56 stitches ; work 2 rows on the 56 stitches. From the 3rd row, always miss the last stitch, so that each row is decreased 1 stitch. Continue in this manner till the 39th row, when there will be but 19 stitches left. From the 40th row, miss 2 stitches at the end of each row. The ground is completed with the 46th row. The 1st row of the work is the *cross-way side ;* the last, the *point at the bottom ;* fasten on the blue silk to the 1st stitch of the 1st row, and on a larger mesh work 1 row round the ground of the fichu, not forgetting that the stitch on the outer edge at the sides must always be taken, and 2 stitches made in the 5th, 10th, 14th,

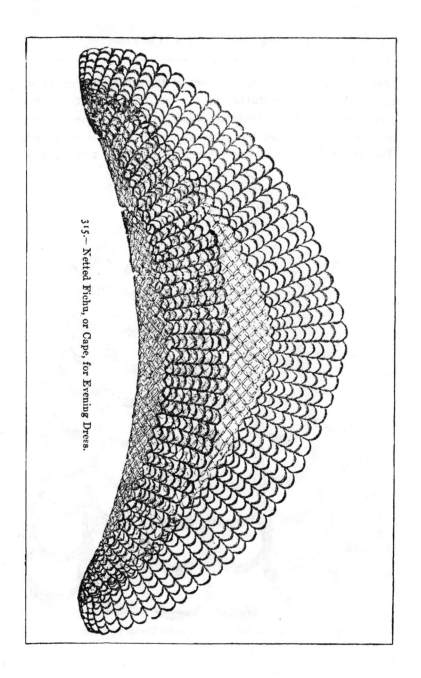

315.—Netted Fichu, or Cape, for Evening Dress.

18th, 21st, 23rd, and 25th stitches at the sides, as well as in each of the 2 middle stitches of the last row; in each of the other stitches 1 stitch should be made. On the corners of the sides increase *once*, on the cross-way side, seven times in all. This forms the 1st round of the edging or lace. 2nd round of

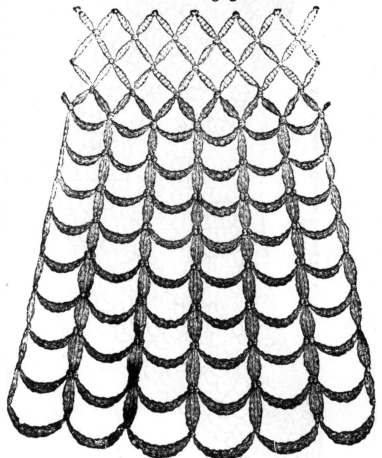

316.—Showing the Netting full size for Border of Fichu.

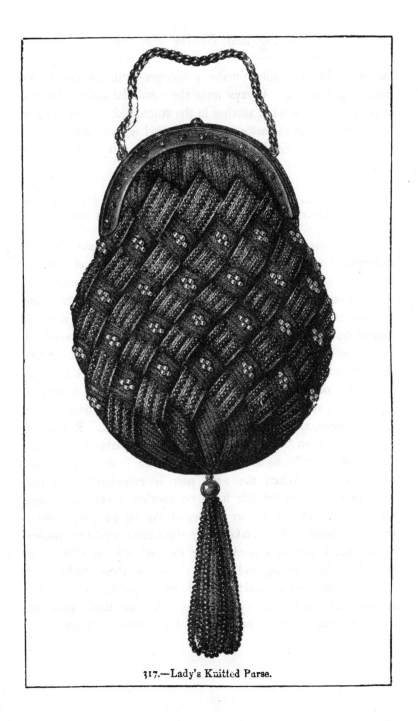

317.—Lady's Knitted Purse.

the lace : In each stitch make 2 stitches—still on the larger mesh. 3rd round : Always miss the small flat scallop formed in last row, and work 2 stitches in the stitch which forms a tight loop. Keep thus the same number of stitches, with which work 6 more rounds. For the last round, work 1 stitch in each *tight* loop.

317.—*Lady's Knitted Purse.*

Materials: 2 skeins of black purse silk; 2 skeins of scarlet ditto; black jet beads; a steel clasp with chain; a tassel of black beads; 5 steel knitting-needles.

This purse is knitted with black and scarlet purse silk, and ornamented with black beads and a black bead tassel. Begin the purse with the black silk in the centre of the bottom part, and cast on for one part of it 7 stitches. Knit 14 rows on these backwards and forwards, in such a manner that the work is knitted on one side and purled on the other. The 1st stitch of every row is slipped, the 1st row of this part is purled. * On that side where hangs the thread with which you work take the back chain of the 7 selvedge stitches of the part you have just knitted on a separate needle, and knit another part, which must have 15 rows, and the 1st row of which is knitted. Repeat 10 times more from * The stitches of several parts can be taken on the same needle, so as not to be hindered in working by too many needles. When the 12th part is completed, take the selvedge stitches on the left hand on another needle, cast them off together with the cast on stitches of the 1st part, and fasten the silk thread. Then take the 7 right-hand selvedge stitches of one black part on a needle, take the red silk on which the beads have been strung and work 15 rows on these stitches, the 1st row from the wrong side, and therefore purled; in the 1st, as well as in all the other purled rows, the last stitch must be purled together with the next stitch of the next black part. In the purled rows, moreover, excepting in the first and last one, a bead must be worked in after casting off the 2nd, 4th, and 6th stitches. The stitch must be worked by inserting the needle into the back part, and in drawing through the silk which has been thrown forward, let the bead slide through the stitch so that it is on the right side of the work. In the following knitted row, the needle must also be inserted into the back part of the bead stitch. When 12 such red parts have been completed, work again 12 black parts on the selvedge stitch of the same, in which the beads are not knitted in, but sewn on afterwards, when the purse is completed. Then work 3 times more alternately 12 red and 12 black parts; when the last 12 black parts have been completed cast off the stitches of the last black part together with the selvedge stitches, the 1st on the wrong side; the stitches of the 6th part are cast off in the same manner together with the selvedge stitches of the 7th. The red parts which remain to be worked on the black part are thus lessened by 2 : the 2nd, 3rd, and 4th, and the 7th, 8th, and 9th of these parts must be by 6 rows longer. Then gather all the stitches and selvedge stitches of the 10 parts on 2 needles, in such a manner that the 2 black parts, the stitches and selvedge stitches of which have been cast off together, are placed on the sides of the purse, and knit as follows with black silk, first on the stitches of the one needle, and then on those of the other :—1 row knitted, knitting together every 3rd and 4th stitch; then work 3 rows backwards and forwards on the same number of stitches, which must be knitted on the right side; then work 8 rows more in the same manner, casting off the 2 first stitches of the 8 rows. Then cast off all the remaining stitches, sew the beads on the black parts from illustration; also the clasp and bead tassel.

318 *to* 320.—*Knitted Antimacassar or Berceaunette Cover.*

Materials: Grey and violet fleecy wool.

This antimacassar, part of which is seen on No. 320, smaller than full size, is made of rosettes and small squares, which are knitted separately with violet and grey fleecy wool with fine knitting-needles. In the middle of each rosette sew on a tatted circle of grey wool. The edge of the antimacassar is ornamented with a grey woollen fringe. For each rosette cast on 6 stitches with violet wool, and knit 12 rows backwards and forwards in such a manner that the work is knitted on one side and purled

318.—Square for Antimacassar.

on the other : the first of these 12 rows is purled, the first stitch of every row is slipped ;* then take the first five selvedge stitches of the knitted part on a separate needle (on the side where the end of wool hangs down, leaving it unnoticed for the present), inserting the needle into the back chain of the stitch (the selvedge stitch which is next to the cast-on stitch remains, therefore, unworked upon), and knit on these a new part, which must have 13 rows ; the first row is knitted, and in this row work 2 stitches in the first stitch, one purled and one knitted, so that this new part is equally six stitches wide. Repeat 8 times more from *. After having worked several parts, the stitches can, of course, be taken on the same needle, so as not to increase the number of needles. When the 10th part is completed, take the selvedge stitches of the left-hand side of the same on a separate needle, cast them off with the cast-on stitches of the first part, and fasten the wool. Then take the 6 selvedge stitches on the right hand of one part on a separate needle; take the grey wool, and work on these stitches 13 rows backwards and forwards; the first row is knitted; it is worked on the right

319.—Rosette for Antimacassar.

side of the work; in this, and in every following *knitted* row, knit the last stitch together with the next stitch of the next violet part. When 10 such grey parts are completed (each of the remaining 9 parts consists of 13 rows, and begins with one knitted row), take all the stitches and the selvedge stitches of these parts on four needles and knit with these stitches, also

with grey wool 1 row knitted, in which the 6 selvedge stitches
must be decreased to 3 by knitting always 2 stitches together as
1 stitch ; each of the other stitches is knitted as usual.   Then
purl 2 rows with violet wool, and cast off.   For the tatted circle

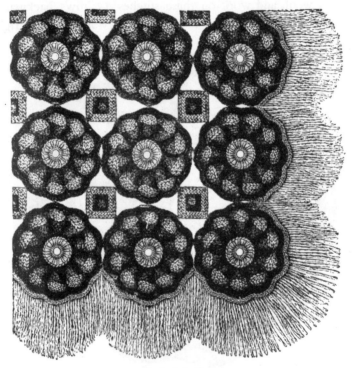

320.—Part of Antimacassar.

in the centre of the rosette, work with grey wool a circle
consisting of 1 double, and 11 times alternately 1 purl 3-10ths
of an inch long, 2 double, then 1 purl and 1 double.   The
circle is sewn on the rosette, from illustration, with grey wool.
No. 319 shows such a rosette full size.   The small squares (*see*
No. 318) are worked with grey wool ; cast on 36 stitches, join

the stitches into a circle, and purl 2 rows. To form the corners, knit together 4 times 2 stitches after every 7 stitches in the first of these two rounds, in the second round knit together 2 stitches after every 6 stitches ; these decreasings and those of the other rounds must always take place at the same places as in the preceding round. Then take the violet wool, and knit 7 rows ; in the first of these knit 4 times 2 stitches together after

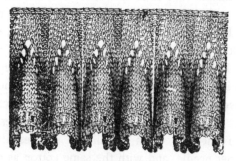

321.—Knitted Border.

intervals of 5 stitches ; no decreasings take place in the 2nd, 4th, and 6th rows ; in the 3rd row knit together 4 times 3 stitches as 1 stitch, and in the 5th and 7th rows 4 times 2 stitches as 1 stitch. After the 7th round, the remaining stitches are cast off together as 1 stitch. Then fasten the wool and cut it off. Lastly, sew the rosettes and squares together from No. 320 for a cover, and edge it round the border with a fringe of grey wool.

321.—*Knitted Border.*

Material : Messrs. Walter Evans and Co.'s No. 10 or No. 50 knitting cotton.

If knitted with thick cotton, this border will be suitable for trimming a quilt or berceaunette cover ; if, on the contrary, fine cotton is used, the pattern will form a very pretty collar for a little boy or girl.

To make a collar, begin by a chain of 220 stitches, and work 6 rows backwards and forwards alternately, knitting 4 stitches and purling 2. In the 2nd, 4th, and 6th rows the 4 stitches are purled, and the 2 are knitted. 7th row : * Purl 2, make 1, knit 2, purl 2. Repeat from *. 8th row : Alternately purl 5, knit 2. All the rows with *even* numbers are knitted like this, except that the number of the knitted stitches are increased by 2 in each of them. We will not, therefore, henceforth mention these rows. 9th row : * Knit 2, make 1, knit 1, make 1, knit 2, purl 2. Repeat from *. 11th row : * Knit 2, make 1, knit 3, make 1, knit 2, purl 2. Repeat from *. 13th row : * Knit 2, make 1, knit 5, make 1, knit 2, purl 2. Repeat from *. The pattern is continued in the same manner. The small gores formed between the ribs are increased by 2 stitches in every second row. Each of these gores has 13 stitches in the 21st row, which is the last. Cast off all the stitches after this row. Take a crochet needle, and with the same cotton as that used for the knitting work 1 stitch of double crochet in every stitch of the selvedge, then the 2 following rows for the edging. 1st row : Alternately 1 treble, 1 chain, under which miss 1. 2nd row : Alternately 1 double over 1 treble of preceding row, 1 purl (that is, 5 chain and 1 slip stitch in the first), under which miss 1. Over the first row of the knitting work 1 row of close double crochet. The border is now completed.

322.—*Knee-cap in Knitting*

Materials : For 1 pair, 4 oz. pink 4-thread fleecy wool, and a small quantity of white ditto.

Begin each knee-cap by casting on with pink wool 114 stitches, equally divided upon 4 needles, and joining them into a circle. Upon this number of stitches work 47 rounds, alternately knitting and purling 2 stitches. In the 48th round begin the

322.—Knee-cap in Knitting.

gore which covers the knee ; it is worked separately backward
and forwards, always alternately knitting and purling 2 stitches.

After 2 rows change the pattern, so as to form small squares

Knit the first row of this gore upon 26 stitches slipped off from the last row on to a separate needle.   At the end of each following row knit the nearest stitch of the nearest needle, so as to increase 1 stitch in each row of the gore.

Continue in this way until only 42 stitches remain of the ribbed part.   After this work the remainder of the gore separately, decreasing once at the beginning and end of each row till only 26 stitches remain ; then take up 23 stitches of the selvedge on each side of these 26 stitches, and work 47 rounds, alternately knitting and purling 2 stitches.

The edging at the top and bottom of the knee-cap is worked in crochet.   With white wool make a chain of 50 stitches ; turn and work 1 row of crochet *à tricoter ;* then work a second row thus : the first part, as usual, with white, but coming back, with pink make 4 chain between each stitch, work in the same way on the other side of the foundation chain, thus forming a small ruche, and sew it on to the edge of the knitting.

323.—*Knitted Neckerchief in Black Shetland Wool.*

Material : Black Shetland wool.

This three-cornered neckerchief is knitted in the following pattern (commencing at the corner).   1st row : slip 1, make 1, knit 2 together, inserting the needle into the back part of the stitch, slip 1, make 1, knit 2 together.   2nd row : Knit 1, purl 1 in the stitch formed by throwing the wool forward in the preceding row ; the other stitches are purled.   In the next row the holes are alternated ; the neckerchief must of course be increased at the beginning and end of every other row.   It measures at the upper edge 1 yard 16 inches across from one corner to the other ; the lower corner is rounded off.   The neckerchief is edged with

522.—Knitted Neckerchief in Shetland Wool.

a knitted lace. The lace is worked in rows backwards and forwards, the cross way. Cast on 22 stitches and work the 1st row as follows :—Slip 1, knit 11, knit 2 together, throw the wool forward, knit 2 together, knit 6. 2nd row : Slip 1, purl 18, knit 1 and purl 1 with the stitch formed in the preceding row by throwing the wool forward. 3rd row ; Slip 1, knit 2 together, knit 9, knit 2 together, throw the wool forward, knit 2 together, throw the wool forward, knit 2 together, knit 5. 4th row : Slip 1, purl 5, knit 1, purl 1, knit 1 in the stitch formed in the preceding row by throwing the wool forward, purl 13. 5th row : Slip 1, knit 2 together, knit 6, knit 2 together, throw the wool forward, knit 2 together, throw the wool forward, knit 2 together, throw the wool forward, knit 2 together, knit 4. 6th row : Slip 1, purl 8, knit 1, purl 1 in the stitch formed by throwing the wool forward in preceding row, purl 9. 7th row : Slip 1, knit 2 together, knit 4, knit 2 together, throw the wool forward 4 times alternately, knit 2 together, knit 4. 8th row : Slip 1, purl 3, knit 1, purl 1 in the stitch formed by throwing the wool forward in the preceding row, purl 13. 9th row : Slip 1, knit 2 together, knit 2, 5 times alternately ; knit 2 together, throw the wool forward, knit 2 together, knit 2. 10th row : Slip 1, knit 1, purl 1 in the stitch formed by throwing the wool forward in preceding row, purl 5. 11th row : Slip 1, knit 2 together, 6 times alternately knit 2 together, throw the wool forward, knit 2 together, knit 1. 12th row : Slip 1, knit 1 in the stitch formed by throwing the wool forward in preceding row, purl 13. 13th row : Slip 1, throw the wool forward, knit 2, knit 2 together, 5 times alternately throw the wool forward, knit 2 together, knit 2. 14th row : Slip 1, purl 10, knit 1, purl 1 in the stitch formed by throwing the wool forward in preceding row, purl 5. 15th row: Slip 1, throw the wool forward, knit 4, knit 2 together, 4 times alternately throw the wool forward, knit 2 together, knit 3. 16th row: Slip 1, purl 3, knit 1, purl 1 in the stitch formed by throwing the wool forward in preceding row, purl 13. 17th row: Slip 1, throw the wool forward, knit 6, knit 2 together, 3 times alternately throw the wool forward, knit 2 together, knit 4. 18th row: Slip 1, purl 8, knit 1, purl 1 in the stitch formed by throwing the wool forward in preceding row, purl 9. 19th row: Slip 1, throw the wool forward, knit 8, knit 2 together, twice alternately throw the wool forward, knit 2 together, knit 5. 20th row: Slip 1, purl 5, knit 1, purl 1 in the stitch formed by throwing the wool forward in preceding row, purl 13. 21st row: Slip 1, throw the wool forward, knit 10, knit 2 together, throw the wool forward, knit 2 together, knit 6. 22nd row: Slip 1, purl 6, knit 1, purl 1 in the stitch formed by throwing the wool forward in preceding row. 23rd row: Slip 1, throw the wool forward, knit 12, knit 2 together, knit 7. 24th row: Purled. Repeat from the 1st row till the lace is sufficiently long. Then sew on the lace round the edge; the lace can be knitted somewhat narrower for the upper edge. One of the ends of the neckerchief is knotted, as seen in the illustration, and the other end is drawn through the knot.

324 *and* 325.—*Knitted Bodice without Sleeves.*

Materials: 4 ounces black, 3½ ounces purple fleecy; black silk elastic; a steel buckle; 9 black bone buttons.

This bodice is knitted in brioche stitch with black and purple wool, so that the raised ribs appear black on one side and purple on the other. The bodice fits quite close. It is fastened in front with black bone buttons and a steel buckle. Two strips of silk elastic are knitted in at the bottom. Begin at the bottom of the bodice with black wool, and cast on 170 stitches. The

324.—Knitted Bodice without Sleeves (Back).

needles must be rather fine, and the knitting not too loose. Work backwards and forwards 24 rows as follows :—Slip the 1st stitch, alternately throw the wool forward, slip 1 as if you were going to purl it, and knit 1. In the next row knit together the stitch which has been slipped and the stitch formed by throwing the wool forward, slip the knitted stitch, after having thrown the wool forward. In the 25th row take the purple

wool and work 1 row as before. Now work alternately 1 row
with black wool and 1 row with purple, but as the wool is not
cut off, the brioche stitch must be alternately knitted and purled.
Work always 2 rows on the same side from right to left. The
following 26th row is worked with black wool in common

325.—Knitted Bodice without Sleeves (Front).

brioche stitch, only the slipped stitch of the preceding row is
purled together with the stitch formed by throwing the wool
forward. 27th row : Turn the work, with purple wool purled
brioche stitch. 28th row : On the same side with black wool
knitted brioche stitch. After having worked 40 rows all in the
same manner, begin the front gore. Divide the stitches upon
three needles, 82 stitches on one needle for the back, and **44**

stitches for each front part on the two other needles. Then
work the first 11 stitches of the left front part (this row must be
worked on that side of the work upon which the ribs appear
purple) in knitted brioche stitch; the 11th stitch must have a
slipped stitch, with the wool thrown forward, therefore it is a
purple rib. After this stitch begin the gore with the following
13 stitches. The ribs are then worked so that a purple one
comes over a black one, and a black one over a purple one. Do
not work upon the following black stitch; knit the following
stitch with the one formed by throwing the wool forward.
Throw the wool forward, and then only slip the black stitch
which had been left, so that it comes behind the stitch which has
just been knitted. This crossing of the stitch is repeated once
more, then knit the following stitch together with the one
formed by throwing the wool forward, throw the wool forward,
slip the crossed black stitch and the two following single black
stitches. The slipped stitch and the stitch formed by throwing
the wool forward before the 3rd single black stitch are then
knitted together, so that the crossed stitches are placed in opposite directions. The three black stitches which are knitted off
together as 1 stitch in the next row form the middle line of the
front gore, and are continued in a straight line to the point of
the gore. The crossing takes place twice in this row, but now
the black stitch is slipped first. After the 24th stitch knit
together the following stitch with the stitch formed by throwing
the wool forward. Then continue to work in common
brioche stitch to the other front part, where the gore begins
before the 24th stitch from the end. In the next row, which is
worked in purled brioche stitch with black wool, take up the
black loop between two purple ribs after the 11th stitch; purl it
so as to form the stitch which is missing at that place. The 3

slipped stitches in the preceding row are purled together as one stitch with the stitch formed by throwing the wool forward between the ribs. The loop is also taken up on the other side of the front gore in the same manner, as well as on the other front part. Then work 6 rows without increasing or decreasing. The crossing of the stitch is repeated after every 7 rows, always on the knitted brioche stitch side, with purple wool. In the 18th row of the gore the 3 middle stitches are not knitted together, but separately, so that the pattern must be decreased in 26 rows. In the back 30 stitches only must be decreased, two in every 6th row. After the 60th row another decreasing takes place on the outer edges of the front parts for the neck; they decrease 2 stitches (1st rib) after the 5th stitch from the front edge in every 3rd row. The 5 stitches which close to the neck are cast off together with the 5 stitches on the shoulders. Then cast off loosely the stitches of the back; take all the selvedge stitches of the front on the needles, and knit 24 rows of brioche stitch with black wool, making 9 button-holes on the right front part. On the wrong side of this part sew on a strip of black silk, with slits worked round in button-hole stitch, stitching at the same time into the knitting. The following scallops are knitted round the top of the jacket and round the armholes with black wool:—Take the selvedge stitches on the needles, work 4 rows alternately, 1 stitch knitted, 1 stitch purled, thread the wool into a Berlin wool-work needle, * cast off 3 stitches together, draw the wool through the needle, and take the 2 following stitches on the wool in the worsted-needle; repeat from *. Sew on the buttons the strips of silk elastic on either side of the black stripe at the bottom, and fasten the ends of the latter with the steel buckle.

326.—*Baby's Boot.*

Materials for one pair: ½ ounce red, ½ ounce white, Berlin wool; steel knitting-needles.

This pretty boot consists of a shoe knitted in red wool, and a sock in white wool ornamented with red. Begin the knitting with the upper scalloped edge of the latter. Cast on 96 stitches with red wool, divide them on four needles, and knit in rounds as follows :—1st and 2nd rounds : With red wool, purled. 3rd to 8th round : With white wool. 3rd round : Knitted. 4th round : * Knit 4, throw the wool forward, knit 1, throw the wool forward, knit 4, knit 3 together. Repeat 7 times more from *. 5th round : Knitted ; the stitches formed by throwing the wool forward are knitted as one stitch. Knit 3 stitches together at the place where 3 stitches were knitted together in the 4th round, so that the decreasing of the preceding round forms the middle stitch of the 3 stitches to be decreased in this round. 6th and 7th rounds : Like the 5th. 8th round : Knitted ; you must have 48 stitches left. 9th to 11th round : With red wool. 9th round : Knitted. 10th and 11th rounds : Purled. 12th to 30th round : With white wool. 12th round : Knitted. 13th round to 30th round : Alternately purl 1, knit 1, inserting the needle in the back part of the stitch. 31st to 33rd round : With red wool. 31st round : Knitted. 32nd round and 33rd round : Purled. 34th and 35th rounds : With white wool. 34th round : Knitted. 35th round : Alternately throw the wool forward, knit 2 together. Each stitch formed by throwing the wool forward is knitted as one stitch in the next round. 36th to 38th round : With red wool. 36th round : Knitted. 37th and 38th rounds : Purled. 39th to 47th round : With white wool. Alternately purl 1, slip 1, as if you were going to purl it ; the wool must lie in front of the slipped stitch ;

in the following rounds take care to purl the slipped stitches
Take now 18 stitches for the front gored sock part (leave
30 stitches untouched), and work backwards and forwards with

326.—Baby's Boot.

red wool. 48th to 50th row : With red wool. 48th row :
Knitted. 49th row : Purled. 50th row : Knitted. 51st to 85th
row : With white wool in the pattern described in the 39th
round. But as you work backwards and forwards you must
alternately knit and purl the stitches. Decrease 1 stitch at the

beginning and at the end of the 84th and 85th rows ; decrease 1 stitch in the middle of the 85th row, so that the 85th row has 13 stitches left.   After this work with red wool.   86th row : Knitted.   87th row: Knit 1, purl 2, knit 1, purl 2, knit 1, purl 2, knit 1, purl 2, knit 1.   Repeat these last 2 rows 3 times more and knit plain to the 94th, decreasing one, however, on each side.   Now work with the whole number of stitches, taking up the selvedge stitches of the gored part and dividing them with the 30 other stitches on four needles.   Knit once more in rounds ; the next 20 rounds are alternately 1 round knitted, 1 round purled.   In the 2 last knitted rounds decrease twice close together in the middle of the back part of the shoe. Knit 8 rounds ; in every other round decrease twice in the middle of the front of the shoe, leaving 9 stitches between the two decreasings.   The number of stitches between the decreasings decreases with every round, so that the decreasings form slanting lines meeting in a point.   Cast off after these 8 rounds, by knitting together 2 opposite stitches on the wrong side.   The sock part is edged with a raised red border, which is worked by taking all the red stitches of the 1st round of the shoe on the needle and knitting 4 rounds, so as to leave the purled side of the stitch always outside ; then cast off very tight. Draw a piece of braid through the open-work row in the sock part. and finish it off at either end with tassels to match.

327.—*Knitted Border for a Bedquilt.*

Materials: Messrs. Walter Evans and Co.'s No. 8 white knitting cotton; thick steel pins.

Cast on a sufficient number of stitches for the length of the border, which must be able to be divided by 31; knit 4 plain

rows; 5th row: Alternately make 1, knit 2 together.   Then 5
more plain rows.

327.—Knitted Border for a Bedquilt.

Now begin the pattern:—1st row: * Make 1, knit 1 *slantways* (to knit a stitch slantways, insert the needle from the front
to the back and from right to left); † purl 5; knit 1 slantways.
Repeat from † 4 times more than from * to the end of the row.

2nd row : Purled.   3rd row : Knit 2, * make 1 ; knit 1 slantways ; † purl 5 ; knit 1 slantways.   Repeat from † four times
more.   Repeat from * to the end of the row.   4th row : The
same as the second.

The continuation of the work is clearly shown in our illustration.   The increasing caused by knitting the *made* stitches is
regularly repeated in each second row, so that the stitches
between the striped divisions increase, and form large triangles ;
the striped divisions, on the other hand, are narrowed so as to
form the point of the triangles.   To obtain this result, decrease
five times in the 6th, 12th, 18th, and 24th rows, by purling
together the two last stitches of one purled division, so that each
division has but eleven stitches left in the 25th row.   In the
28th row knit together one purled stitch with one knitted slantways, so that there will be only 6 stitches left for each division ;
these stitches are knitted slantways in the 29th and 30th rows.
In the 31st row they are knitted together, two and two.   There
remain in each division three more stitches, which are knitted
together in the 34th row.   Two rows entirely purled complete
the upper edge of the border.

328.—*Knitted Quilt.*

Materials : 8-thread fleecy wool; wooden needles.

This pattern may be worked in narrow strips of different
colours, and in that case each strip should contain 1 row of
patterns ; or the quilt may be composed of wide strips with
several rows of patterns, those of one row being placed between
those of the preceding.   In the first case, that is if you work
narrow strips, you may use several colours ; but if wide strips
are preferred, they should be of two colours only.   Our pattern

was worked in wide strips, alternately grey and red. Each strip is knitted the short way.

328.—Knitted Quilt.

For a strip with five raised patterns in the width cast on 20 stitches. 2nd row · Right side of the work. Slip 1, purl 1,

* make 1, purl 4. Repeat from * 3 times more; make 1, purl 2. 3rd row: Slip 1, knit all the stitches that were purled in the preceding row, and purl all those that were made. 4th row: Slip 1, purl 1, * knit 1, make 1, purl 4. Repeat from * 3 times more; knit 1, make 1, purl 2. 5th row: Slip 1, knit all the purled stitches, purl all the rest. 6th row: Slip 1, purl 1, * knit 2, make 1, purl 4. Repeat from * 3 times more; knit 2, make 1, purl 2. 7th row: The same as the 5th. 8th row: Slip 1, purl 1, * knit 3, make 1, purl 4, and so on. 9th row: The same as the 5th row. 10th row: Slip 1, purl 1, * slip 1, knit 1, pass the slipped stitch over the knitted one, knit 2, purl 4, repeat from *. 11th row: Knit all the purled stitches, purl all the rest. 12th row: Slip 1, purl 1, * slip 1, knit 1, pass the slipped stitch over, knit 1, purl 4, and repeat from *. 13th row: The same as the 11th. 14th row: Slip 1, purl 1, * slip 1, knit 1, pass the slipped stitch over, purl 4, and repeat. 15th row: Slip 1, * knit 2 together, knit 3. Repeat from * 3 times more; knit 2 together, knit 2. The second row of patterns begins with the 16th row. There are only 4 in this 2nd row, so that after the 1st slipped stitch you purl 3 stitches instead of 1, and in the 2nd row, after the 4th made stitch, you purl 4 more stitches. Repeat alternately these 2 rows of raised patterns, and when you have a sufficient number of strips sew them together. Trim the quilt all round with a knotted fringe.

329.—*Stitch in Knitting, for Couvrettes, Comforters, Opera Caps, Carriage Shawls, Jackets, &c.*

Materials: Messrs. Walter Evans and Co.'s knitting cotton No. 20, or fine wool.

Cast on an uneven number of stitches. 1st row: Slip 1, * make 1, knit 1, make 1, knit 1. Repeat from *. 2nd row: Slip 1, * knit 2 together, and repeat from * to the end of the row.

330 *and* 331.—*Knitted Veil.*

Material : Fine Shetland wool.

Illustration 330 represents a knitted veil in reduced size. The original was worked with fine Shetland wool in an open

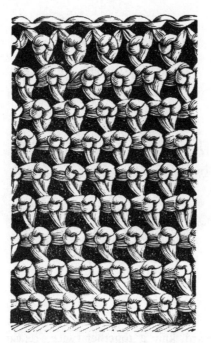

329.—Stitch for Couvrettes, Comforters, &c.

pattern ; it is edged with a knitted lace. Its length is 24 inches, its width 18 inches. Work the veil from a paper pattern of a shape corresponding to that of illustration 330. Compare the paper shape often with the knitting in the course of the work, and try to keep them alike. Knit the veil in the pattern of the original, or in the pattern of illustration 331. For the former one begin at the lower edge of the veil, cast on 45 stitches upon thick wooden needles, and work the 1st row : * Knit 2, throw

330.—Knitted Veil.

the wool forward, knit 2 together twice, repeat from *. 2nd row : Purled. 3rd row : Knit 1, throw the wool forward, knit 2 together, * throw the wool forward, knit 2 together twice, and repeat from *. 4th row : Purled. 5th row : Like the 2nd row. The pattern must be reversed. The pattern figures increase with the increasings at the beginning and at the end of each row. The pattern of illustration 331 consists of the 2 following rows :—1st row : Slip 1, then alternately throw the wool forward, and knit 2 together. 2nd row : Entirely knitted ; make 1 stitch of the wool thrown forward in the last row. When the veil is finished, wet it, and stretch it over paper or pasteboard ; let it dry, and then edge it with the following

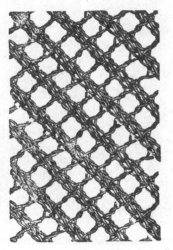

331.—Pattern of Veil.

lace :—Cast on 10, knit the 1st. 2nd row : Knit 1, throw the wool forward, knit 9. 3rd row : Knitted. 4th row : Knit 1, throw the wool forward, knit 2, throw the wool forward, knit 2 together twice, knit 4. 5th row : Knitted. 6th row : Knit 1, throw the wool forward, knit 2, throw the wool forward, knit 2 together 3 times, knit 3. 7th row : Cast off 3 stitches, knit 10. 8th row : Knitted.

2 A

332.—*Knitted Pattern with Raised Embroidery.*

Materials: Messrs. Walter Evans and Co.'s knitting cotton No. 8 or 20.

This pattern is worked in rows going backwards and forwards with thick or fine cotton according to the use you wish to make of it. The star-like figures on the knitted squares are worked

332.—Knitted Pattern with Embroidery.

with soft cotton in *point de poste.* Cast on a number of stitches long enough (19 stitches are necessary for the two squares), work the 1st row : * Knit 11 stitches, alternately 4 times knit 2 together, throw the cotton forward. Repeat from *. The 2nd row is worked like the 1st, only purled ; in this row, as well as in the following ones, the stitch must be knitted with the cotton thrown forward *after* the stitch ; the last stitch of a plain square with the first cotton thrown forward of the open-work figure. The number of stitches in the last must always be 8. The pattern consists alternately of these two rows. Each pattern contains 12 rows, with the 13th the squares are reversed. The star figures are embroidered with double cotton by working 5 chain stitch in the middle of each square; draw the needle underneath the knitting to the next centre of a square.

333 and 334. – Knitted Table Cover. (see page 578.)

Materials: Messrs. Walter Evans and Co.'s coarse knitting cotton; thick steel knitting-needles.

This cover is suitable for either a large or a small table, as the pattern may be increased as much as required. It is suitable

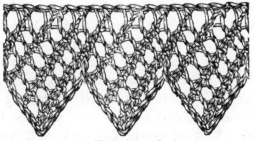

333.—Table-Cover Border.

for antimacassars. Cast on 4 stitches, join them into a circle, and work the 1st round four times alternately. Throw the cotton forward, knit 1. 2nd round: Entirely knitted. 3rd round : * Throw the cotton forward, knit 1. Repeat 7 times more from *. After every pattern round knit 1 round plain. Until after the 21st round, we shall not mention this any more. 5th round : * Throw the cotton forward, knit 2 *. From the 7th to the 12th round the knitted stitches in every other round increase by 1 stitch, so that in the 12th round there are 7 stitches between those formed by throwing the cotton forward. 13th round : * Throw the cotton forward, knit 2 together, knit 4, knit 2 together *. 15th round : * Throw the cotton forward, knit 1, throw the cotton forward, knit 2 together, knit 2, knit 2 together *. 17th round. * Throw the cotton forward, knit 3, throw the cotton forward, knit 2 together, knit 2 together *. 19th round : * Throw the cotton forward, knit 5, throw the cotton forward, knit 2 together, *. 21st round : * Knit 1, throw the cotton forward, knit 5, throw the cotton forward, knit 2 *. 22nd round : * Knit 2, knit 2 together, knit 1, knit 2 together, knit 3 *. 23rd round : * Knit 2, throw the cotton forward, knit 3, throw the cotton forward, knit 3 *. 24th round : * Knit 3, knit 2 together, knit 5 *. 25th round : * Knit 3, throw the cotton forward, knit 2 together, throw the cotton forward, knit 4. 26th round : Entirely knitted *. 27th round : * Throw the cotton forward, knit 9, throw the cotton forward, knit 1 *. 28th round : Entirely knitted. 29th round : * Knit 1, throw the cotton forward, knit 9, throw the cotton forward, knit 2 *. 30th round : Entirely knitted. 31st round : * Knit 2, throw the cotton forward, knit 9, throw the cotton forward, knit 3 *. 32nd round : Entirely knitted. 33rd round : * Knit 3, throw the cotton forward, knit 9, throw the cotton forward, knit 4 *. 34th round : * Knit 4, knit 2 together, knit 5, knit 2 together, knit 5 *. 35th round : * Knit 4, throw the cotton forward, knit 7, throw the cotton forward, knit 5 *. 36th round : * Knit 5, knit 2 together, knit 3, knit 2 together, knit 6 *. 37th round : * Throw the cotton forward, knit 5 three times, throw the cotton forward, knit 1 *. 38th round : * Knit 7, knit 2 together, knit 1, knit 2 together, knit 8 *. 39th round : * Knit 1, throw the cotton forward, knit 6, throw the cotton forward, knit 3, throw the cotton forward, knit 6, throw the cotton forward, knit 2 *. 40th round : * Knit 9, knit 3 together, knit 10 *. 41st round : * Knit 2, throw the cotton forward, knit 15, throw the cotton forward, knit 3 *. 42nd round : * Knit 3, knit 2 together, knit 11, knit 2 together, knit 4 *. 43rd round : * Knit 3, throw the cotton forward, knit 13, throw the cotton forward, knit 4 *. 44th round : * Knit 4, knit 2 together, knit 9, knit 2 together, knit 5 *. When the cover is completed, edge it all round, with the following border worked the short way :— Cast on 5 stitches and knit the 1st row, slip 1, throw the cotton forward, knit 2 together, throw the cotton forward, knit 2. 2nd row : Slip 1, knit the rest. Repeat this row after every pattern row. 3rd row : Slip 1, throw the cotton forward, knit 2 together, throw the cotton forward, knit 2 together, throw the cotton forward, knit 1. 5th row : Slip 1, throw the cotton forward, knit 2 together, throw the cotton forward, knit 2 together, throw the cotton forward, knit 2. 7th row : Slip 1, throw the cotton forward, knit 2 together, throw the cotton forward, knit 2 together, throw the cotton forward, knit 2 together, throw the cotton forward, knit 1. 9th row : Slip 1, throw the cotton forward, knit 2 together, throw the cotton forward, knit 2 together, throw the cotton forward, knit 2 together, throw the cotton forward, knit 2. 11th row : Slip 1, throw the cotton forward, knit 2 together, throw the cotton forward, knit 2 together, throw the cotton forward, knit 2 together, throw the cotton forward, knit 2 together, knit 1. 13th row : Slip 1, throw the cotton forward, knit 2 together, throw the cotton forward, knit 2 together, throw the cotton forward, knit 2 together, throw the cotton forward, knit 2 together, throw the cotton forward, knit 2. 15th round : Cast off 8 stitches, throw the cotton forward, knit 2 together, throw the cotton forward, knit 1. 16th round : Entirely knitted. Begin again at the 1st row, knit a sufficient length of the border, and then trim the cover with it on the outer edge.

335.—*Looped Knitting.*

Materials: 4-thread fleecy wool; 2 wooden knitting-needles; 1 flat
wooden mesh.

Cast on a sufficient number of stitches, and knit the 1st
row plain.

2nd Row.—Slip the 1st stitch ; insert the needle into the

335.—Looped Knitting.

next stitch, and throw the cotton forward as if you were going
to knit the stitch ; place the mesh behind the needle in the
right hand, and turn the wool which is on this needle upwards,
bring it back again on the needle so that it is wound once round
the mesh, and twice round the needle. Then only the
double stitch through the second stitch, knit it, and insert the
needle into the next stitch, and repeat what has been explained.
Knit the last stitch without a loop.

3rd Row.—Before drawing out the mesh, turn the work and

knit one plain row. Every double stitch is knitted as one stitch, so as to attain the same number of stitches as in the 1st row.

4th Row.—Like the 2nd row. Repeat these rows as often as required.

This knitting is chiefly used for borders of mats.

336.—Pattern for Comforters.

336.—*Knitted Pattern for Comforters.*

Materials: 4-thread fleecy; 2 wooden knitting-needles.

Cast on a sufficient number of stitches. 1st row: * 3 stitches in the first stitch, knit 1, purl 1, knit 1, knit 3 stitches together, repeat from *. 2nd row: Plain knitting. 3rd row: Purled. 4th row: Knitted. Repeat these four rows, only in the next row the 3 stitches knitted together are worked on the 3 stitches worked in 1 stitch, and the 3 stitches to be worked in 1 stitch are to be placed on the one formed by knitting 3 stitches together.

337. – *Knitted D'Oyley. (See page 579.)*

Materials: Messrs. Walter Evans and Co.'s crochet cotton No. 36; glazed
embroidery cotton No. 10; steel knitting-needles.

This pattern is knitted with very fine crochet cotton. The
middle part as well as the lace border are worked separately;
the latter is sewn on to the middle part. The spots in the thick
parts are worked in afterwards with coarser cotton. Commence
the pattern in the centre, cast on 6 stitches, join them into a
circle, and knit 2 plain rounds. 3rd round: Alternately knit 1,
throw the cotton forward. 4th and 5th rounds: Plain. 6th
round: Alternately knit 1, throw the cotton forward. 7th
round: Plain. Every other round is plain. We shall not
mention these plain rounds any more. 8th round: Knit 2, *
throw the cotton forward, knit 1, throw the cotton forward,
knit 3; repeat from * to the end of the round; lastly, throw
the cotton forward, knit 1, throw the cotton forward, knit 1.
10th round: * Throw the cotton forward, knit 1, throw the
cotton forward, knit 2 together. 12th round: * Throw the
cotton forward, knit 3, throw the cotton forward, knit 2 together,
throw the cotton forward, knit 1, throw the cotton forward,
knit 2 together. 14th round: * Throw the cotton forward,
knit 5, throw the cotton forward, knit 2 together, throw the
cotton forward, knit 1, throw the cotton forward, knit 2
together. 16th round: * Throw the cotton forward, knit 7,
throw the cotton forward, knit 2 together, throw the cotton forward, knit 1, throw the cotton forward, knit 2 together. The
18th, 20th, 22nd, and 24th rounds are worked like the 16th
round; only the middle plain part of the pattern figures increases
by 2 stitches in every pattern round, so that there are 15 plain
stitches in the 24th round between the 2 stitches formed on either
side of the same by throwing the cotton forward. 26th round:

* Throw the cotton forward, knit 6, knit 2 together, throw the cotton forward, knit 1, throw the cotton forward, knit 2 together, knit 6, throw the cotton forward, knit 2 together, knit 1, knit 2 together. 28th round : * Throw the cotton forward, knit 6, knit 2 together, throw the cotton forward, knit 3, throw the cotton forward, knit 2 together, knit 6, throw the cotton forward, knit 2 together, knit 1. 30th round : * Knit 1, throw the cotton forward, knit 2 together, knit 6, throw the cotton forward, knit 3 together, throw the cotton forward, knit 6, knit 2 together, throw the cotton forward, knit 1, throw the cotton forward, knit 2 together, throw the cotton forward. 32nd round : * Knit 2 together, throw the cotton forward, knit 2 together, knit 13, knit 2 together, throw the cotton forward, knit 2 together, throw the cotton forward, knit 3, throw the cotton forward. 34th round : * Knit 2 together, throw the cotton forward, knit 2 together, knit 11, knit 2 together, throw the cotton forward, knit 2 together, throw the cotton forward, knit 5, throw the cotton forward. 36th round : * Knit 2 together, throw the cotton forward, knit 2 together, knit 9, knit 2 together, throw the cotton forward, knit 2 together, throw the cotton forward, knit 1, throw the cotton forward, knit 2 together, knit 1, knit 2 together, throw the cotton forward, knit 1, throw the cotton forward. 38th round : * Knit 2 together, throw the cotton forward, knit 2 together, knit 7, knit 2 together, throw the cotton forward, knit 2 together, throw the cotton forward, knit 3, throw the cotton forward, knit 3 together, throw the cotton forward, knit 3, throw the cotton forward. 40th round : * Knit 2 together, throw the cotton forward, knit 2 together, knit 5, knit 2 together, throw the cotton forward, knit 2 together, throw the cotton forward, knit 1, throw the cotton forward, knit 2, knit 2 together, throw the cotton forward, knit 1, throw

the cotton forward, knit 2 together, knit 2, throw the cotton forward, knit 1, throw the cotton forward. 42nd round : * Knit 2 together, throw the cotton forward, knit 2 together, knit 3, knit 2 together, throw the cotton forward, knit 2 together, throw the cotton forward, knit 3, throw the cotton forward, knit 3 together, throw the cotton forward, knit 3, throw the cotton forward, knit 3 together, throw the cotton forward, knit 3, throw the cotton forward. 44th round : * Knit 2 together, throw the cotton forward, knit 2 together, knit 1, knit 2 together, throw the cotton forward, knit 2 together, throw the cotton forward, knit 3, knit 2 together, throw the cotton forward, knit 1, throw the cotton forward, knit 2 together, knit 3, throw the cotton forward, knit 1, throw the cotton forward, knit 5, throw the cotton forward. 45th and 46th rounds : Plain, then cast off loosely.

For the lace border, which is worked in the short way backwards and forwards, cast on 22 stitches and knit as follows :—1st row : Slip 1, knit 1, throw the cotton forward, knit 2 together, throw the cotton forward, knit 2 together, throw the cotton forward, knit 2 together, knit 4, knit 2 together, throw the cotton forward, knit 2, knit 2 together, throw the cotton forward, knit 1, throw the cotton forward, knit 2 together. 2nd row : Slip 1, throw the cotton forward, knit 3, throw the cotton forward, knit 2 together, knit 2, throw the cotton forward, knit 2 together, knit 11. 3rd row : Slip 1, knit 9, knit 2 together, throw the cotton forward, knit 2, knit 2 together, throw the cotton forward, knit 5, throw the cotton forward, knit 1. 4th row : Slip 1, throw the cotton forward, knit 7, throw the cotton forward, knit 2 together, knit 2, throw the cotton forward, knit 2 together, knit 9. 5th row : Slip 1, knit 1, throw the cotton forward, knit 2 together, throw the cotton forward, knit 2 together, throw the cotton forward, knit 2 together, knit 2 together, throw the cotton forward, knit 2, knit 2 together, throw the cotton forward, knit 9, throw the cotton forward, knit 1. 6th row : Knit 2 together (knit together the stitch and the next stitch formed by throwing the cotton forward), throw the cotton forward, knit 2 together, knit 5, knit 2 together, throw the cotton forward, knit 2, knit 2 together, throw the cotton forward, knit 10. 7th row : Slip 1, knit 10, throw the cotton forward, knit 2 together, knit 2, throw the cotton forward, knit 2 together, knit 3, knit 2 together, throw the cotton forward, knit 2 together (stitch formed by throwing the cotton forward and the next stitch). 8th row : Knit 2 together, throw the cotton forward, knit 2 together, knit 1, knit 2 together, throw the cotton forward, knit 2, knit 2 together, throw the cotton forward, knit 12. 9th row : Slip 1, knit 1, throw the cotton forward, knit 2 together, throw the cotton forward, knit 2 together, throw the cotton forward, knit 2 together, knit 5, throw the cotton forward, knit 2 together, knit 2, throw the cotton forward, knit 3 together, throw the cotton forward, knit 2 together. 10th row : Knit 2 together, throw the cotton forward, knit 1, throw the cotton forward, knit 2, knit 2 together, throw the cotton forward, knit 14. 11th row : Slip 1, knit 11, knit 2 together, throw the cotton forward, knit 2, knit 2 together, throw the cotton forward, knit 1, throw the cotton forward, knit 3 together. Then begin again on the 2nd row, and work on till the border is long enough ; sew the lace on to the centre, slightly gathering the former. Lastly, work in the spots with glazed or coarse embroidery cotton.

338.—*Knitted Braces.*

Material: Messrs. Walter Evans and Co.'s knitting cotton No. 8 or 12.

These braces are knitted with coarse white cotton, taken double ; the braces themselves are worked in brioche stitch, the lappets are knitted plain. Begin at the bottom of the front lappet, make a foundation chain of 14 stitches, knit 5 rows plain backwards and forwards, then divide the stitches into two halves to form the button-hole ; knit 15 rows on each of the halves consisting of 7 stitches ; then take the 14 stitches again on one needle and work 17 rows on them. Then work a second button-hole like the first one ; knit 6 more rows plain, increasing 1 at the end of every row, so that the number of stitches at the end of the lappet is 20. Then begin the pattern in brioche stitch ; it is worked as follows :—Knit first 1 row, then slip the first stitch of the first following pattern row, * throw the cotton forward, slip the next stitch (slip the stitches always as if you were going to purl them), knit 2 together ; repeat 5 times more from * ; the last stitch is knitted. 2nd row of the pattern : Slip the 1st stitch, * knit 2 ; the stitch which has been formed in the preceding row by throwing the cotton forward is slipped after the 2nd knitted stitch ; repeat 5 times more from * ; knit the last stitch. 3rd row : Slip the 1st stitch, * decrease 1 (here, and in all the following rows, knit the next stitch together with the stitch before it, which has been formed in the preceding row by throwing the cotton forward), throw the cotton forward, slip 1 ; repeat from * ; knit the last stitch. 4th row : Slip the 1st stitch, * knit 1, slip the stitch which has been formed in the preceding row by throwing the cotton forward, knit 1, knit the last stitch. Repeat these 4 rows till the braces are long enough. The pattern is 19 inches long. Then knit 6 rows plain, decreasing I at the end of every row, then work each lappet separately, dividing the stitches so that each lappet is 7 stitches wide. Each lappet has 72 rows; after the first 18 rows make a button-hole as described for the preceding one. Work 18

338.—Knitted Braces.

rows between the 1st and 2nd button-hole. The lappets are rounded off by decreasing after the 2nd button-hole.

339.—*Pattern for Knitted Curtains, &c.*

Material: Messrs. Walter Evans and Co.'s knitting cotton No. 8.

This pattern is suitable for knitting different articles, according to the thickness of the cotton used.

The number of stitches must be divided by ten. The pattern is knitted backwards and forwards.

1st row: All plain. 2nd row: * Knit 1, make 2, slip 1, knit 1, pass the slipped stitch over the knitted one, knit 5, knit 2 together, make 2. Repeat from *. 3rd row: Purl the long stitch formed by making 2 in preceding row, * make 2, purl 2 together, purl 3, purl 2 together, make 2, purl 3. Repeat from *. (By *make* 2 is meant twist the cotton twice round the

339.—Pattern for Knitted Curtains.

needle, which forms one long stitch, and is knitted or purled as such in next row.) 4th row: Knit 3, * make 2, slip 1, knit 1, and pass the slipped stitch over, knit 1, knit 2 together, make 2, knit 5. Repeat from *. 5th row: Purl 3, * make 2, purl 3 together, make 2, purl 7. Repeat from *. 6th row: Knit 3, * knit 2 together (1 stitch and 1 long stitch), make 2, knit 1, make 2, slip 1, knit 1, pass the slipped stitch over (the knitted stitch is a *long stitch*), knit 5. Repeat from *.

Continue the pattern by repeating always from the 2nd to the 5th row; the 6th row is the repetition of the 2nd row, but it is begun (compare the two rows) about the middle of the 2nd row, so as to change the places of the thick diamonds in the following pattern. This will be easily understood in the course of the work.

340.—*Knitted Insertion.*

Material: Messrs. Walter Evans and Co.'s knitting cotton No. 20 or 30.

Cast on 14 stitches, and knit in rows, backwards and forwards, as follows :—1st row : Slip 1, knit 2 together, throw cotton forward, knit 2, knit 2 together, throw cotton forward, knit 2, knit 2 together, throw cotton forward, knit 3. This row is repeated 18 times more; the stitch formed by throwing

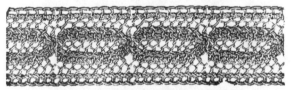

340.—Knitted Insertion.

the cotton forward is knitted as 1 stitch. 20th row : Slip 1, knit 2 together, make 1, knit 1; place next 3 stitches upon another needle behind the cotton, and leave them alone; knit 1, knit 2 together, throw cotton forward, now knit the first 2 of the 3 stitches which have been left; knit the last of the 3 together with the next stitch on the needle, throw cotton forward, knit 3. Repeat these 20 rows till strip is long enough.

341 and 342.—*Knitted Cover for Sofa Cushion.*

Materials : Messrs. Walter Evans and Co.'s knitting cotton No. 12; eight ply fleecy wool.

This cushion (15 inches wide, 12 inches high) is made of grey calico; it is covered on one side with knitting, worked with grey crochet cotton. The knitted cover has an open-work pattern, worked backwards and forwards on a number of stitches which can be divided by 2, and which must suit the width of the cushion, in the following manner :—1st row : Alternately throw the cotton forward, knit 2 together. 2nd row : Slip 1, knit the other stitches. The stitch formed by throwing the cotton forward is knitted as 1 stitch. 3rd row : Knit 1, * throw the cotton forward, knit 2 together. Repeat from *; after the last decreasing knit 1. 4th row : Like the 2nd row. These

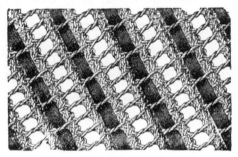

341.—Stitch for Sofa Cover.

four rows are repeated till the cover is sufficiently large. Draw a narrow piece of red worsted braid through every other open-work row of the pattern, as can be seen in illustration 341. When the cushion has been covered with the knitting, it is edged all round with a border knitted the long way, in the above-mentioned open-work pattern ; it is 14 rows wide, and also trimmed with worsted braid : a fringe of grey cotton and red wool, 3¼ inches wide, is sewn on underneath the border at the bottom of the cushion ; to this is added a thick red worsted cord, by which the cushion is hung on over the back of an arm-chair. The cushion, on account of its simplicity, is especially suitable for garden chairs.

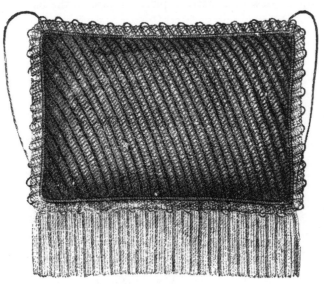

342.—Sofa Cushion.

343.—*Netted Nightcap.*

Material: Messrs. Walter Evans and Co.'s crochet cotton No. 12.

This cap is netted with crochet cotton over a mesh measuring three-quarters of an inch round; work first a long square for the centre of the crown, cast on 28 stitches, and work backwards and forwards 27 rows with the same number of stitches. Then work 34 rounds round this square, and fasten the cotton. Then count 43 stitches for the front border, and 24 stitches for the back border, and leave them for the edge of the cap. On the remaining stitches on each side work the strings in 95 rows

2 B

backwards and forwards on the same number of stitches ; each string is pointed off at the lower end by decreasing 1 stitch in every row.   Sew in a narrow piece of tape in the back border

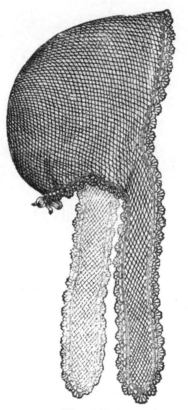

343.—Netted Nightcap.

of the cap ; the remaining part of the border, as well as the strings, are trimmed with crochet lace or with netted edging, No. 311.

344.—*Netted Nightcap.*

Material : Messrs. Walter Evans and Co.'s knitting cotton, 3-thread, No. 30.

This nightcap is very simple and practical. It consists of two similar three-cornered pieces, sewn together so as to form a

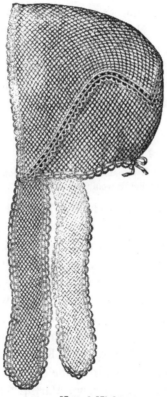

344.—Netted Nightcap.

double triangle ; the point of the triangle is turned back, as seen in illustration, and fastened on the lower half of the same. The cap is edged with a lace ; a similar lace covers the seam between both parts of the cap. The pattern is worked with crochet cotton over a mesh measuring three-quarters of an inch round. Begin each half in the corner ; cast on 2 stitches, and work backwards and forwards, increasing 1 stitch at the end of every row, till the number of stitches is 60. Then sew both halves together, and trim the cap and strings (the latter are worked as on the cap No. 343) with the following lace : work 2 rows of open-work treble stitches—the treble stitches are divided by 1 chain—then work 1 row of double, always working 4 double round the chain stitches which divide 2 treble in the preceding row, or with netted edging No. 311.

345.—*Knitted Pattern.*

Materials : Messrs. Walter Evans and Co.'s knitting cotton No. 20 for couvrettes, or Berlin wool for sofa quilts.

This pattern can be worked either in wool or cotton, and is suitable for many purposes. Cast on a sufficient number of stitches, divided by 18, for the 1st row : Knit 4, throw the cotton forward, knit 2 together, throw the cotton forward, knit 2 together, knit 4, purl 6, repeat from *.   2nd row : The stitcnes knitted in the 1st row are purled as well as the stitches formed by throwing the cotton forward ; the purled stitches are knitted. This row is repeated alternately, therefore we shall not mention it again.   3rd row : * Knit 6, throw the cotton forward, knit 2 together, throw the cotton forward, knit 2 together, knit 6, purl 2.   5th row : Purl 4, * knit 4, throw the cotton forward, knit 2 together, throw the cotton forward, knit 2 together, knit 4, purl 6.   7th row : Knit 2, * purl 2, knit 6, throw the cotton forward, knit 2 together, throw the cotton forward, knit 2 together, knit 6.   9th row : Knit 2, * purl 6, knit 4, throw the cotton forward, knit 2 together, throw the cotton forward, knit 2 together, knit 4. 11th row : * Knit 6, purl 2, knit 6, throw the cotton forward, knit 2 together, throw the cotton forward, knit 2 together. 13th row : Throw the

345.—Knitted Pattern.

cotton forward, knit 2 together, * knit 4, purl 6, knit 4, throw the cotton forward, knit 2 together, throw the cotton forward, knit 2 together. 15th row : * Throw the cotton forward, knit 2 together, throw the cotton forward, knit 2 together, knit 6, purl 2, knit 6 The knitting can now be easily continued from illustration.

346 *to* 348.—*Knitted Shawl.*

Materials: Shetland wool, white and scarlet; steel needles.

This shawl is knitted in the patterns given on Nos. 346 and
347 Both illustrations show the patterns worked in coarse
wool, so as to be clearer. Begin the shawl, which is square,
on one side, cast on a sufficient number of stitches (on our
pattern 290); the needles must not be too fine, as the work

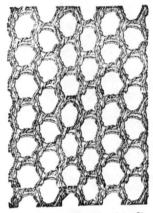

346.—Pattern for Shawl (348).

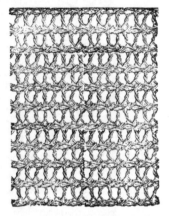

347.—Pattern for Shawl (348).

should be loose and elastic. Knit first 2 rows plain, then 3 of
the open-work row of pattern No. 346, which is worked in the
following manner :—1st row : Slip the first stitch, * knit 2
together, inserting the needle into the back part of the stitch, slip
1, knit 2 together, throw the wool twice forward ; repeat from *.
2nd row : Knit 1 and purl 1 in the stitch formed by throwing
the wool forward in the preceding row ; the other stitches are
purled. In the next row the holes are alternated—that is, after
the 1st slipped stitch knit 1, throw the wool forward, and then
knit twice 2 together. When 3 such open-work rows are com-

pleted, knit 1 row plain, and then work the pattern seen on
No. 347, which forms the ground, and is worked in the following way :—1st row : Slip the 1st stitch, alternately throw the
wool forward, and decrease by slipping 1 stitch, knitting the
next, and drawing the slip stitch over the knitted one. 2nd
row, entirely purled : When 6 such rows have been worked in
this pattern, work again 9 rows of the open-work pattern, but
work on each side of the 2 stripes, each 6 stitches wide, in

348.—Knitted Shawl.

the pattern of the ground (No. 347) ; each first stripe is at a distance of 4 stitches from the edge, and each second stripe at a
distance of 20 stitches. After the 9th open-work row, work
again 6 rows in the pattern of the ground, then again 8 open-
work rows, and then begin the ground, only continue to work
on both sides of the shawl the narrow stripes of the ground
pattern, the narrow outer and the two wide inner stripes of the
border in the open-work pattern. When the ground (pattern
No. 347) is square, finish the shawl at the top with two wide

and one narrow open-work row, as at the bottom, divided by stripes in the ground pattern. Knot in, all round the shawl, a fringe of scarlet wool ; the fringe must be $3\frac{1}{2}$ inches deep.

TABLE OF SIZES of Messrs. WALTER EVANS & Co.'s KNITTING COTTON, 3 THREADS.

	No.
Borders	20, 80
Couvrettes	8
D'Oyleys	80, 100
Edgings	16, 30
Insertions	30, 50
Nightcaps	20
Quilts	4, 8, 12
Socks	20
Table Covers	16

MONOGRAMS AND INITIALS.

MONOGRAMS AND INITIALS.

ALPHABETS.

349.—*Alphabet.*

Material: Messrs. Walter Evans and Co.'s Embroidery Cotton No. 18.

These letters are embroidered in overcast stitch and in satin stitch, and are the capitals for the alphabet No. 350. Stars ornament this very effective alphabet

349.—Alphabet (Capitals).

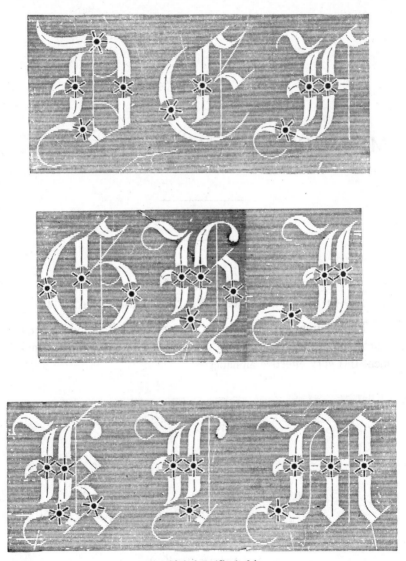

349.—Alphabet (Capitals).

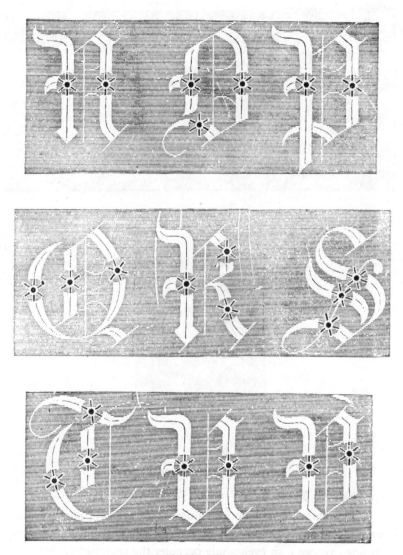

349.—Alphabet (Capitals).

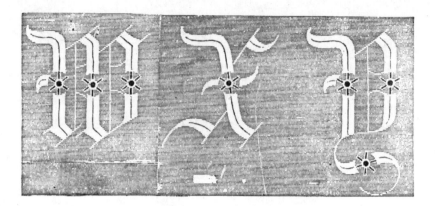

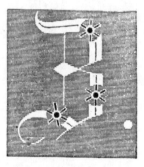

350.—*Alphabet* (*Small Letters*).

Material: Messrs. Walter Evans and Co.'s Embroidery Cotton No. 20.

This alphabet will be found useful for marking linen as well as pocket-handkerchiefs. It is worked in satin stitch, the stars in fine overcast ; an eyelet-hole occupies the centre of each star.

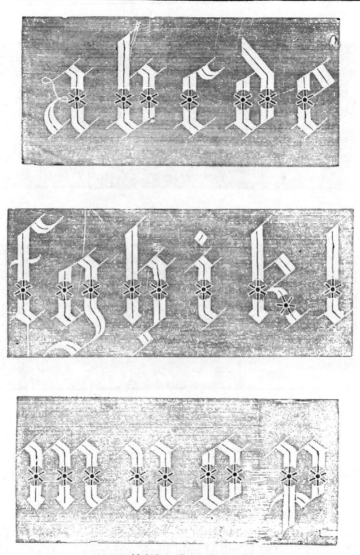

350.—Alphabet (Small Letters.)

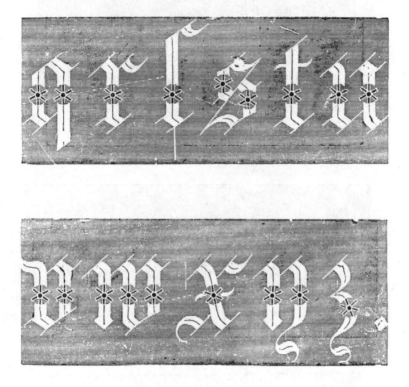

351.—*Alphabet of Small Capitals.*

Materials: Messrs. Walter Evans and Co.'s Embroidery Cotton No. 12 for linen, No. 18 for handkerchiefs.

These letters will be found useful for marking table-linen ; they may be worked either in green, red, or white cotton. The letters are worked in raised satin stitch with raised dots and open eyelet-holes.

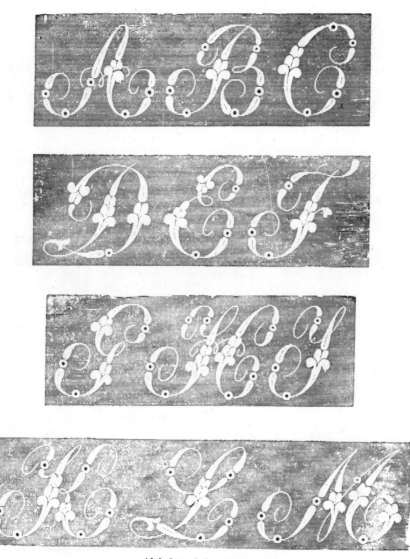

351.—Alphabet of Small Capitals.

2 C

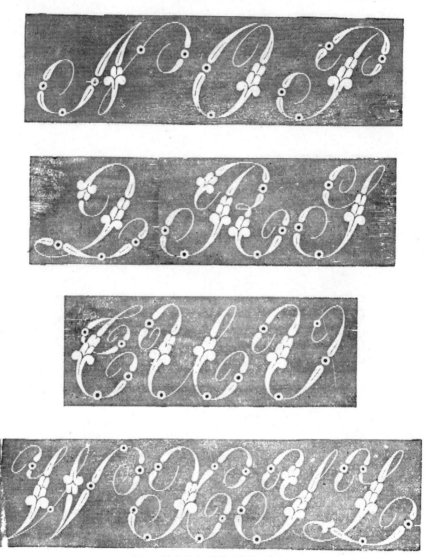

351.—Alphabet of Small Capitals.

352.—*Alphabet.*

Material: Messrs. Walter Evans and Co.'s Embroidery Cotton No. 12.

This pretty alphabet is worked in satin stitch, both raised and veined; the design is composed of forget-me-not blossoms and leaves. Raised dots worked in satin stitch form all the fine lines.

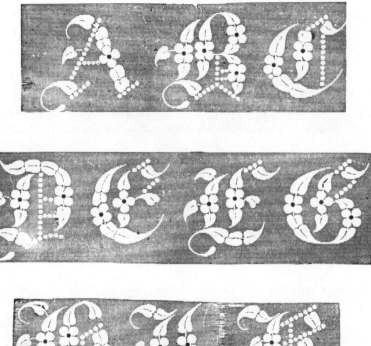

352.—Alphabet in Satin Stitch.

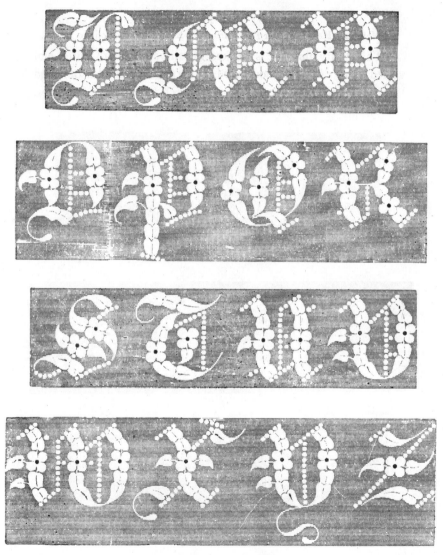

352.—Alphabet in Satin Stitch.

353.—*Alphabet in Coral Stitch.*

Material: Coloured ingrain marking cotton, or black sewing silk, or filoselle.

The letters of this alphabet are particularly suitable for pocket-handkerchiefs. The embroidery is worked either with marking cotton, or coloured or black sewing silk; the long white lines are worked in overcast stitch, the small white spots in satin stitch, the remaining parts of the letters in coral stitch, as can be distinctly seen in illustration.

353.—Alphabet in Coral Stitch.

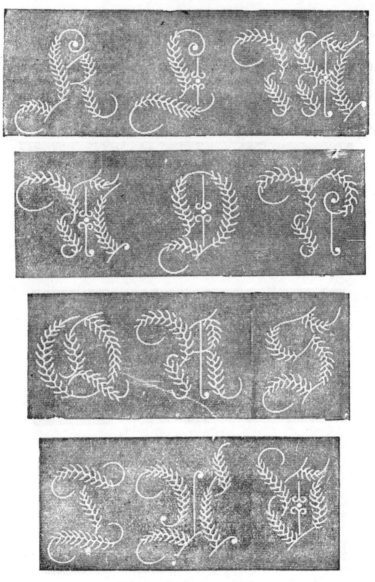

353.—Alphabet in Coral Stitch.

354.—*Small Alphabet.*

Material: Messrs. Walter Evans and Co.'s Embroidery Cotton No. 16.

This useful alphabet is worked in satin stitch, veined in parts and ornamented with tendrils. As the alphabet of capitals (page 377, No. 351) and that of these small letters correspond, any name may be worked from them.

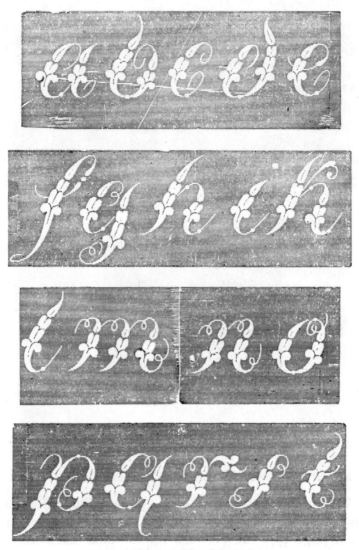

354.—Alphabet of Small Letters.

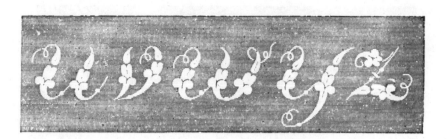

355.—*Alphabet (Capitals).*

Materials: Messrs. Walter Evans and Co.'s Embroidery Cotton Nos. 12 and 20.

This alphabet is worked in raised satin stitch, the outlines being partly scalloped; for the fine lines, which should be worked in overcast, embroidery cotton No. 20 should be employed.

355.—Alphabet in Satin Stitch.

355.—Alphabet in Satin Stitch.

356. *Alphabet (Capitals).*

Material: Messrs. Walter Evans and Co.'s Embroidery Cotton No. 16.

The alphabet here illustrated is in the florid style; the graceful flowing lines are worked in raised satin stitch, as well as the variously-sized dots which ornament the letters.

356.—Alphabet (Florid Capitals).

356.—Alphabet (Florid Capitals).

356.—Alphabet (Florid Capitals).

356.—Alphabet (Florid Capitals).

357.—*Alphabet.*

Materials: Messrs. Walter Evans and Co.'s Embroidery Cotton Nos. 12 and 16.

The letters are worked in point d'or, or dotted stitch, with an outline in fine overcast, and large raised spots in satin stitch. The ornamental wreaths round the first five letters can of course be worked round any of the others. It is very fashionable to work one letter only upon handkerchief corners.

357.—Alphabet in point d'or.

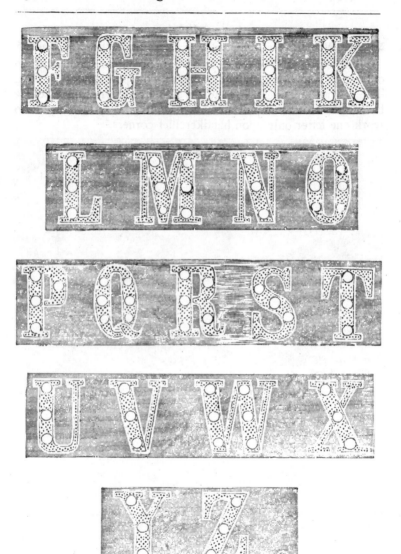

357.—Alphabet in point d'or.

358.—*Alphabet in White Embroidery.*

Material: Messrs. Walter Evans and Co.'s Embroidery Cotton No. 16

This alphabet is worked in appliqué ; the ears of corn only are worked in overcast, satin, and knotted stitch.   These letters look particularly well on transparent materials.   The ears may be omitted by beginners, though they and much to the beauty of the alphabet.   To this alphabet are added the ten numerals, which will be found exceedingly useful.   By means of the whole alphabet and all these figures, any combination of initials and numbers can be made.

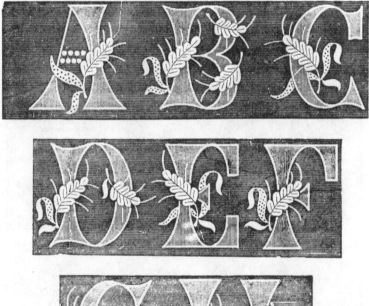

358.—Alphabet in White Embroidery.   2 D

358.—Alphabet in White Embroidery.

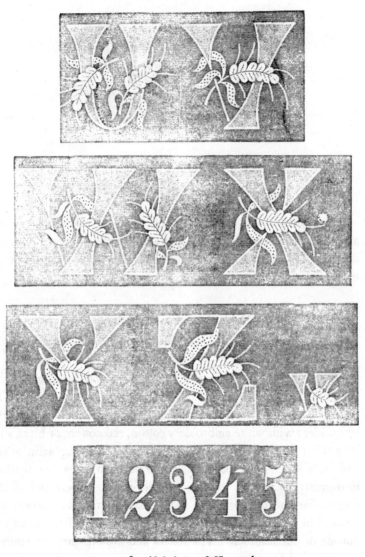

358.—Alphabet and Numerals.

359.—*Alphabet* (*see page* 402).

Materials: Messrs. Walter Evans and Co.'s Embroidery Cotton No. 20;
very fine black silk.

The vine-leaves and grapes of this graceful and fanciful
alphabet are worked in veined and slightly raised satin stitch, the
tendrils in point russe; for these the fine black silk is
employed.

360.—*Sampler* (*Frontispiece*).

Materials: cambric muslin or fine linen; Messrs. Walter Evans and Co.'s
Embroidery Cotton Nos. 16, 18, and 20; red cotton and black silk.

This illustration shows a sampler which will be found
useful for learning to embroider letters for marking linen.   The
material used is cambric muslin or fine linen.   Work the
embroidery with white embroidery cotton, red cotton, or black silk.
The thick parts of the letters are worked in slanting satin stitch
and back stitch; the outlines of the stitched parts are worked
in overcast, as well as the fine outlines of the letters and all the
fine outlines of the patterns.   The monograms and crowns are
worked in a similar manner.   Work button-hole stitch round the
outside of the sampler.   The letters and crowns may, of course,
be employed for other purposes.

361.—*Alphabet (Capitals)*.

Material: Messrs. Walter Evans and Co.'s Embroidery Cotton No. 20

This effective alphabet is very easily worked, the stitches employed being raised and veined satin stitch, and overcast. The raised dots are worked in satin stitch, care being taken to preserve their position in the *centre* of each open space.

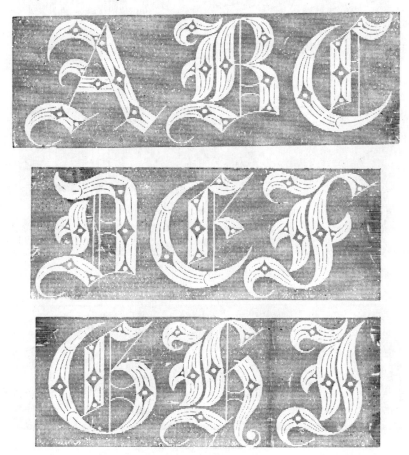

361.—Alphabet (Capitals).

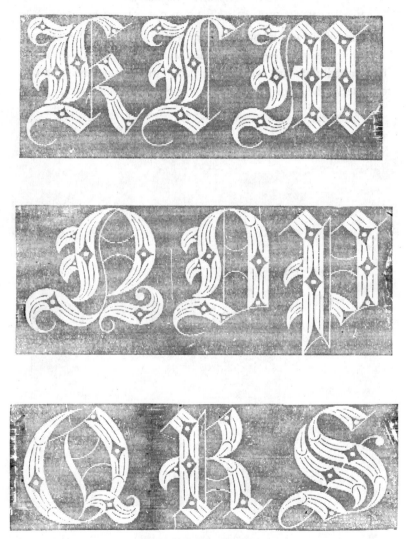

361.—Alphabet (Capitals).

361.—Alphabet (Capitals).

MONOGRAMS AND INITIALS.

362.—Alice.

362.—Alice.

Material: Messrs. Walter Evans and Co.'s Embroidery Cotton No. 20.

The letters of this name, except the initial letter, are very simple, being worked in plain satin stitch, while the initial letter is worked in raised satin stitch, point de poste, and overcast.

363.—*Amalie.*

Materials : Messrs. Walter Evans and Co.'s Embroidery Cotton Nos. 16 and 20.

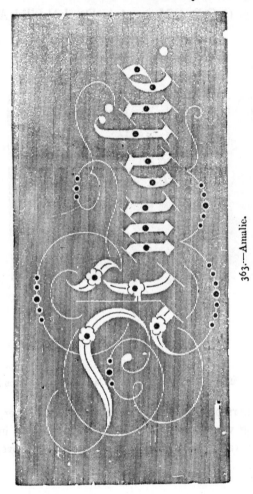

363.—Amalie.

The highly-ornate initial of this name is not difficult to work, requiring only great regularity and evenness in embroidering the tendrils and eyelet-holes. The veinings of the letter must be carefully defined. The remainder of the name is executed in plain satin stitch, a few eyelet-holes being introduced.

"Amalie" can easily be altered into "Amelia" by changing the place of the *a* and *e*. In the centre of each letter a large eyelet-hole is placed; smaller eyelet-holes of graduated sizes occupy parts of the overcast scrolls, which should be worked with No. 20 cotton. The initial letter is worked in raised satin stitch.

3 4.—Amy.

364.—*Amy.*

Material: Messrs. Walter Evans and Co.'s Embroidery Cotton No. 16.

This pretty name is worked in delicately raised satin stitch and point de pois; the dots in dotted satin stitch, and the elegant little design beneath is worked in point russe.

365.—*Annie.*

Material: Messrs. Walter Evans and Co.'s Embroidery Cotton No. 16.

The letter *A* of this name is rather elaborate, and is worked in point de pois or back stitching, the outlines in fine overcast,

365.—Annie.

the letters in satin stitch. The ornaments surrounding the word "Annie" are worked in overcast.

366.—*A. M. K.*

Material: Messrs. Walter Evans and Co.'s Embroidery Cotton No. 16.

This name is worked in satin stitch, with small dots of raised satin stitch. The eyelet-holes in the middle letter to be worked in overcast.

366.—A. M. K.

367.—*B. R.*

Material : Messrs. Walter Evans and Co.'s Embroidery Cotton No. 16.

367.—B. R.

These initials are worked in appliqué in the centre of a medallion in satin stitch, overcast, and lace stitches.

368.—*Carrie.*

Material: Messrs. Walter Evans and Co.'s Embroidery Cotton No. 20.

This name is very easy to work, being very clearly and simply

368.—Carrie.

embroidered in overcast and satin stitch. The thick dots may be worked without the eyelet-holes if preferred.

359.—Caroline.

369.—*Caroline.*

Material: Messrs. Walter Evans and Co.'s Embroidery Cotton No. 18.

This pretty name requires care in working; the leaves which adorn the letters must be very well defined; they, as well as the letters, are embroidered in satin stitch, the initial letter being veined, and the ornaments workd in overcast and eyelet-holes.

370.—Charlotte.

370.—*Charlotte.*

Material: Messrs. Walter Evans and Co.'s Embroidery Cotton No. 16.

This name is worked in satin stitch and overcast, the small and elegant dots in point de russe and graduated satin stitch; the large ones are worked in raised satin stitch.

371.—*Cornelie.*

Material: Messrs. Walter Evans and Co.'s Embroidery Cotton No. 18.

This word is worked in plain satin stitch, the ornamentation in overcast stitch.

371.—Cornelie.

372.—C. M.

Material : Messrs. Walter Evans and Co.'s Embroidery Cotton No. 18.

This design is simple, is worked in graduated satin stitch, and is most elegant.

372.—C. M.

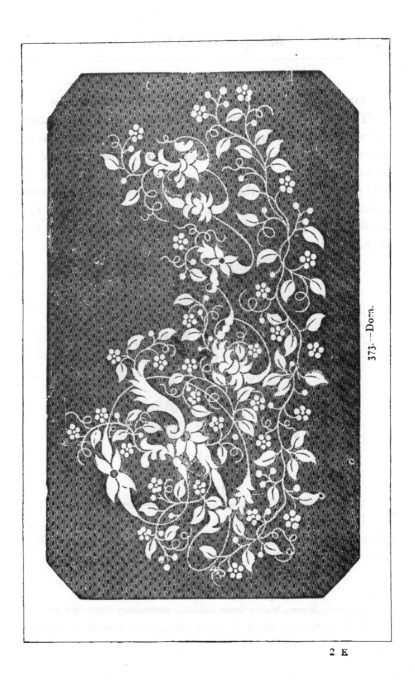

373.—Dot.

373.—*Dora.*

Material: Messrs. Walter Evans and Co.'s Embroidery Cotton No. 30.

This elaborate design should not be attempted by beginners in the art of embroidery; it is worked in overcast stitch, raised and veined satin stitch; the tendrils are entirely worked in graduated overcast; the name is placed over a graceful spray of wild flowers worked in the above-named stitches. This pattern, although originally designed to be worked on net or fine muslin, is far more effective when worked on cambric or fine lawn.

374.—D. C.

374.—*D. C.*

Material: Messrs. Walter Evans and Co.'s Embroidery Cotton No. 16.

These letters are worked in satin stitch and veined satin stitch; the forget-me-nots are worked in raised satin stitch, with a small eyelet-hole in the middle worked in overcast stitch.

375.—*Emily.*

Material: Messrs. Walter Evans and Co.'s Embroidery Cotton No. 16.

This name is worked in satin stitch, the dots in the middle

in point de poste, the rest of the letters in satin stitch and in dotted satin stitch.

376.—*Ernestine.*

Material: Messrs. Walter Evans and Co.'s Embroidery Cotton No. 16.

This elegant design is most effective; the first letter very elaborate; the rest of the letters simply worked in satin stitch. The small stars are worked in overcast stitch, and the initial letter itself in veined satin stitch.

375.—Emily.

377.—*Etta.*

Material: Messrs. Walter Evans and Co.'s Embroidery Cotton No. 20.

The letters which compose this name are formed entirely of leaves, flowers, and tendrils, worked entirely in satin stitch and overcast; the tendrils which surround the name are worked in overcast, and have a few eyelet-holes placed among them.

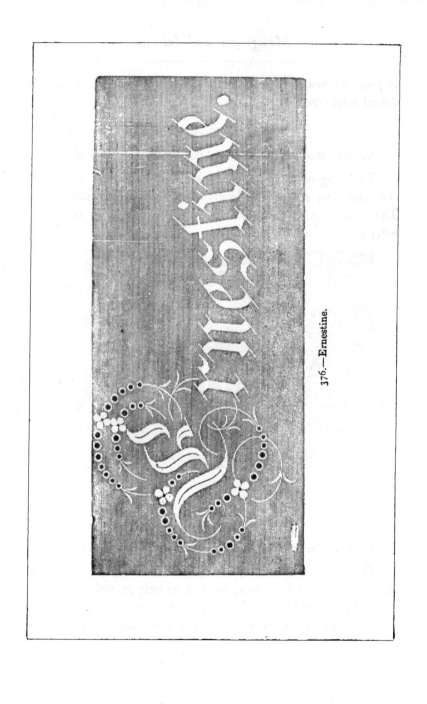

376.—Ernestine.

377.—Etta.

378.—*Eva.*

Materials : Messrs. Walter Evans and Co.'s Embroidery Cotton Nos. 16 and 20.

This name is worked in satin stitch, the leaf in point de sable ; the veinings are worked in raised satin stitch.

378.—Eva.

379.—*E. A.*

Material : Messrs. Walter Evans and Co.'s White and Red Embroidery Cotton No. 30.

This very pretty monogram is worked quite in a new style of embroidery. The design represents the emblems of Faith, Hope, and Charity. The outlines of the shield and cross are worked in overcast, the initials " E. A.," the torch, and the anchor in satin stitch with white cotton, the leaves partly in satin stitch with white and partly in point d'or with red cotton, with only a fine outline in overcast. The cross and the flames of the torch are embroidered in the same manner.

379.—E. A.

380.—*E. A. P.*

Material : Messrs. Walter Evans and Co.'s Embroidery Cotton No. 18.

These pretty initials are worked in satin stitch, the middle letter in point russe and point de poste.

380.—E. A. P.

381.—*E. P.*

Material : Messrs. Walter Evans and Co.'s Embroidery Cotton No. 16.

These elegant letters are worked in veined and raised satin stitch.

381.—E. P.

382.— E. R.

382.—*E. R.*

Material: Messrs. Walter Evans and Co.'s Embroidery Cotton No. 30.

The ovals are worked in overcast and point de pois, the letters in satin stitch, the ornamentation in satin stitch and overcast.

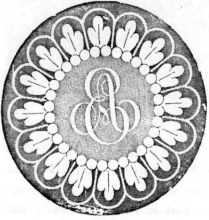

383.—E A.

383.—*E. A.*

Materia.: Messrs. Walter Evans and Co.'s Embroidery Cotton No. 16.

These initials are placed in a medallion ; they are worked in satin stitch and overcast, and in appliqué on muslin. For that part of the pattern in which the name is to be embroidered the material is taken double.

384.—*Elisabeth.*

Material: Messrs. Walter Evans and Co.'s Embroidery Cotton No. 20.

This word is embroidered in satin stitch and overcast. A few small eyelet-holes break the monotony of the outlines, and give lightness to this name.

384.—Elisabeth.

385.—*Elise.*

Materials: Messrs. Walter Evans and Co.'s Embroidery Cotton Nos. 12 and 16.

The open part of these letters is ornamented by one or more dots ; the thick work is raised over chain stitches worked in No. 12, a rather coarser cotton.

385.—Elise.

386.—*Emma.*

Material: Messrs. Walter Evans and Co.'s Embroidery Cotton No. 16.

This name is worked in satin stitch; the large dots may be worked with the eyelet-holes in fine overcast, the smaller dots in satin stitch. The remaining letters in raised satin stitch and point de sable.

386.—Emma.

387.—*F. B.*

Material: Messrs. Walter Evans and Co.'s Embroidery Cotton No. 18.

This elegant monogram is worked in raised satin stitch, the inside embroidered with lace. The leaves and tendrils are worked in satin stitch and point de sable.

387.—F. B.

388.—*F. S.*

Materials: Messrs. Walter Evans and Co.'s Embroidery Cotton Nos. 16 and 20.

The initials " F. S." are placed in the pages of an open book, the outlines of which are worked in overcast, the sides in point de pois. The wreath of flowers which surrounds the book is embroidered in satin stitch, the tendrils and veinings are in overcast. The initials are worked in fine satin stitch.

388.—F. S.

389.—*Fanny.*

Material: Messrs. Walter Evans and Co.'s Embroidery Cotton No. 16.

This name is simply worked in satin stitch and overcast.

389.—Fanny.

390.—*Francis.*

Material: Messrs. Walter Evans and Co.'s Embroidery Cotton No. 16.

The initial letter of this elegant design is worked in fine over-

casting ; the centre star in raised satin stitch with lace in the
middle ; the leaves surrounding it in veined satin stitch ; the

390.—Francis.

other letters are worked in plain satin stitch ; and the dots of
the line in point de poste.

391.—*E. C.*

Material: Messrs. Walter Evans and Co.'s Embroidery Cotton No. 20.

The initials " E. C." are worked within a frame of overcast outlines and satin stitch dots. Vine-leaves and grapes worked in

3)1.—E C.

point de pois and eyelet-holes are placed as ornaments around the frame.

392.—*Gordon.*

Material: Messrs. Walter Evans and Co.'s Embroidery Cotton No. 16.

This pretty name being worked in raised satin stitch, is **very** suitable for gentlemen's handkerchiefs.

392.—Gordon.

393.—*Helene.*

Material: Messrs. Walter Evans and Co.'s Embroidery Cotton No. 16.

We give the French version of this pretty name, it being easily changed to English "Helen" by omitting the final *e* in

393.—Helene.

working. The name is worked in plain satin stitch, slightly raised at the thickest parts of the letters.

394.—*H. D. G.*

Material: Messrs. Walter Evans and Co.'s Embroidery Cotton No. 18.

This elegant design is worked in fine overcast and satin stitch, and point de russe.

394.—II. D. G.

395.—*Jessie.*

Material: Messrs. Walter Evans and Co.'s Embroidery Cotton No. 16.

This design is very simple to work, the letters being so clear and well defined. The thick satin stitch is scalloped in parts.

395.— Jessie.

396.—*J. C.*

Material: Messrs. Walter Evans and Co.'s Embroidery Cotton No. 12.

The letters " J. C." are worked in raised satin and overcast stitch, the thickest part of each letter being worked in scallops.

2 F

396.—J. C.

397.—*Lina.*

Material : Messrs, Walter Evans and Co.'s Embroidery Cotton No. 18.

This name is worked in raised veined satin stitch ; the sm ll stars are worked in point russe round eyelet-holes.

39,. – L....it.

398.—*Lizzie.*

Material : Messrs. Walter Evans and Co.'s Embroidery Cotton No. 16.

This name is worked partly in satin stitch, partly in raised dots and fine overcast ; the letters are in the Greek style, and have an excellent effect if well worked.

398.—Lizzie.

399.—*L. G. A.*

Materials : Messrs. Walter Evans and Co.'s Embroidery Cotton No. 20, and Linen Thread No. 16.

Lace stitches are introduced in the medallion which incloses these letters, the outlines being worked in overcast and point de

pois, the pens and initials in raised satin stitch, as also the flowers.
The open portion is filled in with Mechlin wheels, which are
thus worked :— A number of single threads cross each other in
the space to be filled up ; these are placed about a quarter of an
inch from each other.   All the bars in one direction must now
be worked in fine button-hole stitch, then the opposite bars must

359.—L. G. A.

be worked, and the button-hole stitch must be continued about
six inches past the point where the two lines cross.   The thread
must be slipped loosely round the cross twice, running over and
under alternately, so as to form a circle ; then work in button-
hole to the centre of a quarter of the circle ; make a dot by
inserting a pin in the next button-hole and working three stitches
in the loop thus formed by the pin.   These dots may be omitted
from these wheels.

400.—*L. C.*

Material: Messrs. Walter Evans and Co.'s Embroidery Cotton No. 16.

The effect of this design when well worked is excellent, for, although simple, the contrast between the letters and stars throws each into relief. Veined and raised satin stitch, with very small eyelet-holes, are the stitches used here.

400.—L. C.

401.—*Marie.*

Materials: Messrs. Walter Evans and Co.'s Embroidery Cotton Nos. 20 and 36.

This name is embroidered in satin stitch ; the veinings are well defined, and the tendrils should be worked with No. 30 cotton, as they require very fine work. Stars of overcast and eyelet-holes are the only ornaments.

401.—Marie.

402.—*Maria.*

Material: Messrs. Walter Evans and Co.'s Embroidery Cotton No. 30.

The initial letter of this name is worked in overcast and point de pois, the remaining letters in satin stitch, the ornamentation in satin stitch and overcast.

402.—Maria.

403.—*Maude.*

Material: Messrs. Walter Evans and Co.'s Embroidery Cotton No. 18.

This name is worked in veined satin stitch ; the small stars in raised satin stitch, and the elegant tendrils are worked in overcast. This work is peculiarly adapted for the marking of a trousseau.

403.—Maude.

404.—*M.*

Material: Messrs. Walter Evans and Co.'s Embroidery Cotton No. 16.

This elegant design can be worked in coloured silk if preferred, or the coronet omitted at will. The letter " M " is worked in raised and veined satin stitch ; the centre stars are worked in fine overcast round an eyelet-hole ; the coronet is worked in very fine satin stitch and point de pois, and stars to correspond with those worked in the letter and in the wreath below, the leaves of which are worked in satin stitch and overcast stitch.

404.—M.—Handkerchief Corner.

405.—*M. B. D.*

Material: Messrs. Walter Evans and Co.'s Embroidery Cotton No. 20.

These initials are worked in satin stitch and overcast, the open work in fine overcast round eyelet-holes.

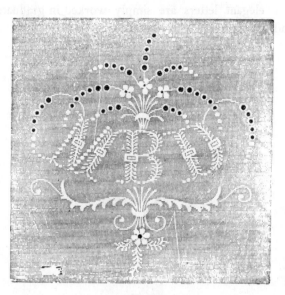

405.—M. B. D.

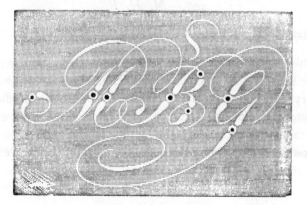

406.—M. B. G.

406.—*M. B. G.*

Material: Messrs. Walter Evans and Co.'s Embroidery Cotton No. 16.

These elegant letters are simply worked in graduated satin stitch and fine overcast with eyelet-holes.

407.—M. H. E.

407.—*M. H. E.*

Material: Messrs. Walter Evans and Co.'s Embroidery Cotton No. 18.

This elegant design is worked in graduated satin stitch, the middle letter is done in point croisé. This stitch is only worked on very thin and transparent materials. Insert the needle into the material as for the common back stitch, draw it out underneath the needle on the opposite outline of the pattern so as to form on the wrong side a slanting line. Insert the needle again as for common back stitch.

408.—*Natalie.*

Material : Messrs. Walter Evans and Co.'s Embroidery Cotton No. 30.

The initial letter of this word contains all those following, and is surrounded by a wreath of roses and other flowers ; these are worked in satin stitch, the leaves in point de pois, the letters

408.—Natalie.

in raised satin stitch. The dots which are represented on the groundwork of the initial are worked in back stitching ; these may be worked in scarlet ingrain cotton if desired for morning handkerchiefs.

409.—*O. R.*

Material : Messrs. Walter Evans and Co.'s Embroidery Cotton No. 18.

This monogram is worked in satin stitch, and the oval is worked in eyelet-holes of graduated sizes.

409.—O. R.

410.—*Phoebe.*

Material: Messrs. Walter Evans and Co.'s Embroidery Cotton No. 20.

The first letter of this word is very elaborate; it is worked in satin stitch, point de sable, and point de pois, the rest of the letters in satin stitch.

410.—Phoebe.

411.—*Monogram for Pocket Handkerchiefs.*

Material: Messrs. Walter Evans and Co.'s Embroidery Cotton Perfectionné
No. 20.

This monogram is worked partly in appliqué, partly in satin

411.—Monogram for Marking Handkerchiefs

stitch. For the middle part of the medallion sew on the pattern
in appliqué of cambric with button-hole stitch ; the remaining
part of the embroidery is worked in satin stitch and point
russe.

412.—*Monogram for Pocket Handkerchiefs.*

Materials: Messrs. Walter Evans and Co.'s Embroidery Cotton No. 20, and Linen Thread No. 20.

This monogram is also worked in appliqué and satin stitch. The circle all round the medallion is worked in appliqué ; in the

412.—Monogram for Marking Handkerchiefs.

middle work lace stitches from illustration. The edge of the medallion is worked round with button-hole stitch.

413.—*Rosa.*

Material: Messrs. Walter Evans and Co.'s Embroidery Cotton No. 20.

Here the name is inclosed in a medallion of overcast and back stitching, the lower part having a graceful wreath of leaves worked in satin stitch. The letters which form the name are worked in raised and scalloped satin stitch and point de pois.

413.—Rosa.

414.—*Rosina.*

Material: Messrs. Walter Evans and Co.'s Embroidery Cotton No. 20.

The stars round this graceful initial letter are worked in raised satin stitch round an eyelet-hole, the leaves in graduated satin stitch, the stems overcast, the wreaths of flowers worked in satin stitch and open eyelet-holes, the stems and veinings in overcast, and the stars on the stems to correspond with those worked in the letter: the rest of the letters in simple satin stitch rather thickly raised.

415.—*R. S.*

Materials: Black china silk; Messrs. Walter Evans and Co.'s Embroidery Cotton No. 16.

These letters are worked in raised satin stitch with a design of point russe worked in black silk.

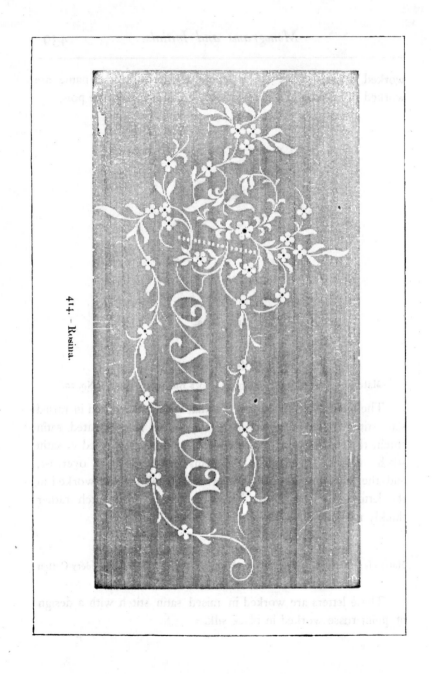

414. - Rosina.

415. - R. S.

416.—*S. E. B.*

Material: Messrs. Walter Evans and Co.'s Embroidery Cotton No. 16.

These letters are worked in graduated satin stitch, the centre star is worked in raised satin stitch, and the four surrounding it as eyelet-holes.

416.—S. E. B.

417.—*L. E. P.*

Material: Messrs. Walter Evans and Co.'s Embroidery Cotton No. 18.

These initials are worked in plain satin stitch, and the elegant stars are worked in point russe worked round an eyelet-hole.

2 G

417.—L. E. P.

418.—*Victoria.*

Material: Messrs. Walter Evans and Co.'s Embroidery Cotton No. 20.

This name is most elaborately worked in satin stitch, over-casting, and eyelet-holes. The initial letter is worked in satin stitch, and the stars in fine overcast round an eyelet-hole.

418.—Victoria.

POINT LACE WORK.

POINT LACE WORK.

—◦◦◦—

LACE is of two kinds—pillow lace, which is made upon a cushion or pillow, and point lace, which is made of stitches or *points* worked in patterns by hand, which are joined by various stitches forming a groundwork, also the result of the needle above.

Pillow lace is entirely worked on the pillow or cushion, the pattern and ground being produced at the same time. Pillow lace is sometimes correctly called bone or bobbin lace, but it appears that the distinction has never been very nicely observed either by lace-workers or lace-traders, many sorts which are really pillow lace being called point, on account of some peculiarity in the stitch or pattern.

The requisites for producing lace in perfection are the dexterity and taste of the workers, and the goodness of the material. To produce many beautiful fabrics a mechanical dexterity alone suffices, but in lace-making the worker must have some artistic talent, even when supplied with designs, for any one can perceive that deviations from the design are easily made, and that the slightest alteration by a worker wanting in taste will spoil the whole piece of workmanship.

The following illustrations are specimens of ancient and modern laces from Mrs. Bury Palliser's collection :—

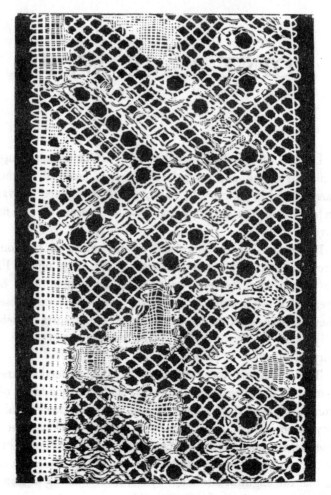

419.—Dalecarlian Lace.

420.—Old Mechlin.

421.—Mechlin Lace (Queen Charlotte's).

No. 419 shows Dalecarlian lace, made by the women of Dalecarlia. This is a coarse kind of lace, and is sewn on caps, &c., and, although highly starched, is never washed, for fear of

422.—Buckingham Point Trolly, 1851 (Black Lace).

destroying its coffee-coloured tint, which, it appears, is as much prized now by the Swedish rustics as it was by English ladies in the last century.

Both these specimens of Mechlin belonged to Queen Charlotte, who much admired this elegant lace.

No. 423.—The Bedford plaited lace is an improvement on the old Maltese.

Honiton guipure lace is distinguished by the groundwork being of various stitches, in place of being sewn upon a net ground. The application of Honiton sprigs upon bobbin net has been of late years almost superseded by this modern guipure.

423.—Bedford Plaited Lace (1851).

The sprigs, when made, are sewn upon a piece of blue paper and united on the pillow with "cutworks" or "purlings," or else joined with the needle by various stitches—lacet, point, réseau, cutwork, button-hole, and purling.

Those who wish to study lace and lace-making should read Mrs. Bury Palliser's *History of Lace* (Sampson Low and Marston).

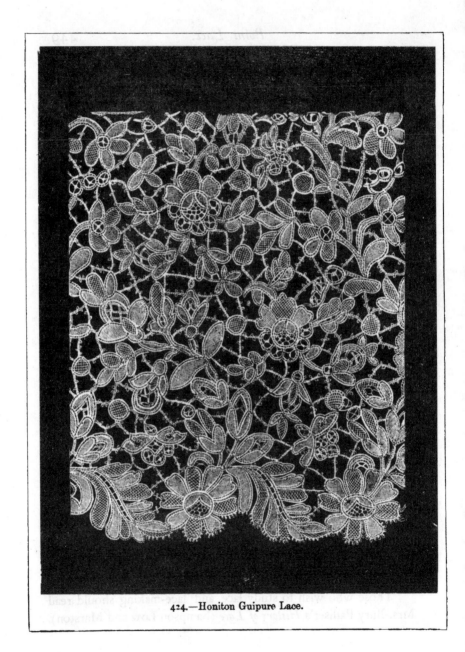

424.—Honiton Guipure Lace.

POINT LACE.

THE materials required for this elegant branch of needlework are neither numerous nor expensive. TRACING CLOTH, LEATHER, or TOILE CIRÉE, various BRAIDS and CORDS, LINEN THREAD and two or three sizes of needles, scissors and thimble. TRACING

425.—Point Lace Scissors.

CLOTH is required when ladies copy point lace patterns, and is the most convenient mode of taking them, as the design can be worked upon the tracing cloth, which, though transparent, is very strong ; the price is 1s. 6d. per yard. Fine LEATHER is the material upon which bought patterns are usually traced, and is decidedly more pleasant to work on than is any other material. In selecting patterns ladies should choose those traced upon green leather in preference to scarlet or buff, as green is better for the eyesight than any other colour.

TOILE CIREE is only a substitute for leather, and is not as pleasant to work upon in warm weather.

The needles employed are usually Messrs. Walker's needles, Nos. 9 and 10. The scissors should be small, sharp, and pointed, as in illustration No. 425. An ivory thimble may be safely employed in this light work.

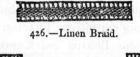

426.—Linen Braid.

427.—Linen Braid.   428.—Linen Braid.

429.—Linen Braid.

430.—Linen Braid.   431.—Linen Braid.

The BRAIDS are of various widths and kinds. None but pure linen braid should be employed ; those with machine-made edgings are eschewed by many lace-workers, the plain, loose-woven linen braid of various widths and qualities being alone acceptable to experienced hands.

But all ladies do not care to be at the trouble of edging the braid, and will find Nos. 426, 428, 430, and 431 very useful. No. 429 is a plain linen braid with a vandyked edge, which works out very prettily. No. 431 is an edged braid with open holes, in imitation of the point lace work of the fifteenth century

Point lace cords resemble the satin stitch embroidery in their close, regular smoothness ; the price is 1s. per hank, and they are of various thicknesses, from the size of a coarse crochet thread up to that of a thick piping cord. These cords are used to ornament the braid, and are closely sewn on the braid, following its every outline, and serve as *heading* to the edging, being always sewn on the outer edge alone. The finer kinds of this cord are used in place of braid where very light work is needed, as in the point lace alphabet which forms the frontispiece of this work. Directions for laying on the cord when employed as braid are given on page 500. When used as a finish only, and to impart the raised appearance of Venice and Spanish lace, it is fixed on the braid by plain, close sewing. The thread used should be Mecklenburg linen thread ; that of Messrs. Walter Evans and Co. we strongly recommend as being of pure linen, washing and wearing well ; it is pleasant to work with, from the regularity and evenness of the make. The numbers run thus :—2, 4, 6, 8, 10, 12, 14, 16, 18, 20, 24, 30, 36, and 40—and will be found adapted for every kind of lace stitch. No. 2 is the coarsest, No. 40 the finest, size.

In working point lace the following directions must be attended to :—Begin at the left hand, and work from left to right, when not otherwise directed, as in reverse rows. Before cutting off the braid run a few stitches across it to prevent it widening. Joins should be avoided, but when a join is indispensable, stitch the braid together, open and turn back the ends, and stitch each portion down separately. When passing the thread from one part to another, run along the centre of the braid, allowing the stitches to show as little as possible. In commencing, make a few stitches, leaving the end of the thread on the wrong side and cutting it off afterwards. In fastening off,

make a tight button-hole stitch, run on three stitches, bring the
needle out at the back, and cut off.

Having now completed our list of materials, we can proceed to lay on the braid.

To Place the Braid.—No. 442 shows the design traced
upon paper or tracing cloth, and lightly tacked to a foundation
of leather or toile cirée. Run on a straight line of braid for the

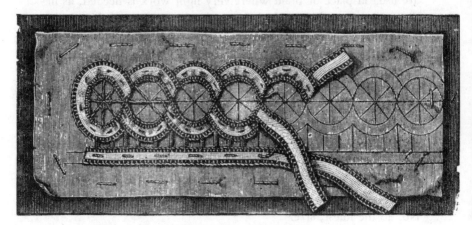

442.—Mode of Placing the Braid.

lower edge, with fine stitches, working as shown from left to
right. Take another piece of braid, or the other end of the
same piece, and begin to lay the braid by " running" stitches in
its centre, keeping it as smooth and even as possible. The
outer edge presents no difficulty, but the inner edge will not lie
evenly without being drawn in by a needle and thread, as follows :—Thread a No. 9 needle with No. 12 Mecklenburg thread
about 20 inches long, fasten the thread to one point, and insert
the needle in and out of the edge of the braid, as if for fine

gathering ; this thread when drawn up will keep the braid in its place. Two or three fastening off stitches should be worked when each circle, half circle, or rounded curve of a pattern is finished, as the drawing or gathering thread remains in the work, and forms an important, though unseen, part of its structure.

As much of the beauty of point lace depends upon the manner of placing the braid, ladies cannot bestow too much pains upon this part of the work, which is a little troublesome to beginners. Many fancy shops now undertake this braid-placing for ladies, who can have their own pattern braided and commenced or braided alone at trifling expense. Among these may be mentioned the following houses :— Goubaud, 30, Henrietta-street, Covent-garden. Boutillier, Oxford-street, W.

The stitches used in point lace may be divided into—

STITCHES PROPER, or *points*.

CONNECTING BARS.

FINISHING EDGINGS.

WHEELS, ROSETTES.

The term point lace, or lace stitches (*points*), has of late been applied to every stitch executed with Mecklenburg thread, and many stitches are erroneously named by modern writers. As there are more than one hundred stitches employed in this beautiful art, much study and opportunity of seeing specimens of old point lace is required to give a novice any idea of the various kinds of point lace ; but by attention to the following stitches the rudiments of the art may be easily acquired and very beautiful lace produced.

The first stitch is POINT DE BRUXELLES, or Brussels lace stitch. This stitch, as may be clearly seen in illustration No. 433, is a simple button-hole stitch worked loosely and with great regularity. The whole beauty of Brussels lace depends upon the evenness of the stitches. This stitch is sometimes employed

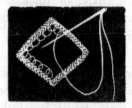

433. Point de Bruxelles
(Brussels Lace).

as an edging, but is more often worked in rows backwards and forwards, either as a groundwork or to fill spaces, as in the point lace collar, No. 496.

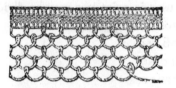

434.—Point de Bruxelles (Brussels Lace
Worked in Rows).

Brussels Point is the foundation of nearly all the lace stitches. POINT DE VENISE (Venetian or Venice Point) is worked from left to right, like Brussels point. Work one loose button-hole,

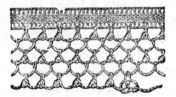

435.—Point de Venise
(Venice Point).

and in this stitch work four button-hole stitches tightly drawn up, then work another loose button-hole stitch, then four more tight button-hole stitches in the loose one, repeat to the end of the row, and fasten off.

PETIT POINT DE VENISE (Little Venice Point) is worked in the same manner as Point de Venise, but one tight stitch only is

436.—Petit Point de Venise
(Little Venice Point).

worked in each loose button-hole stitch. This is a most useful stitch for filling small spaces.

No. 437.—POINT D'ESPAGNE (Spanish Point) is worked from

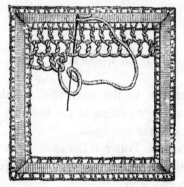

437.—Point d'Espagne (Spanish Point).

left to right as follows :—Insert the needle in the edge of the braid, keeping the thread turned to the right, bringing it out inside the loop formed by the thread (see illustration No. 437); the

2 H

needle must pass from the back of the loop through it. Pass the
needle under the stitch and bring it out in front, thus twice
twisting the thread, which produces the cord-like appearance of
this stitch. At the end of each row fasten to the braid and
return by sewing back, inserting the needle once in every open
stitch

No. 438.—Point d'Espagne (Close) is worked in the same
way as open point d'Espagne, but so closely as to only allow the

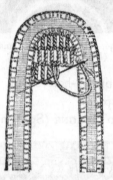

438.—Close Point d'Espagne
(Close Spanish Point).

needle to pass through in the next row. This stitch is also
worked from left to right ; fasten to the braid at the end of each
row, and sew back to the left again.

No. 439.—Treble Point d'Espagne is worked in exactly
the same way as the open and close point d'Espagne, as may be
seen in illustration No. 439.

Three close stitches, one open, three close to the end of each
row. Sew back, and in the next row begin one open, three
close, one open, then close to the end ; repeat the rows as far as
necessary, taking care that the close and open stitches follow in

regular order. Diamonds, stars, and various patterns may be formed with this stitch.

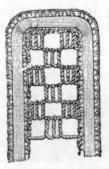

439.—Treble Point d'Espagne
(Treble Spanish Point).

No. 440.—Point de Grecque is begun from left to right, is worked backwards and forwards, and is begun by one stitch in loose point de Bruxelles and three of close point d'Espagne ;

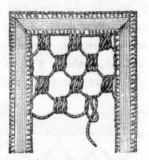

440.—Point de Grecque (Grecian Point).

then one Brussels, three point d'Espagne to the end of the row ; in returning work back in the same manner.

No. 441. Point de Valenciennes (Valenciennes Stitch).— This stitch appears complicated, but is really easy to work. Begin

at the left hand and work six point de Bruxelles stitches at unequal distance, every alternate stitch being larger. 2nd row: Upon
the first large or long stitch work 9 close button-hole stitches,
then 1 short point de Bruxelles stitch under the one above, then
9 close stitches, and so on to the end of row (right to left).

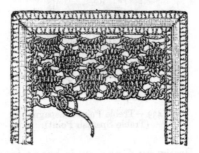

441.—Point de Valenciennes (Valenciennes Stitch).

3rd row : 5 close button-hole in the 9 of previous row, 1 short
point de Bruxelles, 2 close in the Bruxelles stitch, 1 short point
de Bruxelles, 5 close, 1 short point de Bruxelles, 2 close, 1
short, 5 close, 1 short, and repeat. 4th row: 5 close, 1 short
point de Bruxelles, 2 close, 1 short, 5 close, 1 short, 2 close, 1
short, and repeat. Continue the rows until sufficient of the
pattern is worked.

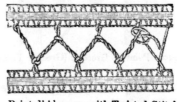

442.—Point d'Alençon, with Twisted Stitch.

No. 442. POINT D'ALENÇON.—This stitch is used to fill up
narrow spaces where great lightness is required. Point d'Alençon

is worked under and over in alternate stitches, like hem stitch. Nos. 442 and 443 show point d'Alençon. In No. 442 a twisted stitch is worked over the plain point d'Alençon, which is clearly shown in No. 443 ; this twist is made by passing the thread three times round each plain bar, and working the knot shown in illustration No. 442 over *both* strands of the bar.

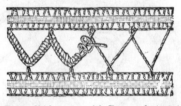

443.—Point d'Alençon, with Button-hole Stitch.

The Point d'Alençon No. 443 is a festoon of close button-hole stitch worked over the plain bars.

444.—Point d'Angleterre
(Open English Lace).

No. 444.—Point d'Angleterre (Open English Lace).— Open English Lace is thus worked :—Cover the space to be filled in with lines of thread about one-eighth of an inch apart, then form cross lines, intersecting those already made and passing alternately under and over them ; work a rosette on every spot where two lines cross, by working over and under the two lines about 16 times round, then twist the thread twice round

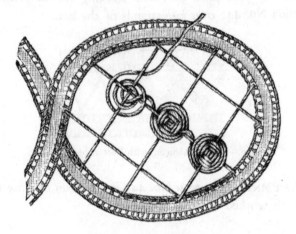

445.—Point d'Angleterre (Enlarged).

the groundwork thread, and begin to form another rosette at the crossing threads. No. 445 shows this stitch much enlarged.

No. 446.—POINT TURQUE (Turkish Stitch).—This easy and effective stitch looks well for filling either large or small spaces ; the thread employed should be varied in thickness according to the size of the space to be filled. 1st row: Work a loop, bringing the thread from right to left, passing the needle through the twist and through the loop, draw up tight and repeat. 2nd row : 1 straight thread from right to left. 3rd row: Work the same as first using the straight thread in place of the braid, and passing the needle through the loop of previous row, as shown in illustration No. 446.

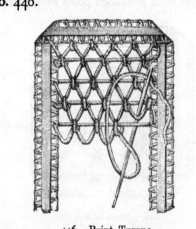

446.—Point Turque.

No. 447.—CORDOVA STITCH is useful for varying other stitches. It resembles the point de reprise of guipure d'art, and

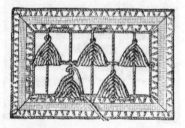

447.—Point de Cordova (Cordova Stitch).

is worked in a similar manner over and under the side of squares formed by straight and parallel lines. (See No. 448.)

No. 448.—POINT DE REPRISE.—This stitch is worked by darning over and under two threads, forming a triangle. The space is filled by parallel and crossway bars, placed at equal distances, and on the triangles thus produced point de reprise is worked.

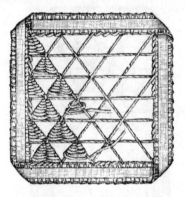

448.—Point de Reprise.

No. 449.—POINT BRABANÇON (Brabançon Lace) is worked as follows :—Left to right.   1st row: 1 long loose, 1 short loose,

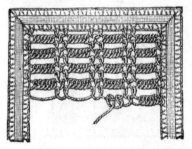

449.—Point Brabançon (Brabançon Lace).

point de Bruxelles alternately to end of row.   2nd row: 7 tight point de Bruxelles in the 1 long loose stitch, 2 short loose point de Bruxelles in the short loose stitch of previous row, repeat. 3rd row: Same as first.

No. 450 is used for groundwork where Brussels net is not imitated, and is very effective. It is begun in the corner or crosswise of the space to be filled. A loose point de Bruxelles

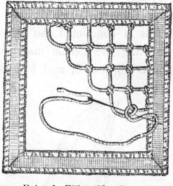

450.—Point de Fillet (Net Groundwork Stitch).

stitch is first taken and fastened to the braid, then passed twice through the braid as shown in illustration, and worked in rows backwards and forwards as follows :—1 point de Bruxelles

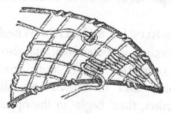

451.—Point de Fillet and Point de Reprise.

stitch; before proceeding to the next stitch pass the needle *under* the knot, *over* the thread, and again *under* it, as shown in illustration No. 450. This stitch is very quickly worked. No. 451

shows point de fillet applied in filling a space, with a few stitches of point de reprise worked upon this pretty groundwork.

No. 452.—POINT DE TULLE.—This stitch is used as a groundwork for very fine work, and is worked in rows backwards and forwards in the same stitch as open point d'Espagne, page 457. When this is completed the work is gone over a second time, by inserting the needle under one twisted bar, bringing it out and inserting it at *, and bringing it out again at

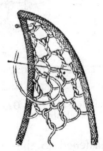

452.—Point de Tulle.

the dot •. This produces a close double twist which is very effective.

No. 453.—MECHLIN LACE (Mechlin Wheels).—This is one of the prettiest stitches in point lace, but also one of the most difficult to work correctly. It is thus worked : — Work a number of diagonal bars in button-hole stitch on a single thread in one direction, then begin in the opposite side the same way, and work 5 or 6 stitches past the spot where the two lines cross, pass the thread round the cross twice under and over the thread to form a circle. Work in button-hole stitch half one quarter, make a dot by putting a fine pin in the loop instead of drawing the thread tight, and work 3 button-hole stitches in the loop held open by the pin, then take it out, and continue as before. Beginners will do well to omit the dot, leaving the loop

453.—Mechlin Lace Wheels.

only on the wheel. Mechlin wheels are also worked in rows upon horizontal and parallel lines of thread.

No. 454.—ESCALIER LACE.—This useful lace may be varied in pattern to any extent by placing the open stitches in any desired order ; it then takes the name of diamond or Antwerp lace, according to the design. True escalier lace is made by working nine button-hole stitches close together ; then miss 3—that is,

454.—Escalier Lace Worked in Diamonds.

work none in the space that 3 stitches would occupy—work 9. miss 3 as before to the end of row, begin the 2nd row 3 stitches from the end, to cause the open spaces to fall in diagonal lines— a succession of steps or stairs (*escalier*), which gives name to this stitch.

No. 455.—SPANISH POINT LACE is adorned with highly-raised scrolls, flowers, &c. This is effected by working over an underlay of coarse white thread or over fine white linen cords. The wheels are worked by winding soft coarse linen thread round pencils or smooth knitting-pins of various sizes, and working over the circle thus obtained a succession of close button-hole stitches. These wheels are sewn on to the lace when completed. The

455.—Spanish Point Lace (Worked à l'Anglaise).

groundwork of Spanish lace is usually worked in what are called Raleigh Bars (see page 477), but this lace has sometimes for groundwork point de Venise. An easy mode of working this handsome lace is to trace the design upon very fine good linen ; raise the thick parts as above directed, and embroider the whole in fine thick scalloped button-hole stitch ; fill the ground with Raleigh bars, or, as shown in illustration No. 455, in treble point de Venise, and cut away the linen from beneath the ground-work.

WHEELS AND ROSETTES.

WHEELS or rosettes are used to fill up circles, or in combination to form lace. The simplest is—

THE SORRENTO WHEEL.—Nos. 456 and 457.—This is worked by fastening the thread in the pattern to be filled up by means of the letters. Fasten it first at the place *a*, then at the place *b*, carrying it back to the middle of the first formed

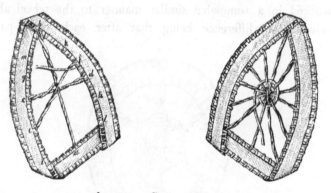

456 and 457.—Sorrento Wheels.

bar by winding it round, fasten the cotton at the place *c*, carrying it back again to the centre by winding it round the bar, and so on ; then work over and under the bars thus formed as in English lace. See page 462, and illustrations Nos. 456 and 457

No. 458.—ENGLISH WHEEL.—This is worked in the same manner as the Sorrento wheel, but instead of *winding* the thread over and under the bars, the needle is inserted under each bar and brought out again between the thread and the last stitch ; this gives a kind of button-hole stitch, and gives the square, firm appearance possessed by this wheel.

458.—English Wheel.

No. 459.—Rosette in Point d'Angleterre.—This rosette is worked in a somewhat similar manner to the wheel above described, the difference being that after each stitch passed

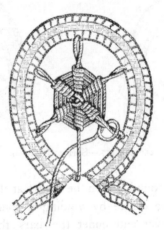

459.—Rosette in Raised Point d'Angleterre.

round and under the bars, the thread is passed loosely round in the reverse direction, as shown in illustration No. 459, before proceeding to make the next stitch.

No. 460 is a rosette or star which is used to fill circles of braid, and forms the centre of many modern point lace patterns.

It is worked upon a pattern traced and pricked in small holes at equal distances. Two threads are employed, one coarse tracing thread, the other of finer thread. The coarse thread is laid on thus :—Pass the needle containing the fine thread, No. 12, through one of the pricked holes, over the tracing thread and back through the same hole ; repeat, following the traced outline until the whole of the coarse thread is laid over the outline, then work

460.—Rosette for centre of Point Lace Circles.

over in tight button-hole stitch witn picots or purls, as on the Raleigh bars (see page 477). This mode of laying on tracing or outlining thread is also applied to fine braid and to point lace cord, as in the alphabet No. 400 (see page 500).

BARS.

THE word *Bar* is applied to the various stitches used to connect the various parts of point lace work, and the beauty of the work depends greatly upon the class of bar and its suitability to the lace stitches used. The simplest bar is—

No. 461.—THE SORRENTO BAR.—It is worked from right to
left, a straight thread being carried across and fastened with a
stitch. The return row consists of a simple twist under and

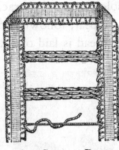

461.—Sorrento Bars.

over the straight thread ; three of these bars are usually placed
close together at equal distances between each group. The

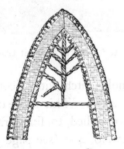

462.— Sorrento Bars.

thread is sewn over the braid in passing from one spot to
another.

Sorrento bars are also applied as shown in illustration No. 462.

No. 463.—D ALENCON BARS are worked upon point de
Bruxelles edging, and are only applied to the inner part of a

pattern, never being used as groundwork bars. The thread is merely passed three times over and under the point de Bruxelles stitches, the length of these bars being regulated by the space to be

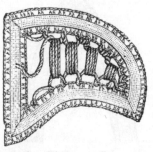

463.—D'Alencon Bars.

filled; when the third bar is completed a tight point de Bruxelles stitch is used to fasten off the bar, the thread is passed through the next point de Bruxelles stitch, and a second bar begun

464.—Venetian Bar.

No. 464.—THE VENETIAN BAR is so simple that it hardly needs description. It is worked over two straight threads in reverse button-hole stitch.

No. 465 shows the Venetian bar applied as the " veining " of leaf, and worked upon Sorrento bars.

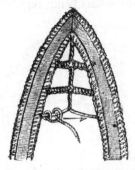

465.—Venetian Bar.

No. 466.—VENETIAN BARS are worked so as to form squares, triangles, &c., in button-hole stitch upon a straight thread. The *arrow* in the illustration points to the direction for working the next

466.—Plain Venetian Bars.

No. 467.—BARS OF POINT D'ANGLETERRE.—These bars may be worked singly or to fill up a space, as in illustration. Work rosettes as in point d'Angleterre, page 461 ; when each rosette is

finished twist the thread up the foundation thread to the top,
fasten with one stitch, then pass it under the parallel line running

467.—Bars of Point d'Angleterre.

through the centre and over into the opposite braid; repeat
on each side of each rosette, inserting the threads as in illustration
No. 468.—POINT DE VENISE BARS (EDGED).—Begin at the
right hand and stretch a line of thread to the left side of the

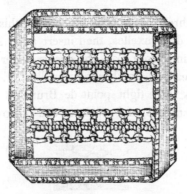

468.—Point de Venise Bars (Edged).

braid, fastening it with one tight stitch of point de Bruxelles.
Upon this line work a succession of tight point de Bruxelles
stitches. In every third stitch work one point de Venise stitch.

No. 469.—We now come to the most important feature of BARS—the *dot, picot,* or *purl,* for by all these names it is known. This dot is worked in various ways upon different lace bars. Dotted point de Venise bars are worked as follow :—

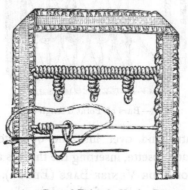

469.—Dotted Point de Venise Bars.

Stretch the thread from right to left, on this work five tight stitches of point de Bruxelles, then insert a pin in this last stitch to hold it open and loose, pass the needle under the loose stitch and over the thread, as clearly shown in illustration No. 469, and in this loop work three tight point de Bruxelles stitches. Then work five more stitches, and repeat to end of row.

470.—Picot or Dot on
Sorrento Bar.

No. 470 shows a dot or picot upon a Sorrento bar worked between rows of point de Bruxelles, three twisted stitches being worked into the loop left by the twisted thread; this forms a picot resembling satin stitch in appearance.

Nos. 471 and 472.—RALEIGH BARS are worked over a foundation or network of coarse thread, twisted in places so as to more easily fall into the desired form.

471.—Raleigh Bars.

By following the numbering from No. 1 to 21, in No. 472, a square place may be easily filled, and portions of this arrangement applied to form groundwork of any shape desired. Upon this groundwork tight point de Bruxelles stitches are worked, and the dot worked upon these in one of the following ways :—

DOT or PICOT.—1st Mode : Five tight point de Bruxelles stitches, one loose point de Bruxelles; pass the needle under the loop and over the thread, as shown in point de Venise bars

No. 469, draw up, leaving a small open loop as in tatting. Work five tight point de Bruxelles and repeat. 2nd Mode : Proceed as above, but instead of continuing the tight stitches work two or three tight stitches in the loop thus formed, and repeat. 3rd Mode : Work four tight point de Bruxelles stitches, one

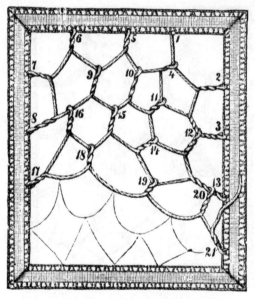

472.—Network for Working Raleigh Bars.

loose, through which pass the needle point, wind the thread three or four times round the point, as shown in illustration No. 473, press the thumb tightly on this, and draw the needle and thread through the twists. This is a quick mode of making the picot, and imitates most closely the real Spanish lace.

Illustration No. 473 also shows how this stitch may be applied as a *regular* groundwork, but the beauty of old point groundwork bars is the variety of form.

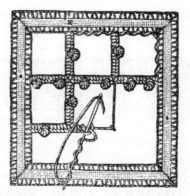

473.—Third mode of making Picots or Dots.

EDGES AND PURL FINISH.

THE correct edging of lace is a most important part of this art, and care should be taken to work a proper edge for each kind of lace. Sorrento edging should be worked upon Limoges lace. Spanish lace requires a full rich edge, as shown in No. 478, &c. The simplest edge is point de Bruxelles, which is

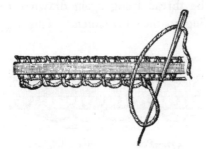

474.—Point de Bruxelles Edging.

worked somewhat like the stitch No. 433, and is secured by a knot worked in the braid. Many lace-workers omit this knot.

No. 475.—SORRENTO EDGING is worked with one short and one long stitch alternately.

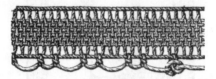

475.—Sorrento Edging.

No. 476.—POINT DE VENISE is worked precisely like that stitch (see page 456), three and even four stitches being worked in the loop.

476.—Point de Venise Edging.

No. 477.—POINT D'ANGLETERRE EDGING is worked in point de Bruxelles, the thread being again drawn through the braid before proceeding to the next stitch. This edging is strong and useful.

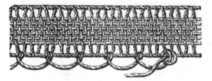

477.—Point d'Angleterre Edging.

No. 478.—POINT D'ESPAGNE EDGING.—This stitch is easily worked. Insert the point of the needle through the braid and

wind the thread round it 20 times, draw the needle through
these windings and draw the picot tight, sew over the braid
the space of 3 stitches, and repeat.

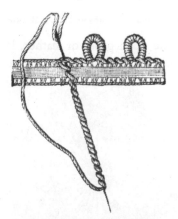

478.—Point d'Espagne Edging.

No. 479.—ANTWERP EDGE.—This edge is only a variety of
point d'Angleterre edging, and differs only in the mode of making

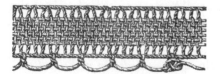

479.—Antwerp Edge.

the knot; the thread is passed over, under, and through the loop
formed by the point de Bruxelles lace.

NOTE.—It will be observed that the stitches here given are much enlarged
for the sake of clearness in showing details.

PATTERNS.

No. 480.—*Star in Point Lace.*

Materials: Braid; Messrs. Walter Evans and Co.'s Mecklenburg thread No. 20.

Trace the outline upon paper or leather, lay the braid on as directed. Work the centre in Sorrento bars, and on these work

480.—Star in Point Lace.

a rosette in point d'Angleterre, the edge in point d'Angleterre edging, and the wheels in open English lace.

No. 481.—*Medallion in Point Lace.*

Materials: Linen Braid; Messrs. Walter Evans and Co.'s Mecklenburg thread No. 14.

This medallion is useful for cravat ends and for a number of purposes, as trimming for sachets, dresses, &c. Having placed the braid as before directed, work an English rosette in the centre, fill in the ground with point de fillet or with point de

Bruxelles. An edging of Spanish point completes this pretty medallion.

481.—Medallion in Point Lace.

No. 482.—*Point Lace Border.*

Materials : Braid ; Messrs. Walter Evans and Co.'s Mecklenburg thread No. 12.

This border represents the completed work shown on p. 454. A point d'Angleterre rosette is worked in each circle. The plain braid is edged by Sorrento edging. Venice bars are worked above the trimming, and treble point de Venise edges the border.

482.—Point Lace Border.

No. 483.—*Point Lace Border.*

Materials : Braid ; Messrs. Walter Evans and Co.'s Mecklenburg thread No. 10.

This border is both easily and quickly worked in Sorrento bars. The edge is worked in two rows of point de Bruxelles.

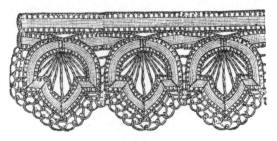

483.—Point Lace Border.

No. 484.—*Insertion in Limoges Lace.*

Materials : Plain linen braid ; Messrs. Walter Evans and Co.'s Mecklenburg thread No. 14.

This insertion will be found very useful, being so quickly

worked. Edge the braid with Sorrento edging, fill up with bars and plain point d'Alençon and Sorrento wheels, No. 456.

484.—Insertion in Limoges Lace.

No. 485.—*Point Lace Border for Handkerchief.*

Materials: Fine lace braid or cord; Messrs. Walter Evans and Co.'s Mecklenburg thread No. 24.

This border is suited for a handkerchief or for trimming a square bodice. The braid is not tacked on by stitches running through the centre, as is usual in point lace braids, but sewn on by passing a thread from underneath over the braid and out through the same hole, as is done by lace-workers with a thick thread; this forms the design. The stitches employed in this pattern are Raleigh bars, which connect the work; Sorrento edging, which finishes the whole outline; English rosettes filling the open spaces. Point lace cord may be used for this in place of braid.

485.—Point Lace Border for Handkerchief.

No. 486.—*Star-Centre for Toilette Cushion in Point Lace.*

Materials : Braid ; Messrs. Walter Evans and Co.'s Mecklenburg thread
Nos. 16 and 12.

This beautiful star will be found useful for other purposes

486.—Star-centre for Toilette Cushion in Point Lace.

than as a toilette cushion cover, and is worked as follows :—
English rosette in centre ; Sorrento wheels in the 4 ovals, worked
with No. 12 thread ; point de Bruxelles ground, worked with
No. 16 ; braid edged by dotted Venetian edges. The eight

487.—Cravat End in Point Lace.

spaces may be filled with 2 or 4 contrasting stitches, taking care that they contrast well, and are placed alternately, and worked in No. 12.

487.—*Cravat End in Point Lace.*

Materials: Fine braid: Messrs. Walter Evans and Co.'s Mecklenburg thread No. 12.

This cravat is worked in Sorrento wheels, point d'Alençon bars, and Sorrento edging.

488.—Point Lace Edging.

488 *and* 489.—*Point Lace Edgings.*

Materials: Braid; Messrs. Walter Evans and Co.'s Mecklenburg thread Nos. 12 and 16.

These edgings can be used as a finish to insertions and other trimmings or for edging couvrettes. No. 488 is worked with

489.—Point Lace Edging.

2 K

Sorrento wheels ; the edge in two rows of point de Bruxelles, a straight thread being drawn from the end to the beginning of each scallop over which the second row is worked. No. 489 is worked with the same materials in treble point de Venise, edged by the same, and finished off with a row of point de Bruxelles, the upper edge being worked in the same way.

490.—*Design in Point Lace for Collar, Lappet, &c.*

Materials : Linen braid ; Messrs. Walter Evans and Co.'s Mecklenburg thread Nos. 10 and 16.

This design may be used for a variety of purposes, and is extremely effective. The principal stitches required are given at the sides of the pattern. *a* is Valenciennes lace, *b* Brussels net, *c* Venetian spotted, *d* Sorrento edging, *e* Mechlin wheel, *f* English rosette, *g* Raleigh bars.

491.—*Oval for Cravats, &c.*

Materials : Point lace cord ; muslin ; embroidery cotton ; Messrs. Walter Evans and Co.'s Mecklenburg thread Nos. 14 and 18.

This beautiful oval is worked in point lace and embroidery. This is begun from the centre on the muslin by overcasting the space filled by a wheel. The eyelet-holes are then worked, and the satin stitch ornament raised and *prepared* for working. The edge, of point lace cord, is then laid on, and the under portion edged in tight and open point de Bruxelles, the centre of the circles being worked in point de Bruxelles. The light ground-work is worked entirely in Mechlin wheels, the satin stitch being

490.—Design in Point Lace for Collar, Lappet, &c.

worked when these are completed. This pattern can be enlarged

491.—Oval Pattern for Ornamenting Cravats, &c.

and applied to many purposes. The muslin is cut away when
the whole work is finished.

492.—*Point Lace Trimming for Square Bodice.*

Materials : Braid ; Messrs. Walter Evans and Co.'s Mecklenburg thread
No. 12 or 20.

We give two sizes of thread, as this design is capable of
many uses, and the size of the thread differs with these. The
pattern is worked in English rosettes and bars (see No. 467).
No. 488 edging looks well with this pattern.

493.—*Point Lace Collar.*

Materials : Fine braid or cord ; Messrs. Walter Evans and Co.'s Mecklenburg
thread No. 22.

Set on the braid or cord by passing a thread through a hole

492.—Point Lace Trimming for Square Bodice.

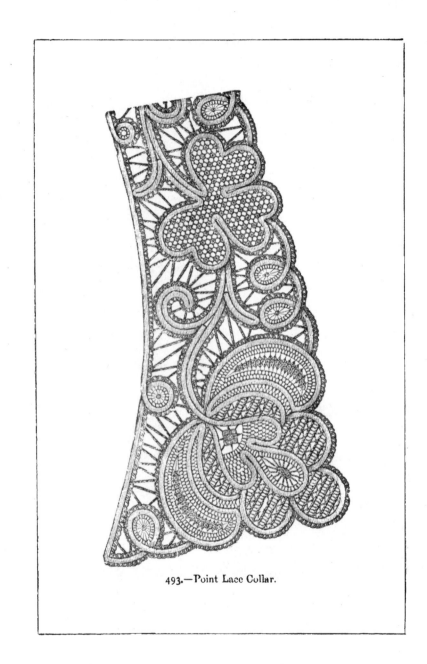

493.—Point Lace Collar.

pricked in the pattern over the braid and out again through the same hole. Edge the braid with point de Bruxelles, the design

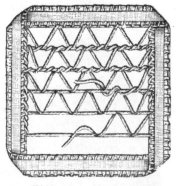

494.—D'Alençon and Sorrento Bars.

being filled by Mechlin wheels, Sorrento wheels, point de feston, and the mixed stitch shown in No. 494, which is composed of d'Alençon and Sorrento bars, and is easily worked. Those

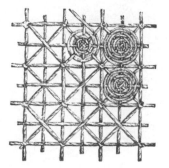

495.—Close English Wheels.

who cannot work Mechlin wheels easily, can substitute close English, as shown in illustration No. 495. The bars are Sorrento.

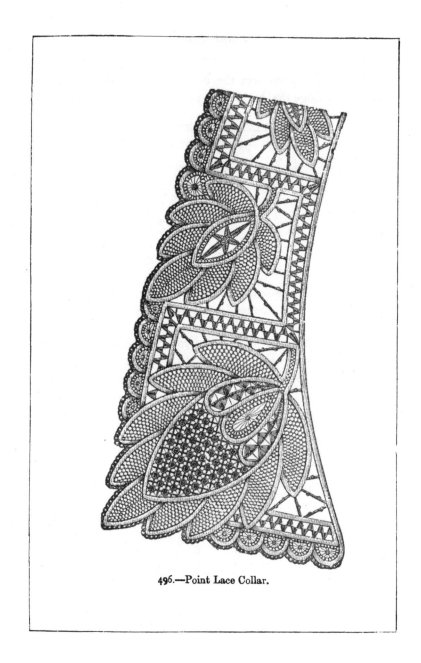

496.—Point Lace Collar.

496.—*Point Lace Collar.*

Materials : Fine braid or cord ; Messrs. Walter Evans and Co.'s Mecklenburg
thread No. 22.

This collar is worked in the same way as No. 493, though
the stitches vary. The Grecian line is worked in point de reprise,
the pattern in close English wheels, point de reprise, point de
Bruxelles, English rosettes, and Raleigh bars.

497.—*Point Lace Lappet.*

Materials : Braid; Messrs. Walter Evans and Co.'s Mecklenburg thread
No. 16 or 24, according to the fineness required.

This lappet is exceedingly pretty. It is composed of the following stitches :—Point d'Alençon, point de tulle, English rosettes,

498.—Point d'Anvers.

499.—Point Grecque.

Sorrento bars, d'Alençon bars, dotted Venise bars, and the fancy
stitch point d'Anvers, which is not a true point lace stitch, but
which is much employed in modern point.

Point Grecque is another useful variety of fancy stitch, **and**
so easily worked as to be a favourite stitch with beginners.

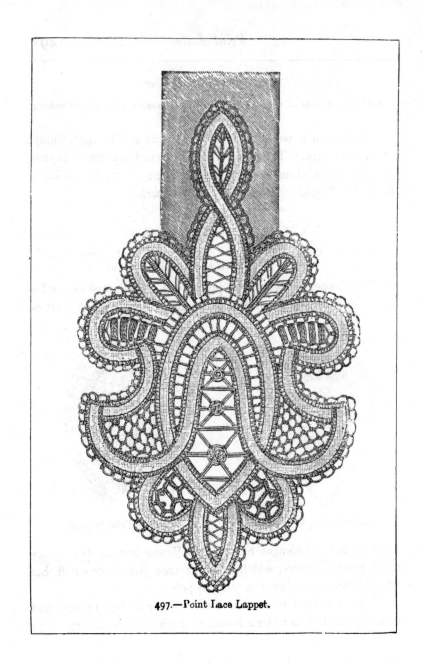

497.—Point Lace Lappet.

500.—Letter A in Point Lace.

501.—Letter A Enlarged.

500 to 502. – Alphabet in Point Lace. (See endpapers.)

Materials : Point lace cord; Messrs. Walter Evans and Co.'s Mecklenburg
thread No. 36.

This alphabet is useful for marking pocket-handkerchiefs,
and for initials for sachets, &c. The cord is laid upon the
pattern and pricked out by passing a thread up through a hole
over the cord, and back through the same hole ; then pass on to
the next hole, and repeat. The holes should be about an eighth
of an inch apart, or nearer when the pattern is finely convoluted.
The letters are worked in point de Bruxelles, point d'Alençon,
and dotted Sorrento bars. No. 501 shows the letter A greatly
enlarged, to show the mode of working.

TABLE OF THREADS SUITED TO VARIOUS ARTICLES WORKED IN POINT LACE.

Caps	36	„	„
Collars	30	;;	„
Couvrettes	2	4	6
Cravats	18	30	„
D'Oyleys	8	10	12
Dress Trimmings	22	30	„
Edgings	14	30	„
Handkerchiefs	30	36	40
Insertions, coarse	6	8	12
„ fine	24	30	„

Point lace cord runs about twelve yards to the hank.
Point lace edged braid runs thirty-six yards on cards.
Plain linen twelve yards in each hank.

GUIPURE D'ART.

INSTRUCTIONS AND PATTERNS

IN

GUIPURE D'ART.

———◆———

ANCIENT Guipure was a lace made of thin vellum, covered with gold, silver, or silk thread, and the word Guipure derives its name from the silk when thus twisted round vellum being called by that name. In process of time the use of vellum was discontinued, and a cotton material replaced it. Guipure lace was called *dentelle à cartisane* in England in the sixteenth century. Various modern laces are called Guipure, but the word is misapplied, since Guipure lace is that kind only where one thread is twisted round another thread or another substance, as in the ancient Guipure d'Art.

In every design where lace can be introduced, Guipure d'Art will be found useful. It looks particularly well when mounted upon quilted silk or satin. The squares, when worked finely, look well as toilet-cushions, or, if worked in coarser thread, make admirable couvrettes, and as covers for eider-down silk quilts are very elegant. Guipure squares should be connected by guipure lace, crochet, or tatting, or they may be edged with narrow guipure lace and joined at the corners only when placed over coloured silk or satin ; thus arranged, a sofa-cushion appears in alternate squares of plain and lace-covered silk ; a ruche of ribbon and fall of lace to correspond completes this pretty mounting.

Not one of the least important attractions of Guipure d'Art is the speed with which it is worked, and the ease with which fresh patterns are designed by skilful workers.

GUIPURE D'ART is an imitation of the celebrated ancient Guipure Lace, and is worked in raised and intersected patterns upon a square network of linen thread, Mecklenburg thread of various sizes being used for this purpose. The needles employed are blunt, and have large eyes, to admit the linen thread.

Materials required : One frame of wire covered with silk ribbon ; one square of Mecklenburg thread net (*fillet*), either coarse or fine ; Mecklenburg thread ; netting-needles and meshes of various sizes.

The netted foundation, or "*fillet,*" upon which this elegant work is embroidered, can be made by ladies very easily, and at much less cost than when bought ready made.

The square is worked by netting with coarse No. 2 or fine No. 10 thread over a mesh measuring three-quarters of an inch or more, in rows backwards and forwards. Begin with 2 stitches, and increase 1 at the end of every row till you have one more stitch than is required for the number of holes. Thus, if a square of 26 holes is required, continue to increase up to 27 stitches, then decrease 1 at the end of every row till 2 stitches only remain. The last 2 stitches are knotted together without forming a fresh stitch.

The completed foundation is laced upon the frame, taking the lacing cotton through the double edge formed by the increased and decreased stitches. If the four corners of the netting are tied at each corner of the frame before beginning the lacing, that operation is greatly facilitated. The netting should be laced as tightly as possible, it being far easier to darn on than when loose.

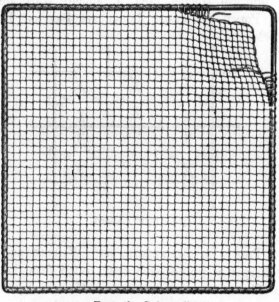

503.—Frame for Guipure d'Art.

Ladies who wish to excel in working guipure d'art should practise each of the stitches until they attain perfect regularity and quickness in their execution. Two or three hours devoted to this in the first instance will not be time wasted, as the most elaborate pattern will be worked with ease as soon as the stitches are mastered.

2 L

The Mecklenburg thread of Messrs. Walter Evans and Co., of Derby, will be found a better colour than any other, as it closely resembles the shade of the ancient guipure lace.

It is sold only in spools of 200 yards each, and the numbers run as follow ; No. 2, 4, 6, 8, 10, 12, 16, 20 ; No. 2 being the coarsest, and No. 20 the finest.

The principal stitches used in guipure d'art are POINT D'ESPRIT, POINT DE TOILE, POINT DE FESTON, POINT DE

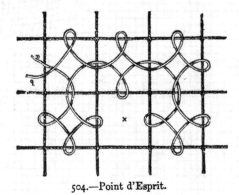

504.—Point d'Esprit.

REPRISE, POINT DE BRUXELLES, and WHEELS and STARS. POINT D'ESPRIT is worked with finer cotton than the foundation, say No. 10 on a foundation of No. 6. It consists of a succession of small loops, as will be seen clearly in the illustration. The learner should begin from the mark * No. 503, and working a row of loops the length required, turn the frame and work loops on the opposite half of each square intersecting the first worked loops in the centre of each intervening bar of netting. A careful examination of Nos. 503 and 506 will explain this more clearly than is possible in words.

POINT DE TOILE, or LINEN STITCH, is plain darning under

and over each thread; this forms a fine close groundwork, and is much used in guipure d'art. Care should be taken to keep the same number of stitches in each square, both along and

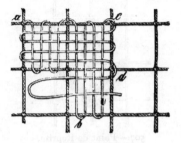

505.—Point de Toile.

across; the number of threads shown in illustration No. 504 is 4 only, but 6 and even 8 are used in many netted foundations in fine patterns.

POINT DE FESTON is worked by a series of overcast stitches, as seen by illustration 506, which clearly shows the manner of

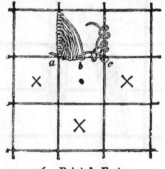

506.—Point de Feston.

working. The frame is turned at each stitch, the stitches are taken across the squares, and increase in length at the top of the square.

POINT DE REPRISE, or DARNING, is worked by stretching 2 or 3 threads over 1, or 2, or more squares. The thread is

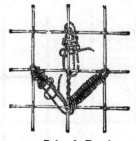

507.—Point de Reprise.

darned over and under, and the needle used to arrange the last stitch while passing through to form the next. This stitch is very easily acquired. It is always worked with coarser thread

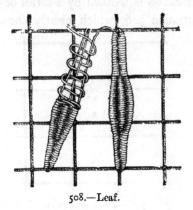

508.—Leaf.

than the foundation; No. 2 thread should be employed for a coarse groundwork. No. 510 shows this stitch used to form stars, figures, &c.

Point de Bruxelles, as shown on pages 506 and 507, is a kind of loose button-hole stitch, and is used for forming various

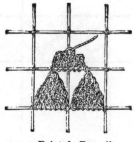

509.—Point de Bruxelles.

patterns and for filling up squares. It also forms "leaves," when the number of stitches is decreased each row until the

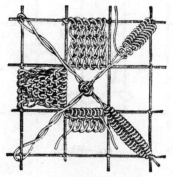

510.—Point de Bruxelles.

leaf finishes off in a point. Nos. 509 and 510 clearly show this stitch.

WHEELS are easy to work, and are begun in the centre. Four threads are taken across, as shown in design No. 511 ; the

511.—Wheel (commenced).

thread is twisted in bringing it back to the centre, and the wheel formed by passing the thread under and over the netting and the

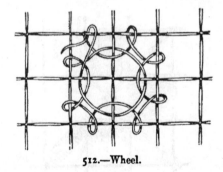

512.—Wheel.

crossing threads. It is fastened off on the back of the several wheels.

Wheel No. 513 is a square wheel, and is worked in the same manner, with the addition of point d'esprit loops, through which,

and under and over the cross-twisted threads, 4 or 5 rows of
thread are passed.

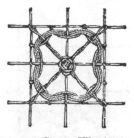

513.—Square Wheel.

STARS are of various form, as shown in Nos. 516, 517,
518, 519, and 520.

No. 516 is worked in point de feston (see page 507) round

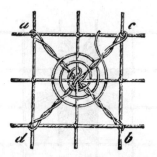

514.—Wheel larger than its real size.

a single square hole, which is filled in by a small wheel or
rosette.

No. 517 is worked in point de feston and point de Bruxelles, alternately round a centre simply crossed by point d'esprit threads.

No. 518 is more elaborate, and is worked thus :—Begin at

515.—Wheel Completed.

the place marked *a;* twist the linen thread 3 times round the nearest thread, draw it on to the knot *b;* repeat this 3 times,

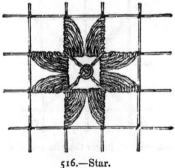

516.—Star.

following the order of the letters ; twist the **linen** thread also between **the** threads, as can be seen from the illustration, and fasten it underneath the knot *a;* for the wheel fasten on the cotton afresh and work the remaining pattern in darning stitch (point de reprise)

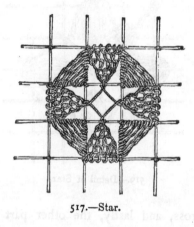

517.—Star.

No. 520 consists of a double cross formed by twisted loops of linen thread. Copy these loops exactly from illustration 520

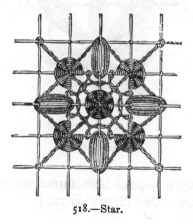

518.—Star.

One part of the straight cross lies underneath, then comes

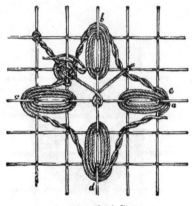

519.—Detail of Star.

the slanting cross, and lastly, the other part of the straight cross.

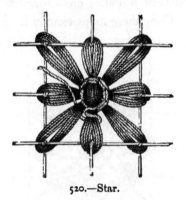

520.—Star.

In the centre the loops of linen thread are fastened with two rounds of stitches. (See illustration 520).

OVERCAST STITCH is worked like embroidery overcast, and forms the stems of the flowers and leaves of guipure d'art ; it is worked over one or two coarse threads. It is employed in No. 530, and forms the triangles in the centre of the middle squares.

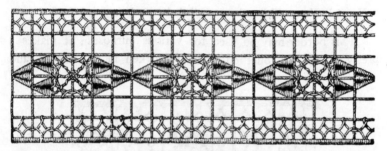

521.—Insertion in Guipure d'Art.

521.—*Insertion in Guipure d'Art.*

Materials: Guipure frame netting of 6 holes wide ; Mecklenburg thread No. 8 or 10 ; needle No. 7.

For the netted foundation, which is six holes wide, begin at one corner with 2 stitches, work 5 rows, at the end of each of which increase 1 stitch, continue to work the strip with the same number of stitches, alternately decreasing 1 at the end of one row and increasing 1 at the end of the next. For decreasing net 2 stitches together, for increasing net 2 stitches in the same hole. When the strip is sufficiently long, complete it by decreasing in the same proportion as the increasing at the beginning. As the pattern is so clearly shown in the illustration, it will be very easy to work from it. It is worked in point de

feston and star wheels ; the border is in point d'esprit. The
insertion is finished on either side with a row of button-hole
stitches.

522.—*Lace Border in Guipure d'Art.*

Material: Messrs. Walter Evans and Co.'s Mecklenburg thread No. 8 or 10.

This border may be used for various purposes ; it makes a
pretty edging for toilet cushions if worked in fine thread, and

522.—Lace Border in Guipure d'Art.

looks equally well for trimming couvrettes, &c., in No. 2 thread
The netting is nine holes wide, the stitches employed are point
d'esprit and point de feston, the edge is in buttonhole stitch, the
netted ground is cut away outside the scallops.

523.—*Square for D'Oyley*

Materials: Frame; 1 square of netting; Mecklenburg reel thread Nos. 8 and 10; needle No. 6.

This square may be used to form part of a couvrette, or a

523.—Pattern of Square for D'Oyley.

d'oyley, or pincushion. The three other corners of the square are worked exactly like the one seen in illustration ; the rosette in the centre is shown in full size. The square is worked in point d'esprit, linen stitch, and point de reprise. Each of the leaves of the foliage is worked in one hole of the netting; they are worked by throwing the cotton three times across the hole, and working darning stitch on them. The stem is worked in overcast on the thread of the netting. The daisy in the centre is worked like the leaves, each leaf taking up one or more holes of the netting.

524.—Corner Border in Guipure d'Art.

524 and 525.—Corner Borders in Guipure d'Art.

Materials: Messrs. Walter Evans and Co.'s Mecklenburg thread No. 2 for couvrettes, No. 8 for pillow-cases, No. 16 for lace edgings.

These corner borders are suitable for pillow-cases or small couvrettes; the stitches worked on these patterns are linen stitch, darning stitch, point de Bruxelles, and wheels. The edge is formed by buttonhole stitches. The netting is cut away after these are worked.

525.—Corner Border in Guipure d'Art.

526.—*Strip of Insertion in Guipure d'Art.*

Material: Messrs. Walter Evans and Co.'s Mecklenburg thread No. 8.

This strip of insertion is 8 stitches wide, and is worked in zigzag lines of point de feston, with a border of point d'esprit and point de toile; a four-point star occupies the centre of the triangle left by the zigzag line. This pattern is so easy to work that it hardly needs description, the only part requiring care being the squares of point de feston; these are begun in the centre, and the thread should be drawn rather tightly so as to form a good square

526.—Pattern for a strip of Insertion in Guipure d'Art.

527.—*Small Square.*

Materials: Frame; Messrs. Walter Evans and Co.'s Mecklenburg thread No. 4, 6, or 8 for the netting, and No. 16 for the pattern.

Work over a mesh measuring $2\frac{1}{10}$ inch round the foundation of each square, which has seven stitches in length, and as many in breadth. It is embroidered in darning stitch, and point d'esprit, and wheels. The outer edge is worked round in button-

527.—Small Square.

hole stitch. Larger squares are worked in the same manner, only a few rows larger in length and breadth. The squares are fastened together with a few stitches, and sewn on the pincushion or any article they are intended to ornament

528.—*Insertion in Guipure d'Art.*

Materials: Messrs. Walter Evans and Co.'s Mecklenburg thread No. 8, or 16 for very fine work.

This strip of insertion is very pretty, and can be used for all kinds of lingeries. The size of the material depends, of course,

2 M

on the use to be made of the insertion. The guipure pattern is worked in linen stitch and point d'esprit, the raised leaves in darning stitch. The edges are worked round with buttonhole stitches.

528.—Insertion in Guipure d'Art.

529.—*Rosette in Guipure d' Art.*

Material : Messrs. Walter Evans and Co.'s Mecklenburg thread No. 6.

This rosette is worked in point de toile and small wheels.

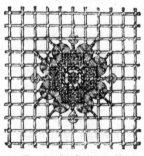

529.—Rosette in Guipure d'Art.

A larger wheel occupies the centre, and is ornamented with a round of overcast.

530.—*Quarter of a Square in Guipure d'Art.*

Materials: One guipure frame; Mecklenburg thread Nos. 6 and 12; needle No. 7.

This pattern shows, in full size, one quarter of a square in guipure d'art. The outer border is in point d'esprit, then comes

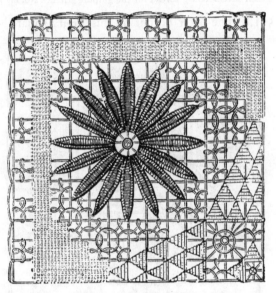

530.—Quarter of a Square in Guipure d'Art.

a border in linen stitch. There are large stars in the corners ; these stars are worked in raised darning stitch only, and fastened on the netting at the points of each brand ; in the centre of the star there is a wheel (see No. 515) edged with buttonhole stitch. The pattern for the centre, one quarter of which only is seen in the illustration, consists of 4 branches forming small triangles in point de Bruxelles, 4 open-worked stars or wheels worked over

4 holes of the netting, and a four-branched centre of point de feston with a wheel in the middle.

531 *and* 532.—*Square Patterns in Guipure d'Art.*

Materials: Messrs. Walter Evans and Co.'s linen thread No. 2 for the netting, and their Mecklenburg thread for the guipure stitches No. 8.

No. 531. The outer border of this pretty square is worked

531.—Square Pattern in Guipure d'Art.

in point d'esprit, the inner border in point de toile; then follows a round of small wheels or rosettes.

For these, fasten the cotton to one of the knots of the first square stitch of this round, work one loop upon each of the three other knots, so as to form a slanting cross; then work round the centre point of the cross, passing alternately under and over its branches, then twist the cotton over the threads of the foundation until the next square is reached, and begin another wheel.

The centre of No. 531 is composed of wheels and point de reprise; the pattern round the centre is worked in point de

532.—Square Pattern in Guipure d'Art.

feston, differing a little from that given on pages 505 and 506, but the illustration clearly shows the difference.

No. 532 has similar borders to No. 531; the centre is occupied by a star (see page 512) in point de feston; four large wheels surround this; the square stitches between are filled with small wheels and with groups of long loops, fastened together in sheaves. Point d'esprit and point de toile, worked one way only, complete this square.

533 *to* 536.—*Four Patterns in Guipure d'Art.*

Material: Messrs. Walter Evans and Co.'s Mecklenburg thread No. 2 or 16,
according to the size of the work.

These four patterns will be found useful for filling up small
squares, or for varying the usual groundwork of point d'esprit.

533.—Pattern in Guipure d'Art.

No. 533 is a succession of point de feston stitches, which half

534.—Pattern in Guipure d'Art.

fill each square of the netting. This pattern must be worked
with great regularity.

No. 534 consists of a kind of double point d'esprit.

No. 535 is a thread twisted and taken *across* each square, and resembles lace stitches.

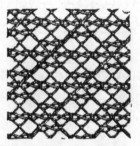

535.—Pattern in Guipure d'Art.

No. 536 is a succession of small close wheels, intermingled with point d'esprit. This grounding is very effective.

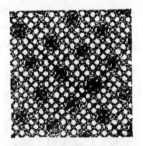

536.—Pattern in Guipure d'Art.

537.—*Lace Border for Veils, &c.*

Materials: Messrs. Walter Evans and Co.'s Mecklenburg thread No. 16; strip of square netting of the required length; oblong frame.

This simple border is easily and quickly worked. The edge is overcast, the ground worked in point d'esprit, the border in point de toile, and the pattern in point de reprise. When completed the netting is cut away from the overcast edge.

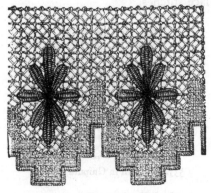

537.—Lace Border for Veils, &c.

538 *and* 538a.—*Squares in Guipure d'Art.*

Materials: 2 squares of netting of 8 holes; Messrs. Walter Evans and Co.'s Mecklenburg thread No. 10 or 16, according to the fineness required.

These squares are very pretty for cravat ends, cuffs, or hand-

538.—Square in Guipure d'Art.

kerchiefs. They are worked on netting with very fine cotton in the usual manner, beginning on two stitches in one corner

The different stitches of the guipure darning can be distinctly seen in illustration, and are point de feston, point de reprise, point

538a.—Square in Guipure d'Art.

de toile, and point d'esprit on No. 538, and the same stitches surround a wheel in No. 538a.

539.—Guipure d'Art Insertion.

539.—*Insertion in Guipure d'Art.*

Materials: Messrs. Walter Evans and Co.'s Mecklenburg thread Nos. 8 to 16; strip of netting length required.

This insertion is worked in point de toile, and wheels worked in point de feston. The ground in point d'esprit.

Materials: Coarse or fine linen; Messrs. Walter Evans and Co.'s
Mecklenburg thread No. 4 or 12.

540.—Square in Point de Venise.

This square is worked in the so-called point de Venise,
together with other squares; it is very pretty for covers, toilet
cushions, &c. It is worked on coarse or fine linen, according to

the use you wish to make of it. Prepare a square piece of linen, by drawing out long and cross threads, so as to form perfect squares. In the pattern No. 540, which is worked on fine linen,

541.—Quarter Square in Reticella Work (Enlarged).

28 threads have been drawn out, both the long and cross way; 8 squares are formed in this way each time that 28 threads have been drawn out; leave 7 or 8 threads of the ground, which form the framework. Then fasten the piece of linen on card-

board, and work close button-hole stitch round the inner edge
Then work with darning stitch over the long and cross threads
of the ground.

From No. 541, which shows the fourth part of the square
4 times larger than full size, it is easy to see how the framework is darned. When the latter is entirely darned, work the
patterns in the different squares in button-hole stitch. The
circular and serpentine patterns consist of 3 rows of button-hole
stitch ; the patterns which imitate whole rosettes and half rosettes
are worked in rows of button-hole stitch. For each row the
thread must be first drawn from one place to the other, as can
be seen in illustration, and fastened on the framework. The
knots in the last button-hole stitched row are made by working
in each stitch when completed, another stitch, and drawing the
cotton again through the first completed knot. It is easy, however, to work all the patterns from No. 541. The dotted lines in
the right-hand corner show the direction of the patterns which
are wanting there. The square is edged all round with an
open-work hem, which can also be worked from No. 541.

542 *and* 543.—*Corner Patterns in Guipure d'Art*

Material: Messrs. Walter Evans and Co.'s Mecklenburg thread No. 14.

These patterns are very pretty for cushions, handkerchiefs, &c.
The netted ground is to be worked from the corner. Cast on
2 stitches, and work in rows backwards and forwards, increasing
1 stitch at the end of every row. The pattern is worked in
point d'esprit, linen, and darning stitch, as can be seen in illustration.

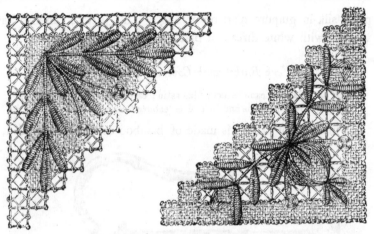

542 and 543.—Corner Borders.

544.—*Flower for Ornamenting Cravats and Caps in Guipure d'Art.*

Materials: Black or coloured silks, or Messrs. Walter Evans and Co.'s
Mecklenburg thread No. 10.

544.—Flower in Guipure d'Art.

This pattern is worked with middle-sized light-coloured

purse silk in guipure d'art on netting. This pattern can also be worked with white thread or black silk in point de reprise.

545.—*Work Basket with Covering of Darned Netting.*

Materials: Bamboo cane basket; blue satin; cardboard; netting; Messrs. Walter Evans and Co's Mecklenburg thread No. 16.

This elegant basket is made of bamboo cane and blue satin,

545.—Work Basket Covered with Guipure d'Art.

fastened on cardboard, and covered with guipure d'art. The stand of varnished bamboo is twelve inches long, seven and a half inches wide, and five and a half inches high. The case inside is made of cardboard, covered on both sides with blue satin, and the guipure d'art on the outside only. The stitches used are point de toile, point de reprise, and point d'esprit.

546 *and* 547.—*Squares in Guipure d'Art.*

Materials : Messrs. Walter Evans and Co.'s Mecklenburg thread No. 12 or 20;
and point d'esprit according to the fineness required.

Both these square patterns are suitable for ornamenting

546.—Square in Guipure
d'Art.

lingerie, cravats, collars, &c. Repeated at regular intervals on a
larger centre, they are likewise suitable for couvrettes, cushions,
pillow-cases, &c.; they are worked in darning and linen stitch

547.—Square in Guipure
d'Art.

548.—*Insertion in Guipure d'Art.*

Materials: Strip of netting 6 holes wide, and of the required length; Messrs.
Walter Evans and Co.'s Mecklenburg thread No. 8 or 12.

This simple insertion consists of double rows of wheels
worked at each side of a strip of point d'esprit, an edge of button-
hole stitches being worked between the rows.

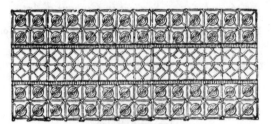

549.—Guipure d'Art Insertion.

550 and 551.—Squares for Antimacassar.

Materials: Square of netting of 12 holes; Messrs. Walter Evans and Co.'s Mecklenburg thread No. 8.

550.—Square for Antimacassar.

No. 550 is very quickly worked. The border and groundwork in point d'esprit, the centre star in point de reprise, the pattern in point de toile.   Wheels fill in the four holes in the centre of the squares.

No. 551 has a border in point d'esprit, the star is worked in point de feston, the other stitches are point de toile.   Wheels in part of star pattern No. 518.

551.—Square for Antimacassar.

552 *and* 553.—*Borders in Guipure a Art.*

Material: Messrs. Walter Evans and Co.'s Mecklenburg thread No. 8 or 16.

These corner borders are very suitable for couvrettes, and, worked with fine thread, for pocket-handkerchiefs.   The netted ground of the borders is to be worked in the size seen in illustration ; for the border No. 553 darn the ground in button-hole stitch, darning stitch, point d'esprit, and point de feston ; the

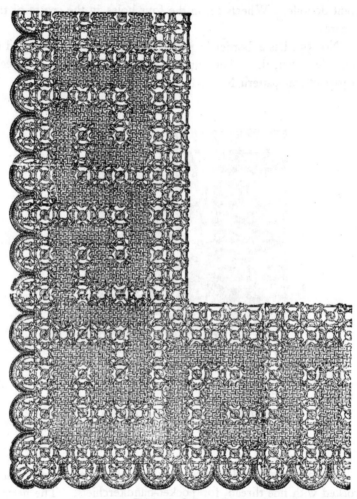

552.—Border in Guipure d'Art.

pattern No. 552 is worked in linen stitch and point d'esprit; small wheels are also to be worked. Both borders are to be

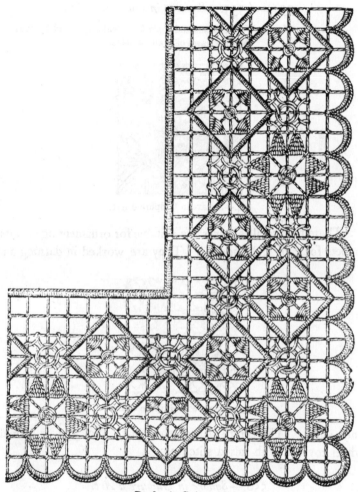

553.—Border in Guipure d'Art.

worked round in button-hole stitch ; the netted ground is cut away along the outside.

554 and 555.—Squares in Guipure d'Art.

Materials: Messrs. Walter Evans and Co.'s Mecklenburg thread No. 20;
netted squares of 7 and 8 holes.

554.—Square in Guipure d'Art.

These two small squares are suitable for ornamenting cravats,
lappets for caps and lingeries.   They are worked in darning and

555.—Square in Guipure d'Art.

linen stitch   The centre part of the square, No. 554, is a small
wheel covered with raised stitches.

556.—Square in Guipure d'Art.

Material: Messrs. Walter Evans and Co.'s Mecklenburg thread No. 12.

The centre of this square is worked in point de feston as well
as the border ; point de toile forms the groundwork of the square

in the centre, round which a row of button-hole stitch is worked.

556.—Square in Guipure d'Art.

557.—*Insertion in Guipure d'Art.*

Materials : Strip of netting of 4 holes in width ; Messrs. Walter Evans and Co.'s Mecklenburg thread No. 12.

The ground of this simple pattern is worked in point d'esprit, square wheels are worked in the centre of the strip.

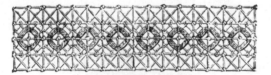

557.—Insertion in Guipure d'Art.

558 *to* 563.—*Different Strips of Insertion, Rosettes and Lace, in Guipure d'Art.*

Materials : Fine white cotton ; Messrs. Walter Evans and Co.'s Mecklenburg thread Nos. 16 and 20.

These strips of insertion, rosettes, and borders are very suitable for ornamenting lingeries, cravats, &c. The ground of

insertion, Nos. 558 and 560, is worked with fine white cotton over
a fine steel knitting-needle, in slanting netting, and darned with
thread in the manner seen in illustrations.   The ground of each

558.—Insertion in Guipure d'Art.

strip is 11 rounds wide, and worked with button-hole stitch along

559.—Insertion in Guipure d'Art.

the edges ; the darned patterns can be worked from illustration.

560.—Rosette in Guipure d'Art.

For the rosette, No. 560, cast on 6 stitches over a fine knitting-
needle, and join the stitches into a circle ; in the 1st round work

2 stitches in every stitch. In the 2nd—5th rounds work 2 stitches in every increased stitch of the preceding round, and in every other stitch 1 stitch. In the 6th round take a steel knitting-needle double the size of the first, and work over it 1 stitch in every stitch of the preceding round. Then work the 7th round over the fine needle as follows :—

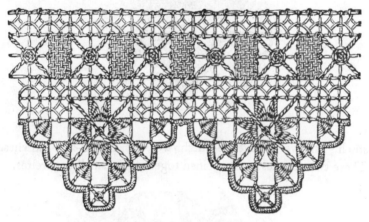

561.—Border in Guipure d'Art.

Draw always the second stitch of 2 stitches through the first, and work 1 stitch in the stitch which has been drawn through the first, and then 1 stitch through the other stitch. In the 8th round work always 2 stitches in the stitch between the 2 crossed stitches, 1 stitch in all the other stitches. Lastly, darn the rosette, from illustration, with fine glazed cotton.

For the ground of the rosettes, illustrations Nos. 562 and 563, cast on 6 stitches, join the stitches into a circle, and work then in the 1st round 2 stitches in every stitch ; in the following 8 rounds 2 stitches in every increased stitch, in all the other stitches 1 stitch. The last (10th) round is worked without increasing. Then darn the rosettes, from illustrations, with thread in darning stitch, linen stitch, and point d'esprit. The edges of the two rosettes are worked round in button-hole

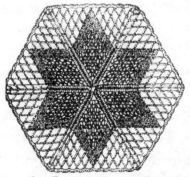

562.—Rosette in Guipure d'Art.

stitch ; in every selvedge stitch work 3 button-hole stitches. These two rosettes can be joined together for small couvrettes.

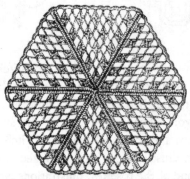

563.—Rosette in Guipure d'Art.

The ground of the border, No. 561, is formed by a strip of straight netting 9 squares wide, cut out in vandykes on one side, and worked round in button-hole stitch, as seen in illustration. This ground is darned, from No. 561, in darning stitch, point d'esprit, linen stitch, and ornamented with bars and wheels (See illustration).

564.—Corner Border in Guipure d'Art.

564 and 565.—*Corner Borders in Guipure d'Art.*

Material: Messrs. Walter Evans and Co.'s Mecklenburg thread No. 20 for handkerchief, or No. 8 for couvrettes.

These corner borders are suitable for handkerchiefs, couvrettes, &c., or as strips of insertion for cushions or pillow-cases. They are worked with more or less fine cotton, according to the use they are meant for. They are edged round with button-hole stitch on the outside, and finished off with a row of crochet purl. Work 1 double in every button-hole stitch; after every other stitch draw out the loop on the needle about one-

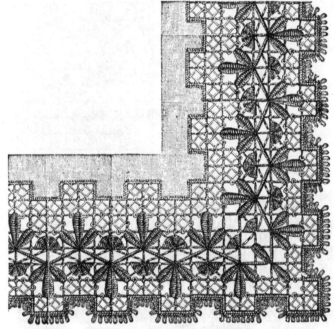

565.—Corner Border in Guipure d'Art.

tenth of an inch; take out the needle and leave the loop as a purl; take up 1 loop in last double stitch, and cast it off with the next double stitch.

566.—*Jewel Case, forming Pincushion.*

Materials: Deal box; satin ruche; satin ribbon; quilted satin and silk cord; guipure netting.

This case consists of a square cardboard or deal box, lined

with satin, and slightly quilted ; it is also covered on the top
with satin, and ornamented all round with a satin ruche four-
fifths of an inch wide, pleated in the manner seen in illustration.
The top of the box is stuffed so as to form a pincushion. It is

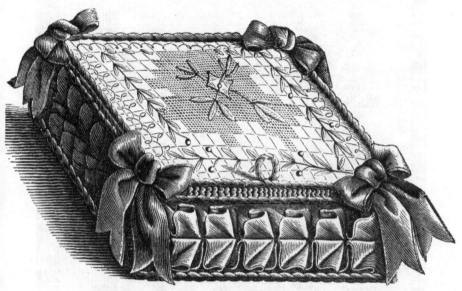

566.—Jewel Case, with Pincushion.

then covered with guipure d'art No. 567. Ornament all round
with silk cords, and at the corners with bows of satin ribbon.

567.—*Guipure Pattern for Jewel Case.*

Materials : Netting 25 holes square ; Messrs. Walter Evans and Co.'s
Mecklenburg thread No. 14.

This cover is worked in point d'esprit, point de toile, point

557.—Guipure Pattern for Jewel Case (No. 566).

de reprise, and point de feston. Thick dots are introduced occasionally.

568. – Parasol Cover in Guipure d'Art. (See page 580.)

Materials: Messrs. Walter Evans and Co.'s Mecklenburg thread No. 20, and cotton No. 80.

For working this cover, one part of which is shown in our illustration two-thirds of its full size, work first a straight strip of netting for the foundation, which must count as many holes in width as are required for the width of the covering. The size of the holes depends on the size of the knitting-needle or mesh which you use. The pattern is worked with cotton No. 80, over a steel knitting-needle which measures two-fifths of an inch round. Begin the strip in one corner. Cast on 2 stitches, and work in rows backwards and forwards, increasing 1 stitch at the end of every row, till you have 1 stitch more than the stripe is to have holes in width, on our pattern 68 stitches ; then work 1 row on the same number of stitches, and then increase alternately 1 stitch at the end of 1 row, and decrease 1 at the end of the next, till the strip is 250 stitches long. The strip is finished off in a straight line at the bottom by working a certain number of rows in which the last stitch remains untouched. At the beginning of the row do not work 1 stitch over the mesh, but only 1 knot in the stitch of the preceding row, so that the cotton is drawn on tight. When the strip is completed, trace from No. 568 the outlines for the pattern of each of the eight parts of the parasol with double thread, in such a manner that two parts lie next to each other, but reversed, that is, the point of one part must lie next to the wide part of the next part. Then work in each part the pattern seen in illustration, and afterwards each part round with button-hole stitch, working over the double outline. Cut out the different parts, and sew them together on the wrong side with close overcast stitch.

569.—Scent Sachet in Guipure d'Art.

569.—*Scent Sachet in Guipure d'Art.*

Materials: Messrs. Walter Evans and Co.'s Mecklenburg thread No. 18; green
satin; poudre d'iris; green satin ribbon; green silk cord.

The size of the netting depends on that of the sachet.　The

netting must be fastened in a frame, and darned with fine thread; the flowers are worked in darning stitch, and the ground in point d'esprit. The cushion is made of green satin, perfumed with poudre d'iris. When the netting has been fastened on, it is edged all round with a green satin ruche, and green silk cord, forming loops at every corner.

570.—Square in Guipure d'Art.

570.—*Square in Guipure d'Art.*

Materials: Netted square of 26 stitches; Messrs. Walter Evans and Co.'s Mecklenburg thread No. 12.

This pattern is worked in point d'esprit, edged with an outline of point de reprise. This outline may be worked in close button-hole stitch. Point de toile is used for the groundwork, upon which point de reprise is worked.

571 and 572.—*Work Case in Guipure d'Art.*

Materials: Blue satin; Messrs. Walter Evans and Co.'s Mecklenburg thread
No. 16; blue silk cord.

This little work-case, of darned netting and blue satin, is five inches and four-fifths long, four inches wide, and is fastened

571.—Work Case in Guipure d'Art (Back).

with a loop and button. The back, front, side, and the flap are worked all in one piece. The netting is worked with white thread No. 12, over a mesh measuring at least two-fifths of an inch round. For the flap the netting must be slanted off on both sides; this is done either by decreasings, or by cutting off the corners of the work. The latter is then darned in linen stitch, darning stitch, and point d'esprit, from No. 572, which shows the front of the case, and from No. 571, which shows the back. The netting is then lined with blue satin, and sewn together at the sides with button-hole stitches on the right side. The flap is edged with button-hole stitch ; sew on a small button, and make a small loop to correspond. The case is edged all round with blue silk cord.

572.—Work Case in Guipure d'Art (Front).

573. – *Banner Screen in Guipure d'Art.*

Materials : Netting ; Messrs. Walter Evans and Co.'s Mecklenburg thread No. 12 ; carved oak stand ; glacé silk ; cords ; tassels.

Banner-screens are used in two ways, either suspended from the mantelpiece or mounted as shown in illustration No. 573. The banner is 23 inches long, 19 inches wide, lined with coloured glacé silk, and edged with a lace border of guipure d'art. The design for the banner is given in page 554. Work the netting for the groundwork over a larger or smaller mesh, according to the size you wish it to be. The pattern is worked in point d'esprit, point de reprise, and point de toile. When the

2 o

pattern is completed, line the banner with coloured silk, edge with a gathered border of guipure d'art, finish with coloured

573.—Banner Screen in Guipure d'Art.

silk cords and tassels. The banner may be finished off in close button-hole stitch, instead of adding the lace border.

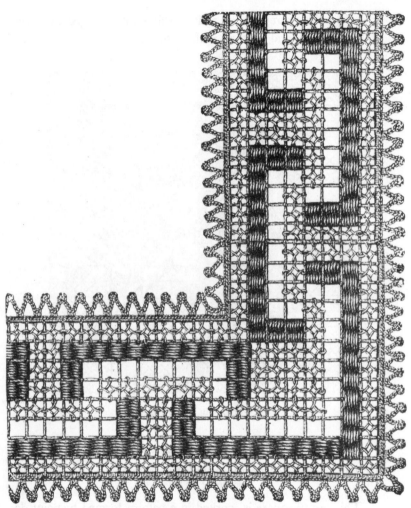

575.—Border in Guipure d'Art.

575.—Border in Guipure d'Art.

Material: Messrs. Walter Evans and Co.'s Mecklenburg thread No. 8.

This border is suited for couvrettes. It is worked in point d'esprit, point de reprise, or plain darning stitch, edged by a row of button-hole, and finished with a crochet edging.

576.—Square in Guipure d'Art.

576.—*Square in Guipure d'Art.*

Materials: Messrs. Walter Evans and Co.'s Mecklenburg thread No. 12; netted square of 20 holes.

This pretty square is worked in a pattern formed by point de feston, point de toile, and point de reprise, the star in the centre as that shown on page 514, omitting the alternate points ; border of point d'esprit, ground worked in simple crossed bars.

Table of the right size of Mecklenburg thread to use in working :—

	No.
Antimacassars	2
Borders	4
Handkerchiefs	20
Insertions	8
Lace edgings and insertions	16
Lamp shades	16
Parasol covers	18
Sachets	12
Sofa cushions	8
Toilet cushions	10
Toilet mats	10

FRAMES

May be obtained for large, middle-size, and small squares Oblong frames are used for working insertions and lace edgings.

BERLIN WORK

INSTRUCTIONS.

◆

BERLIN WORK includes every kind of stitch which is made upon canvas with wool, silk, or beads. The principal stitches used are common cross stitch, Gobelin stitch, leviathan stitch, raised or velvet stitch, tent stitch, and others. The materials and needle must always be carefully chosen of a corresponding size. For common cross stitch and raised stitch Penelope canvas must be used; for small articles, such as slippers, bags, or borders, single Berlin wool is preferable; for larger ones fleecy wool or double Berlin wool (the latter, however, is much more expensive). For Gobelin stitch and tent stitch undivided canvas (not Penelope) is required. Purse silk is often used for the latter; it is more brilliant than floss silk or filoselle. Floss silk is generally used for other stitches because it covers the thread of the canvas better than purse silk; it is, however, often replaced by filoselle, which is a much cheaper material. Moss wool is hardly ever used. Before beginning to work upon a piece of canvas the raw edges must be hemmed or sewn over with wool. Care must be taken not to crumple the canvas in the course of the work. It is best to roll one end of the canvas upon a round piece of deal while the other end is kept down upon the table with a lead cushion. Handsome artistic patterns should always be worked in a frame. When you undertake to work a large pattern begin in the centre, and complete one half before you commence the other. Always work the stitches in the same direction, from the top downwards—this is very essential to the beauty and regularity of the pattern.

Always begin with the colour which is used the oftenest; those colours that lose their dye in working must be put in last. When the pattern is finished begin the grounding. The wool must not be drawn too tightly, otherwise the threads of the canvas appear. If the wool is too coarse for the canvas, one long stitch is to be made from left to right as far as the particular colour is to be worked, and over this long stitch, cross back in the usual way.

The plainest stitch in Berlin wool work is the common cross stitch; illustrations 577 to 584 show varieties of the same.

We now proceed in the following pages to show, by description in writing and by most careful illustration, all the stitches which are used in Berlin Work. These are numerous, but neither too great in number nor too simple or too elaborate in execution for those who aspire to become Berlin workers.

577.—Common Cross Stitch.

ILLUSTRATION 577.—The common cross stitch is worked in rows backwards and forwards over 2 threads in height and 2 in width (square of the canvas) in straight lines ; the 1st row is worked from left to right; the 2nd row, which completes the stitches, from right to left. Illustration 577 shows 2 rows of completed stitches and 1 row in course of working.

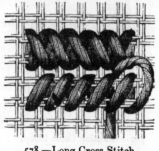

578.—Long Cross Stitch.

ILLUSTRATION 578 shows the long cross stitch. It is worked like the preceding one, only over 4 threads in height and 2 in width.

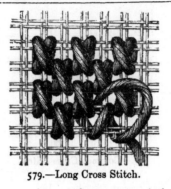

579.—Long Cross Stitch.

ILLUSTRATION 579 shows a long cross stitch, which is worked like the preceding one, except that 2 threads are missed between 2 stitches, and in the next row the stitches are worked between those in the preceding row. This stitch is not worked in rows backwards and forwards ; each stitch is completed before beginning the next.

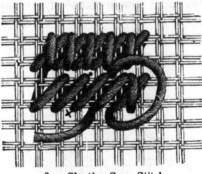

580.—Slanting Cross Stitch.

ILLUSTRATION 580.—The long slanting cross stitch is worked like No. 578, in rows backwards and forwards ; the 1st row is slanting, the 2nd is straight. The places for inserting the needle and for drawing it out are marked on the illustration with a cross and dot.

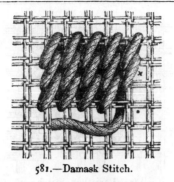

581.—Damask Stitch.

ILLUSTRATION 581.—-The damask stitch is worked in single rows from left to right, over 4 threads in height and 2 in width. The stitches of one row come between those of the next. The cross and dot shown in illustration are where to insert and draw out the needle.

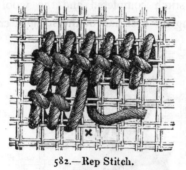

582.—Rep Stitch.

ILLUSTRATION 582 shows the rep stitch—a variety of the preceding. The first half of it is worked slantways over 6 threads in height and 2 in width, the second half, like the common cross stitch, from right to left over the 3rd and 4th of the 6 canvas threads; each stitch is completed at once. The illustration shows the last stitch being worked; the first half of the stitch is completed; the dot shows where the needle must be inserted for the second half; it is drawn out where the cross is placed on illustration.

583.—Leviathan Stitch.

ILLUSTRATION 583.— The leviathan stitch consists of 1 slanting and 1 straight cross stitch over 4 threads in height and 4 in
width. Each stitch is completed immediately. No. 583 shows
one half of the stitch completed and the wool as it must be
placed for working the first half of the straight cross stitch.

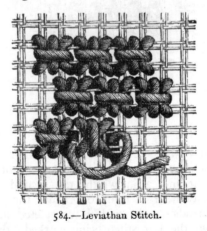

584.—Leviathan Stitch.

ILLUSTRATION 584.— The leviathan stitch is worked exactly
like the preceding, only the stitches are not worked on the same
threads in the different rows, as may be seen from illustration.

585.—Double Leviathan Stitch.

ILLUSTRATION 585.—The double leviathan stitch is a variety of the preceding; it is worked over 6 threads in height and as many in width. Make a common cross stitch over these 6 threads, then a long cross stitch in height and a long cross stitch in width. Illustration 585 shows 2 stitches completed and 1 being worked.

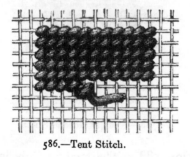

586.—Tent Stitch.

ILLUSTRATION 586.—Tent stitch. Each stitch is worked over 1 stitch in height and 1 in width, and is worked in rows form left to right.

587.—Slanting Gobelin Stitch.

ILLUSTRATION 587.—The slanting Gobelin stitch is worked on undivided canvas; each stitch is worked over 3 threads in height and 2 in width, divided from the next stitch only by an interval of 1 thread.

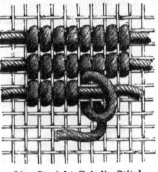

588.—Straight Gobelin Stitch.

ILLUSTRATION 588.—The straight Gobelin stitch is worked over 2 threads in height with 1 thread between, so that the stitches appear more raised; they are worked over thin cord or a thick piece of wool

ILLUSTRATION 589.—The raised or velvet stitch is worked over small round wooden meshes, and forms small raised loops. Take 2 similar meshes and as many threaded needles as there are colours in the work; make first a slanting stitch, as for the beginning of the common cross stitch, but instead of drawing out the needle straight under the place where it was inserted, draw it out exactly at the same place, so as to form a slanting stitch on the right and on the wrong side; then begin to work over 1 mesh; insert the needle above it and draw it out in a slanting

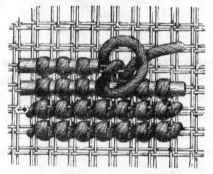

589.—Raised or Velvet Stitch.

direction underneath. On the wrong side of the work a regular cross stitch is formed. Illustration 589 shows 2 rows of velvet stitch completed and 2 rows being worked; the first of the latter is yet on the mesh, the second being worked so as to show the position of the wool upon the mesh. Observe that the rows of the velvet stitch are worked upwards, and that 2 meshes are necessary, because the lower one must not be drawn out before the next row is completed. The loops may be cut open if preferred.

590.—Plaited Stitch.

ILLUSTRATION 590.—The plaited stitch is worked like the herring-bone stitch. Each stitch is worked over 4 threads in height and 4 in width. Illustration 590 shows one part of the plaited stitch completed, and the place where the needle is to be inserted for the next stitch is marked by a dot. For the next stitch the needle is carried under the 2 threads below the stitches of the preceding row.

ILLUSTRATION 591.—The plush stitch is also worked upwards. Begin to work a common cross stitch, then insert the needle through the canvas over 2 threads in height and 2 in width, downwards in a slanting direction. Do not draw the wool close up, but leave a loop hanging down about four-fifths of an inch long, and make 1 more common cross stitch to fasten the loop. This stitch can also be worked over flat meshes. Work a common cross stitch at the end of every row. When the work is completed the loops are cut open and clipped, as may be seen from illustration.

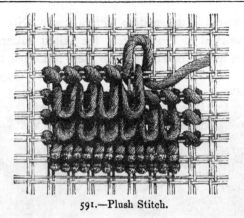

591.—Plush Stitch.

ILLUSTRATIONS 592 to 594.— Three Berlin wool work borders for trimming baskets, &c. No. 592.—The 2 outer rows which edge the border are worked in long straight cross stitch ; each stitch is crossed in the centre with a back stitch.

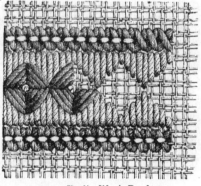

592.—Berlin Work Border.

The grounding consists of 2 rows of vandykes placed opposite each other, which are formed of long straight stitches of different lengths. The squares in the centre are formed in the same way,

2 P

and are completed in the middle with a knot. No. 593.—The ground is worked in cross stitch, the raised patterns in satin stitch ; in the middle of each pattern there is a cross stitch. The

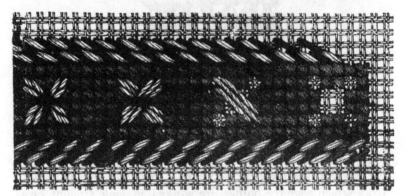

593.—Berlin Work Border.

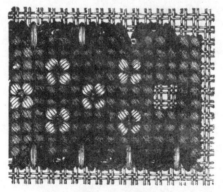

594.—Berlin Work Border.

outer rows are worked in half cross stitch over 2 threads in height and 4 in width in 2 different shades. No. 594.—The petals of the flowers are worked over 4 threads in height and in width, and consisting of 4 slanting stitches. In the centre the flower is completed by a knot ; the ground in cross stitch is completed on either side by a narrow border of scallops, formed of slanting stitches divided in the centre by 1 slanting stitch. It is easy to work these stitches from illustration. The choice of colours depends upon what use the border is intended for and upon personal taste.

PLATES

TATTED ANTIMACASSAR (*see page* 80).

214.—PATTERN FOR COUVRETTE (213).

213.—COUVRETTE IN APPLIQUÉ.

215.—Pattern for Couvrette (213).

334.—KNITTED TABLE COVER (*see page* 347).

337.—KNITTED D'OYLEY (*see page* 352).

568.—PARASOL COVER IN GUIPURE D'ART (*see page* 549).

INDEX.